YOU'RE
DOING IT
WRONG

OTHER BOOKS BY KAZ COOKE

Girl Stuff 8-12

Girl Stuff 13+

Up The Duff

Babies & Toddlers

Ada

KAZ COOKE

YOU'RE DOING IT WRONG

A History of Bad & Bonkers Advice to Women

VIKING
an imprint of
PENGUIN BOOKS

For Vi.

This book includes images of Aboriginal people who have died.

It was researched and written on Ngunnawal country
and the land of the Wurundjeri Woi Wurrung peoples.

CONTENTS

We've been told a load of nonsense.

WELL, HELLO. Shall we talk about how women are still challenging the 'down, girl' advice given to them in every industry, in art, religion, politics, home life, medicine, science, and from hordes of clergy, governments, advertisers, influencers, problem pages, wellness monetisers, blokey philosophers, and moustachioed mansplainers centuries apart? I think we ought. It's hilarious and horrifying; it's bad and it's bonkers; and it just keeps coming.

For centuries we've absorbed this nonsense that women are inferior and have to follow more rules than men, but when it comes in newer forms sometimes it's harder to recognise. We're hard-wired to look to other humans for lessons on how to be, so it is often easier to perpetuate advice without questioning.

When growing up, and through grown-up life, we're so busy, and tired and often a bit furious, sometimes we forget to ask *why* we're being given advice, where it comes from, who's telling it, whether it's useful and what 'leading philosopher' even means. (Jean-Paul Sartre had himself injected with mescaline and spent weeks thinking he was in a chorus line with some Moreton Bay bugs, and Sigmund Freud only removed a phallic cigar from his cat's-bum mouth long enough to be wrong on everything from vaginal orgasms to penis envy.)

I've been interested in advice to women for a long time. One of my most fun jobs as a journalist was reviving the 'agony aunt' column idea, which became *Keep Yourself Nice* in *The Age* newspaper in the late 1980s. My first 'big' book, *Real Gorgeous: The Truth About Body and Beauty* tried to debunk the advice given to women about how they should look; and my other books are designed to give girls and women confidence and reassurance with reliable information, from interpreting public health advice for pregnant women (*Up The Duff*) and new parents (*Babies & Toddlers*); and pre-teen girls (*Girl Stuff 8-12*) and teen girls (*Girl Stuff 13+*)

Because I update those books each year, I'm almost constantly worried I'll miss an important change in medical or other advice. I lose sleep when somebody posts on social media that they're using a second-hand copy because I know it will be outdated advice on the safest sleep positions for pregnant mums and for babies. I know an old copy won't tell women of South Asian or African heritage their normal length of pregnancy might be 38, not the 40 weeks assumed for others.

That started me thinking about which advice for women over the centuries we can trust, which advice has changed, and what had stayed the same. Is a 19th-century corset any different from celebrity-branded shapewear, leaving aside the whalebones v. hospital-beige-coloured latex debate?

Move along, ladies. Victoria Market, 1970s. (John Collins, State Library Victoria)

Australian etiquette, hierarchy and instructions to women are the product of attitudes imposed by the sort of British aristocrat who blithely lectured other people about vulgarity as they bounced downstairs for dinner in clanking assemblages of pearl and diamond necklaces with matching tiara and seven brooches that could buy a ship, while barking instructions at servants over a shoulder weighted down by unearned epaulettes.

Many themes are explored in the book, but the overarching one is this: most of what we've been told to do, and say, and feel, hasn't been about morality and practical help at all; it's about keeping women quiet and off-balance and judged inferior and doing the boring stuff so men can do the interesting stuff. And of course the underlying hatred and exploitation of women is always intensified when crossed with racism and class war. Brutal colonial attitudes and laws are still used against Aboriginal and Torres Strait Islander women, and I'll talk about the role my own family has played in this.

We've been given bad advice by the churches and governments, and then through the boom in printing and books of the 19th and 20th century, and public health campaigns, and politicians and social media. We've been told how to get chooks to lay eggs in the right place and curtsey to the Queen (not simultaneously). Variously, we've been instructed which chemical to use when scrubbing other people's gussets, what speed to put a vibrator on, and to walk in shoes on little stilts.

We've been told our bosoms shouldn't wobble, how many inches a fork should be from a knife on the table, to quietly move away when men put their hand up our skirt on public transport. We've been advised that we can't fly planes, jumping causes a uterus to fall out, and what sort of wire to stick through our cervixes to end a pregnancy.

We're reminded we have to look good (the definition of which changes) from cradle to grave; change shape; buy stuff which can't possibly do what it claims, to make us morally improved, more beautiful, more worthy. Politicians have told us to have more children if we're the right class, and fewer if we're poor.

This book is full of terrible advice – every heading is a lie that women have been told. Bad advice has been given for all sorts of motives by different people: the misguided evangelical, the clueless, the arrogant, the money-grubbing, those who want to seem 'in the know' or be admired as a leading-light revealing conspiracy theories. A piece of advice might even represent several motives on its way to us: from a profit-driven cosmetics company with an 'anti-ageing' cream dodging consumer laws, through a sponsored 'beauty editor' recommendation and a mention from a social media 'influencer' who wants more likes.

Humans are bad at change. Word-of-mouth advice can persist for centuries. As a whole, we're bad at listening carefully and challenging what we already think. We've been bad at going 'Hello, you're different, would you like a cup of tea, tell me a story' instead of 'You're weird, stand still while I hit you with a stick.' I hope we're getting better at it.

This isn't a scholarly book, mostly because I wanted to burst into tears every time I thought about handling the software that wrangles footnotes, but also because I am trained as a journalist, not an academic. I admit that while researching, the almost omnipresent phrase 'as Michel Foucault observed,' causes me to bark out a strangled cry of anguish, and feel about myself for a sandwich.

I've often used examples in the book of women in my own family history as emblematic of their own eras. Convict-era

Sarah, my grandmother six generations back who had the first pre-nup in Australia, and my mum, coming off a farm to the city, and becoming a mother and mature-age student during the Women's Lib era of the 1970s.

In some ways I've been working on this book my whole life (oh, they all say that), collecting thousands of images and reading hundreds of books and essays, especially over the past few years, first incidentally while a fellow at State Library Victoria on another project a few years ago; more recently doing 12 weeks' focused research for this book at the National Library of Australia. In the end, I veered off and crashed into the history of misogyny, shouted at the moon a bit, wrote enough words for three books, and had to hack my way back to the road with a cutlass and an editor.

Every one of the subjects here could be expanded upon to form its own book, and of course, in many cases, already is the subject of several marvellous volumes. Readers are encouraged, nay, badgered, to seek old and new research and commentary by expert, informed women in their books, blogs, documentaries, films and podcasts. The list goes through history from Christine de Pizan in the 1400s to hordes of more recent feminist historians and LGBTQI+ activists; and the hundreds of emblematic writers, such as Dr Jacqueline Huggins on the forced servitude of Aboriginal women; others on violence and abuse; Ginger Gorman on trolls and Caroline Criado Perez on how health advice and public policy puts women in danger by not including them in research or decisions.

I've used the scaffolding built by the work of such women to write this book.

The themes of advice to women are many: be quiet; don't laugh; you're the wrong shape; do almost all of the housework; find a man, do what the man says, make the men feel clever and important (don't look over there, lesbians aren't real); if you're Aboriginal you're not entitled to the same rights as white women; look sexy but don't want sex; your education won't give you equal opportunities; if you do well in a career you're weird; you must be a 'perfect mother' even though it's literally impossible; look like a beautiful robot; if you don't follow fashion you're a contemptible frump, and if you do you're a trivial chit.

I wanted to write this book for all of us. To say to older women: you haven't imagined it. There's a reason why you're tired and furious: we've been told this nonsense all our lives. And to say to young women: you're going to be told a cavalcade of lies to keep you feeling bad about yourself. Sometimes, it will feel like it's coming at you through a fire hose. But when you can see it coming, you can step out of its way: or stab a hole in the hose with a kitchen knife, screaming.

To put it another way, it's almost as if women have been handed the same pamphlet for about 600 years, but by different people knocking on the door, one after another; each time the pamphlet is getting longer. First there was a bloke in a Friar Tuck haircut waving a Bible, and then Queen Victoria, and then another bloke in a top hat, and then a 1950s Barbie doll in a platinum bouffant and a pencil skirt, then that advertising guy who was in *Mad Men*, and more recently an Instagram influencer in a crop top waving a mango.

It might be time to lock the door for a while, or at least shout, 'Who the bloody hell are you?' before opening it. Because they're not going to stop.

We have to stop *believing* it.

I want us to stop wondering, 'What do I have to do to be a proper woman?' and instead say, 'Ohh, I recognise this. It's just actually a giant lot of hairy historical bollocks with a new hairdo.' And then we can shut the door in its face. It will totter off in its bandage-dress and frighty heels and find another door, of course, but at least it won't be at your place, or in your head.

Advice to women is so often just a way of saying, 'If you're a woman, you're doing it wrong.' It says you don't matter enough, you don't look right, you don't have the right to your own thoughts, feelings, pain and joy, and you should be using an 'anti-ageing cream' on your inside-vagina wrinkles.

This book is my way of saying: don't take any of this utterly crap advice to heart. Your heart, and your appropriately rumpled vagina, deserve better.

EVERY HEADING IN THIS BOOK IS A LIE.

Nellie Sanderson, 8, in a witch costume with the lot – pointy hat, broom and demonic house pet – at the Children's Fancy Dress Ball, 1887. (State Library South Australia)

1

SIT DOWN & SHOOSH

DO YOU REMEMBER THE FIRST TIME YOU FELT IT? Maybe you were 10, or 12, or 13. I still wince as I remember it now: a sickening realisation that I was in the grip of intense, paralysing, visible self-consciousness, and there was nothing I could do to stop it. I blushed so hard that it seemed to sweep over and consume my whole body. My face felt like it was literally burning; my ears pulsed so hot I wondered if they would blow off the sides of my head, like in a cartoon.

It was an agony of self-perpetuating mortification; the more I wanted it to stop, the more I stood still and longed to disappear, the more the blush went on. Decades later, I can't even tell you why I was blushing. I just remember the feeling of being desperately ashamed.

At some point we all stopped being a little girl galumphing about having fun and became hyper-aware that we didn't stand up to even imaginary scrutiny. Each one of us, darling-hearted, perfectly individually gorgeous, clever girls, starts a transition into young womanhood feeling that we're not up to scratch. And when did it become normal for women to live full-time with some version of those peak moments of mortified self-consciousness? When did we start thinking that we were, all the time, at least partly but probably mostly, and maybe totally... *wrong*?

'Oh, God, don't look at me (and whatever you do, don't look at my parents dancing). I'm probably too fat, or thin in the wrong places, or accidentally wearing something terrible. Did my laugh sound like a bark? Is everyone staring at me? How can I make myself invisible? But also decorative, at the same time? But not vain. Am I even supposed to have bosoms yet, and if so why are they the wrong size? I've mispronounced that word, haven't I? I'm not an expert so I shouldn't say anything. And if I am an expert I'd better listen to some dude's windbag explanation, just to be polite.'

We've been given so many contradictory, stupid rules and unattainable definitions of perfection, that getting it right is literally impossible. No wonder we constantly feel like we've turned up to a knife-fight in a netball uniform.

But all the religions and every alleged philosopher in the entire world have been telling us how awful and wrong we are, for hundreds of years, so it must be true, right? Well. Deep breath in.

Aristotle was a fuckwit. He said that women had brains and bodies that were lesser versions of men – at a time when the whole of medical science was based on the baffling idea that women are cold and moist while men were hot and dry: 'We should look upon the female state as being as it were a deformity, though one which occurs in the ordinary course of nature.'

Writing in Latin didn't make Virgil sound any smarter: 'A woman is always a shifty and changeable thing.' I expected better of you, Plato, saying that women's genitals are the stunted versions of men's. I mean, honestly, Galen, telling us that women were the reincarnation of men who couldn't control their emotions.

As Nancy Tuana says in her 1993 book *The Less Noble Sex*, hardly any one of the famously revered public intellectuals amongst the faffage of philosophers over centuries, nor any religious text, could countenance the idea of women being equal humans. All their theories were twisted to make women look worse. The fact that women have babies was taken to prove they're physically weaker and can't be brainy as well as reproducey. The 'learned' beard-grooming types didn't spend any time thinking about how surviving childbirth showed immense physical resilience and strength, or that women might be intellectual if they had a chance.

Contradictions were ignored. Women were too weak to make their own decisions or opinions, so they had to be told what to do – but they were strong enough to do all the heavy work of carrying water, doing laundry and looking after the sick.

Periods made women so weak they musn't be educated or exercise or do anything physical or they'd go mad, according to a book by a Dr Edward Clarke that was reprinted at least 17 times in the 1800s. And so, in order for them to be categorised as strong enough to be enslaved, the lie was told and accepted that Indigenous and Black women didn't menstruate, or they didn't have the same physiology, or capacity for thought or feelings . . . or whatever else it was convenient to conclude. A divide was always policed between ladies and women.

The first and fastest way to repress us is to control our conduct. Our sexuality, work and childbearing was controlled by the rules of churchmen, kings, fathers and husbands, legally free to beat daughters and wives at will. Chaucer, writing in the 1300s, understood there were different rules for women, and that not all women obeyed them: he wrote about a widow, a category of female considered dangerously independent and probably sexually insatiable.

For her fabulously informative 1983 book *The Lady in the Tower: Medieval Courtesy Literature for Women*, Diane Bornstein looked at the conduct instruction books from the 12th to the 15th century, in French, English, German, Spanish and Italian. Only one was written by a woman before 1500, feminist foremother Christine de Pizan, who proved that women could do as well as men if they were liberated by money and circumstances to make their own way in the world.

What the instruction books did most is bang on about virginity, because they were written by men obsessed with sex, as so many religious fanatics are. Tertullian, writing in 207 AD or so, was among the first to say women were 'the gate of the devil', a concept that stayed all the rage – more than 1500 years later the hatchet-faced baldy Bishop of Adelaide called Aboriginal women 'the bond-slaves of Satan'. St Augustine accepted that women should marry but said lifelong virginity was better.

Christine de Pizan, bless her, didn't care much about whether anyone was a virgin but reckoned not being married, aka practising chastity, meant you could have independence and escape decades of hideous drudgery, abuse and body-breaking, endless pregnancies. (You might have to live in a nunnery, but they had wine.)

Advice on chastity wasn't enough, of course. Bornstein says, 'Courtesy books admonish women to be humble, meek and obedient. They are told to be sweet and gentle and to comply with all of their husband's requests . . . When it comes to deportment they are told to walk daintily, keep their eyes lowered, and keep their bodies still. When it comes to speech, they are told to keep their voices low, not talk too much, and not to laugh, jest or swear.'

As Chaucer expert Margaret Hallissy has pointed out about those times, men believed that the natural state of women required constant scolding and changing. They were basically shrewish, nagging, contrary, gossiping, spendthrift nympho temptresses who needed to be kept from idleness (convenient if you want clothes washed and dinner cooked). The word 'houswifly' in medieval times meant 'busy'. All sacred and secular texts conspired to deny women the right to any authority.

Prospective grooms asked permission from a father to propose to a daughter. On their wedding day, women were walked down the 'aisle' by their fathers and then handed to their husbands at the altar, symbolising the transfer of ownership and supervision, which had guaranteed her virginity. This tradition has proved remarkably tenacious, even if its origins are lost.

"Do what men tell you."

In about 1639 a French bloke called Jean Puget de la Serre wrote a massively impertinent book giving advice to the Queen of England. Translated as *The Mirrour Which Flatters Not*, it was 'dedicated to the queen of "Great Britaine". Rare book curator Dr Anna Welch showed me an original copy at State Library Victoria. (It's quite the treat to gently pat a book that's nearly 400 years old.) She explained that Serre was the official historian to Marie de' Medici, Queen of France and mother of the Queen of England, Henrietta, who'd been married off to Charles I. Perhaps Marie was using her paid historian to keep ordering her daughter around.

The author opens with simpering flattery to Henrietta: *'All the* divine qualities which you possesse of Super-eminence *in all*

things … adorable qualities … the splendour *of your* virtue *dazzles*.' 'Yes, yes,' you can imagine Henrietta muttering, as she riffles through the pages, 'I'm stupendous – and yet I feel a "but" coming.' And there is. Serre urges Henrietta to remember the Bible verse of Deuteronomy 32:29 – like everyone, she's going to die and be judged by God, so she'd better behave or she'll go to Hell.

To hammer his point home the book's engraved frontispiece is pretty ghastly, even by the more-familiar-with-death standards of the day: a long-haired, maggoty skeleton wears a queen's robe and crown and holds a sceptre, surrounded by skulls and bones. And there's an hourglass with sands running through it. Yeah, yeah, we get it.

"Punish the witches (who totally exist)."

Old women, unwanted women, unprotected women, independent and difficult women, inconvenient women, women whose property is coveted by others, all of them were accused and convicted of being witches as part of the craze for 'trials' which began in Europe in the 1400s and spread to the Americas.

16

Witchcraft panic and persecutions raged for about 500 years reaching a middle peak around 1500, with the last executions in the 1700s. Tens of thousands of accused 'witches', the vast majority of them women, were killed.

Most were tortured, psychologically and physically, and their naked bodies inspected by prosecuting men. Diagnosed witchy behaviour included having traditional and respected herbal or midwifery knowledge, the making of medicines, choosing who to have sex with, giving dirty looks, chatting to yourself, having pets, having the markers of being older including facial hair or moles, being independently single or a widow, and being a vulnerable woman who could be blamed for crop failure or illness.

Many town officials and churchmen were all for it, putting 'witches' in stocks and chains, throwing them into freezing ponds as well as setting fire to them. It's nice to know some people weren't having it: when a medical woman in a French village called Françoise Bonvin was denounced as a witch in the mid-1400s, the locals protected her and gave evidence. The gist was she might be a bit of a gossip, but so what, and she was acquitted of causing bad weather. She was re-accused, rearrested, tortured and eventually released, according to *The Oxford Handbook of Witchcraft in Early Modern Europe and Colonial America* edited by Brian Levack. Many women fought back, and sued for slander after the accusations were dropped.

It's quite something to see modern men accused of sexual assault in the workplace claim that they're the victims of a 'witch hunt'. The parallels are difficult to see without an electron microscope, which can see atom-sized chemical reactions (like the one Dame Pratibha Gai perfected in 2009 after 20 years of being the lead researcher).

In 2016, Immigration Minister Peter Dutton accidentally sent a text to a *Daily Telegraph* journalist, in which he called her 'a mad fucking witch'.

His cabinet colleague Simon Birmingham defended Mr Dutton: 'He of course has come out and publicly acknowledged that it was him, to avoid there being a witch-hunt . . .'.

In 2019 and 2020, after a campaign by Mad Fucking Witches, a pressure group that named itself after Mr Dutton's insult, 500 advertisers boycotted shock jock Alan Jones's radio show.

'My favourite thing to do each morning is to go through my mineral collection and choose a few stones to throw in my bra.' – Renee Watt, witch and podcaster, quoted by *Bust* magazine, 2019

'Most of the accusers are men because if you accuse your fellow woman, then tomorrow it will be you.' – Ghanaian Adamu Mahama, accused of being a witch when her son died after they argued, quoted by *Guardian* journalist Tracy McVeigh, 2020

According to the notes for a 2016 exhibition of witch-related artworks at *Musea Brugge* in Belgium, it was the painter Pieter Bruegel the Elder who fixed the image of witches with a cauldron, black cat and broomstick. Centuries before the pointy hat, painters like Hieronymus Bosch really upped the ante: bizzaro fever-dream scenarios of cavorty-bacchanalian group sex between flying crones with fanged tortoise vaginas and bitey demon monster-bats who have horse legs.

By the time Shakespeare's *Macbeth* was performed in 1606 it had witches frolicking about a cauldron, and in the 21st century we got the 'good witch' in *The Wizard of Oz* and the *Wicked* musical, and renewed interest in Wiccan religion and the psychological comfort of spells and rituals. Western women who call themselves witches generally have a better time of it now – although many religious schools have been known to ban witchy books, TV shows and costumes. Meanwhile, we're still dealing with baffling 'slutty-witch' Hallowe'en costumes.

And yet, around the world, from Africa to Papua New Guinea, women and children are still accused of being witches and subjected to physical violence including 'exorcism' rituals. Again, older women, some with dementia, and people with differences including albinism are targeted. Some evangelical Christian Pentecostal pastors have encouraged the persecution.

"You must be perfect."

In 1722 an Englishman in the now defunct job of ball dance choreographer called John Essex wrote *The Young Ladies Conduct; Or, Rules for Education, under Several Heads; with Instructions Upon Dress, Both Before and after Marriage; and Advice to Young Wives*. He had no business or experience in any of it but summed up the advice of the age: Big character flaws included curiosity, anger, and 'Gluttony, Drunkenness, Concupiscence (a fancy word for lust), Madness, Malice, Folly, and Extravagance.' Instead, every woman ought to display 'Modesty, Obedience, Complaisance, Respect, Humility, Temperance, Chastity and Industry' all at the same time. (Not easy unless you're allowed to do an interpretive dance, which you weren't.)

In short, we were required to be angels.

"Don't speak."

John Essex's book also instructed women not to feel proud of any of their accomplishments: best not to open their mouths at all. 'In publick Company avoid much Talk, few Words are best.'

Edward Cole, the founder of the Cole's Book Arcade, successfully advertised for a wife in the newspaper. He later released this sheet music, c1890. (National Library of Australia)

An inquirer to the problem columns of *The Girl's Own Paper* in the 1880s is advised when walking to 'speak low, and look as quiet and sedate as possible.' On the same page, a young woman is told she has made a sad mistake in speaking her mind. 'It is a common excuse for highly unseemly and uncalled for remarks, to call the feeling that dictates them, "straightforwardness".'

Eighteenth-century women condemned to silence (and bored to shrieks) resorted to lists of mythical coded messages that could be sent by the position of a silk fan to express their feelings, from 'come hither' to 'you stinking cad'. By the 19th century they could use 'the language of flowers' and let a daffodil do the talking.

When women do speak, they've been advised to be careful so as not to upset men's sensibilities. More recently, we've been encouraged to be more assertive, and remove 'modifiers' from our way of speaking, such as, 'I think', 'Maybe if we just', 'If I could add . . .', 'Does that make sense?', 'Just a quick note' and 'I'm probably not explaining it very well.' Some women use an app called Just Not Sorry to highlight modifiers in emails and texts, so they can be more aware of it.

The idea that women should be quiet and listen to men feeds into multiple modern phenomena: the vile abuse of trolls who abuse and threaten women journalists and commentators whenever they express their opinion or are quoted – and when people suggest the solution is for women to ignore rape and death threats and graphic abuse or leave social media. We recognise it when men steal a woman's idea in a meeting and take credit for it, as mansplainers lecture women at length on subjects the women are experts in, and in the puzzling feature of first dates at which a man asks no questions.

Women are even now cast in the role of audience, student, handmaiden or subordinate to a man – at parties, on professional panels and in research.

"Watch your tone."

Women have also been disqualified from speaking, not just because they don't have the right, but because they're 'shrill'. Men running commercial radio in the 1990s and early 2000s were still saying that 'the public' didn't like women's voices on radio. (Since I was in the room when the same sort of men tried to convince my friend comedian Judith Lucy to run an on-air competition called 'Celebrity Sperm', in which a winning listener would be impregnated, I can't say I found them persuasive, as a rule.)

In arguing against women having the right to vote in 1869, clergyman Horace Bushnell wrote that women could not thunder. Instead they produce a 'chorus of treble, fluting half the time'. If they did get the vote, it would change their voices, which would become 'more wiry and shrill'; they will become taller and brawnier and get bigger hands and feet and a 'heavier weight of brain'.

A travelling singer called Garin lo Brun in the 1100s sang advice to girls, rocking up to villages in leather pants with a banjolele (I imagine) telling women to keep their face clean, wear shoes that make their feet look smaller, take on the emotional mood of their husband, have a well-modulated voice and walk slowly with small steps (much more likely if your stupid, too-small shoes hurt).

"Smile."

According to that old ninny John Essex, we should keep our faces unlined by not making any expressions and always having what came to be known as a 'pleasant countenance', because even the feelings of disagreeableness, or anger, will ruin our looks.

Presumably if you had any wrinkles caused by spending every night of your life hunched near a sputtering candle squinting at your sewing, or working during all the hours of daylight in the fields, or surviving 12 childbirths before you were 30 it was probably best to throw yourself and your lined face off a rocky outcrop.

I remember Hazel Hawke, the wife of former Prime Minister Bob Hawke. After one of her facelifts she said she

'When you walk, don't turn your head; when you speak, don't open your mouth too wide; when you sit, don't move your knees; when you stand, don't shake your dress; when you are happy, don't laugh aloud; when you are angry, don't shout aloud.'
– Ninth-century Chinese manual, T'ang Dynasty Courtesans, Ladies and Concubines} translated by Howard Levy

'There's nothing sexist about commercial radio. I'd love a woman who could pull an audience . . . I'd hire Jack the Ripper if he could rate.'
– Ian Grace, manager of 2GB radio station, 1996

Too Fat, Too Slutty, Too Loud: The Rise and Reign of the Unruly Woman – Book title by Anne Helen Petersen, 2017

didn't like how the lines on her face had made it look like she was frowning. All those years she spent bringing up the kids on her own, smiling with dignity at endless fundraisers and public appearances, while her alcoholic, unfaithful husband was lauded as a hero. If anyone had earned the right to her own face, it was Hazel Hawke.

Even a dressmaking pattern catalogue – Madame Weigel's July newsletter in 1942 – told us 'Cheerful Countenance is the Fashion'.

"You've got a resting bitchface."

Women whose faces in repose don't suggest a smile were said to have a problem. 'Among the slew of pop culture icons said to be afflicted with so-called Resting Bitch Face,' reported *The Washington Post* in 2016, 'the vast majority are women.' You do surprise me.

"Don't laugh, & if you do, make it quiet."

By the early 1300s Francesco da Barberino wrote (because he was a lawyer who didn't have enough to do) that women should not show their teeth by laughing heartily. Women's laughter was considered dangerous and wrong.

Etiquette books over the next few hundred years rarely failed to reprimand women: they laughed too loud, too much, at too high a pitch, and – hard to imagine how else to do it – with their mouth open.

The Lady's New Year's Gift or Advice to a Daughter by George Lord Saville, Late Marquis and Earl of Saville, printed in 1688, particularly warns against 'doing it loud, which is an unnatural Sound and looketh so much like another Sex, that few Things are more offensive'. 'That boisterous kind of Jollity,' he said, was totes slutty, 'contrary to Modesty and Virtue.'

Girls were made to feel self-conscious about their laugh, and one who wrote to the ever-astringent mean-girl advisor in *The Girl's Own Paper* in 1881 felt she had a horrid one. She was advised to 'laugh very low and gently' so that nobody was disgusted.

"Keep still."

From the 1800s we were told to stay very still, though it was a hard act to keep up unless you were Music Hall artiste Pansy Montague, who performed as the human statue (but more of Pansy later).

"Be meek."

Women were already being warned in the 1700s that they should guard against passion, or certainty, or vehemence or other sins of enthusiasm or volume, by exercising and eating moderately so as not to inflame themselves by scoffing tea, coffee, chocolate, wine, pickles and hot sauces. Before and since, pretty much every conduct and etiquette guide to being a girl or a woman has insisted on meekness.

According to idiotic Alexander Walker in his ludicrous arsery of a book, *Beauty: Illustrated Chiefly by an Analysis and Classification of Beauty in Woman* (1836), 'A single trait of rudeness, a severe air, or even the character of majesty would injure the effect of womanly beauty.'

Many beautiful traditional girls' names often focused on jewels, flowers and virtuous characteristics: Grace, Constanctia, Prudence, Patience, Faith, Verity, Hope, Charity.

'Being able to sit very still is sexy.' *Sex and the Single Girl*, Helen Gurley Brown, 1962

Perhaps it's time to start also naming girl babies Adventura and Wildy. No pressure.

Letters and Advice to Young Girls and Young Ladies: On Dress, Education and Marriage, Selected from the Writings of John Ruskin appeared in 1879: 'A woman must be a pleasant creature . . . women's work is to please people; to feed them in dainty ways; to clothe them; to keep them orderly and to teach them.' Yes, *that* John Ruskin, allegedly rendered incapable of having sex for five years after discovering on his wedding night that his wife's naked body was unlike the smooth marble statues he'd seen in museums (was it her nipples or pubic hair, as rumoured, or perhaps he was terrified she had eyeballs . . .). Anyway, I'm sure it made her feel tremendous. Well done, Effie Ruskin, for running off with John Millais.

The meekness instruction is the basis of the traditional way of dancing, the man must 'lead'.

"Women's brains are inferior to men's."

One of the first reasons given in writing for women's 'natural inferiority' was that God designed it that way, then we were told by doctors that women's 'humours' system were 'cold and moist' (euw) and weak; whereas men were hot and dry, which meant sensible and good at inventing and thinking. Then it was claimed that women have differently developed 'sections' of the brain than men, although it seems no research has actually established anything other than men's brains tend to be bigger than women's, but this is fairly irrelevant because crows and octopuses are nearly as smart as several known people I could mention.

The inventor of the term 'neurosexism', Professor Cordelia Fine, pointed out in her book *Testosterone Rex* that some of the modern assumptions about supposed innate differences between male and female human behavior about women waiting to be chosen by men were based on a 1940s study of (put the kettle on; you'll be needing a cup of tea) . . . fruit flies.

One of the problems with assumptions about hard-wired women's behaviours and the idea of totally girly brains is some of the assigned characteristics are compleeetely contradictory. Post-menopausal women were once considered insatiably inflamed sexpots, but have been more recently characterised as difficult party-poopers putting the mockers on their husband's later-life sex prospects.

Our essential woman-brain makes each of us at once a raving temptress, inflamed by Earl Grey tea in 1882; a timid, hankie-twisting 'frail' in need of protection; a hard-boiled partier who pops a bullet into a private detective while wearing a tight red dress; *and* the fun-killer, 'but-you're-never-home' wife of the hero in Hollywood movies.

Setting the bar low. Let's Drive Better Than Men! *book, by Mary Arnold, published by the Australian and New Zealand Vacuum Oil Company, 1934. (National Library of Australia)*

"Women shouldn't drive."

Driving manuals for women from the 1930s to the 1960s shared the theme of 'driving better than men'. The insult 'woman driver' was common in the 20th and 21st centuries even though women have a safer driving record than men, and therefore cheaper insurance premiums.

Women have been held back – less able to afford to rent or own a car, and banned from driving on the grounds that it creates independence and danger for unsupervised women.

The technical right for women to drive in Saudi Arabia was granted in 2018, but many women's rights activists who advocated it are still beaten and jailed there. Reform activists continue to argue for the implementation of relatively new laws for female adults to have freedom of movement and marriage without the permissions of male 'guardians'.

"Follow a gazillion etiquette rules."

As women in Europe and its colonies became more literate, and the upper class of women were liberated from work, there was suddenly a huge number of etiquette books in the 19th century. (Obviously everyone had more time on their hands having burned all the witches by then.)

Elaborate etiquette advice to women, detailed down to the angle of bugle beads on a mourning cloak and who to curtsey to, was the ultimate requirement to 'stay in your lane'. Even if you'd moved up a lane in more egalitarian America and Australia, you might not know which fork to use at dinner and didn't want to embarrass yourself.

A Philadelphian bachelor girl called Miss Eliza Leslie wrote her *Behavior Book* in 1839, which was pretty brazen given she'd plagiarised her first cookbook from classes at Mrs Goodfellow's culinary school. Her book goes on for an unfeasibly long time, with inexhaustible advice on everything from not mentioning bedbugs to a host, and how many leaves to have in a posy. (I can't remember and I'm not going back in.)

There are a lot of 'don'ts': 'tinking on a piano with your forefinger only'; 'singing as you go up and downstairs'; 'holding the hand of a friend all the time she sits beside you, or kissing and fondling her before company' (no freewheeling lesbians or bisexuals in the parlour, thank you); 'slapping a gentleman with your handkerchief' or 'tapping him with your fan'; reminding servants of 'their unfortunate African blood'. Or being Irish.

"Obey etiquette writers because they are posh."

A pretend cachet of sophistication is useful as an etiquette writer: many appear in dim light to be minor aristocrats. Lady Troubridge sold more books than Laura Troubridge would have.

By the 1920s, *Etiquette* author Mrs Massey, editor of *Queen* magazine, claimed to be a social contact of various royals, and an expert on their jewels and how royalty goes on holiday. The publishers of the 47th edition of *Manners and Rules of Good Society or Solecisms to Be Avoided*, claimed the anonymous author was a 'Member of the Aristocracy'.

Hundreds of books on conduct for women have been written over the years, almost all of them by women. Most of the authors were not united by expertise on how to present a visiting card or a fierce personal interest whether a rear admiral went to dinner before the son of a baronet, but by the necessity to make their own living in a man's world, often as single mums before the advent of any useful government benefit payments.

While telling people how to present their visiting cards, and not to shriek at the servants, they were jobbing authors or writers – minor aristocrat Nancy Mitford had the cred and cleverness and needed the cash when she wrote her famous list of 'U' – for upper class – and 'non-U' language. (Upper class people said ill, loo and table napkin. Lower class folk said sick, toilet and serviette.) US expert Amy Vanderbilt (a distant relative of the rich ones) started as a reporter when she was 16, in the 1920s. Lillian Pyke wrote *Australian Etiquette* after being widowed suddenly in 1914 with three small children.

Emily Post published her first etiquette book when she fell on hard times in the 1920s: her works are still in print, updated by her great-great granddaughters and a great-great-grandson. Miss Manners has also become a dynasty, with her descendants sharing the newspaper byline that still appears syndicated across America.

In the early 1980s Australia had Sheila Scotter, with her plummy English accent, a history of editing *Vogue* and the clever branding of only ever wearing black and white. She was generally described as a doyenne, or, as in her obituary, 'a grand dame of impeccable taste'.

She was vile to waiters and other staff, and disapproved of a long list of things she was rude about, including 'vulgarity, noisy behaviour, sloppy speech, unacceptable and inappropriate standards of dress, incorrect salutations, forgotten thank-you letters . . . and tardiness'.

It's a little startling to find that in her 1998 autobiography she devoted a page to a list of the men (many of them married) who she'd had sex with – coyly billed as 'gentlemen with whom I have enjoyed breakfast'.

But poor old Sheila: she was sent away forever to another continent for school when she was four years old. She fits the bill, after all, of most etiquette writers being women who write because they had to make their own way in the world, while supporting all the rules that kept them out of their own demure debutante-to-wife life.

Each of them capitalised on a desperation to know the rules, and to avoid shame of being lowlier than others. And perhaps to get a leg up the social ladder, for money or status. All of the Australian authors advised on what to do if you were 'presented at court' at Buckingham Palace. Nobody reading the book was likely to be invited; those who *were* invited didn't need a book, being supplied with well-versed, aristocratic aunts.

The 1959 *Manual of Modern Manners* by Judith Listowel was written by a countess who made her own living after studying at the London School of Economics. She survived a plane crash in Uganda in her 70s and a mugging, aged 89 in Budapest, and I wish she'd written about *that*.

"Women belong at the bottom of any society."

The countess's book echoes just about every etiquette guide sold in the 'British Empire' in demanding a gracious reliance on 'good manners, good breeding, and true politeness'. The heart of it is to understand the hierarchy: knowing the 'precedency' in any given room. 'It assigns to everyone his or her place.' Places were assigned by royal families, who returned favours over a few centuries by creating aristocrats and bestowing land on them and ranked titles such as dukes, baronets, earls, marquises, counts and viscounts.

It was important to know what the rules were – and never question them. Because when you do, you realise it's utterly bizarrely fawning to call anybody 'Your Majesty', 'Your Highness', 'Your Grace', or 'Your Eminence' – I mean, why not 'Your Gorgeousness', or 'Your Uppity', or 'Mr Prominent-Pants'? It's part of a system that literally puts women at the bottom,

Princess Alice of Albany, sitting down and shooshing at a coronation wearing priceless jewels, including the Ears of Wheat tiara to denote her fertility, 1911. Phwoarrr.

and Indigenous women and women with dark skin at the very bottom. You can write the rules down, and base generations of laws and politics on them, but it's still a lie.

The etiquette system underpinned racism, sexism, colonialism, misogyny, disrespect of others in the guise of 'manners' and certitude, and general snippiness, reinforced over decades, often by plagiarism. Hierarchy lists were published. For women, the Queen was at the top, then the Queen Mother and the sovereign's daughters, going through reams of various wives and daughters ranked solely by the position in a family of their husband or father (i.e. eldest son of a duke down to 11th son of a baronet), before descending to 'wives of gentlemen'. No woman was above a man of her own station.

"Girls need charm school."

I've been obsessed with 'problem' and etiquette columns since I was that galumphing, gauche suburban teenage girl reading British books during downtime working at a second-hand bookshop, who found herself clueless and employed in a big-city newspaper office. On my first night out with colleagues I was handed a menu in a restaurant and had no idea what the Italian words meant (except spaghetti), or how to order, which implement to use or how to pay.

As a young reporter, I intended to write an undiluted satire of archaic deportment, elocution and etiquette lessons at the Elly Lukas School of Elegance in Melbourne. But I found myself moved by the girls in the class. Although some of the lessons were sexist, and much of it was eminently send-uppable, I recognised that I was another one of these lower-middle-class and working-class girls, trying to make the best of herself. I poked fun at being taught how to sit with one calf laid along the other, stand up and walk with grace or get out of a car without showing your undies. But not showing your undies is not a bad skill to have. You can always decide to show them another time.

I began an advice column myself at *The Age* in the late 1980s, a tongue-in-cheek version called 'Keep Yourself Nice'. The editor, though delighted with its success, assumed I was making up the letters. They were all real: a mix of genuine inquiries, but mostly ones joining in some fun feminism about required hats and which fork to use when you were sexually harassed.

Canberra High School girls balance books on their heads to practise walking during the 'poise and personality course' by the YWCA, 1965. (The Australian newspaper, National Library of Australia)

"English etiquette rules are timeless."

The emphasis on 'Indian and Dominion Etiquette' and calling colonial governors Your Excellency shifted before Noreen Routledge released *Etiquette For Australians* in 1944 which, as you'd expect for the time, contains a list of how to address military men and identify which medals were given for what. Given the scattering hither and yon of men during the war, she added that the tradition of asking a father for his daughter's hand in marriage was over.

Presumed to be going from their childhood family home to a husband's, frugal brides-to-be were advised to hold a 'kitchen, linen or laundry tea' so they could assure a good stock of cannisters, tea towels, and eggbeaters to set their own households. Noreen echoed other advisors in explaining that typewritten letters were vulgar; women were finally allowed to smoke; and all ordinary mortals were presented to people of Royal Blood, much in the way you would offer a sausage roll on a tray.

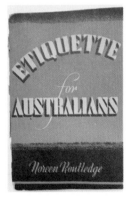

Onya, Noreen. Her 1944 edition.

In 1930, 'An unmarried girl cannot stay at the house of a bachelor, unless she is duly chaperoned' for example, contrasts with *Seattle Stranger* columnist Dan Savage's assured 2012 adjudication that lesbian couples should 'go halvsies' when paying for a new strap-on dildo.

Even modern etiquette advisors have deemed it largely unnecessary to advise women that they ought not send an employee or acquaintance an unsolicited happy snap of their vulva, or masturbate during a work video call.

In the case of Lady Troubridge, being republished post-humously in the 1980s was less about the claim of the subtitle, 'A standard reference for 50 years' than to amuse readers with anachronisms, including motoring etiquette about not using the horn to frighten pedestrians, nor throwing sandwich boxes onto the road.

By 2014, 'kick-arse' advice to women by stunt woman Ky Furneaux in *Girl's Own Survival Guide: How to Deal With the Unexpected – From the Urban Jungle to the Great Outdoors* included how to start a fire without matches, navigate by the stars, tie useful knots, avoid a knife fight and poo in the outdoors. I myself have found use only for, 'Travelling by yourself? Wear sunglasses with dark lenses so that it's hard for people to make eye contact with you'.

June Dally-Watkins almost raising an eyebrow. Look at that posed hand, 1949. (Max Dupain, State Library of NSW)

The etiquette expert and charm school entrepreneur June Dally-Watkins, at 90, was delighted to be informed of the phrase 'slut-shaming' by the co-host of an ABC TV docu-comedy about women and etiquette, in 2017. 'Slut . . . *shaming*,' approved the elegant quote-machine with a twinkle in her eye, 'I love that . . . don't be a slut.'

Miss Dally-Watkins's era emphasised respectability, neatness and fiancé-luring purity. Our era emphasises independence, buying things and fiancé-luring sexiness. Being shamed for being a 'slut' is still more the norm than somebody telling you off for slut-shaming.

"You should out-British the British."

Australian etiquette writers often clung desperately to old ideas to try and 'stay English'. Most white Australians saw themselves as British subjects and wanted to appear classier than convicts – or perhaps to mask convict origins.

Struggling single mum Lillian Pyke's perennial book *Australian Etiquette: The Rules of Good Society* was first published around 1911, then nicked and printed by others, with its last edition in the 1960s, decades after she died.

Early reviews and Press mentions noted Lillian's claim in her intro that, in Australia, a miner might rise to be a politician. This created a new class that needed instructing. There was a Functions at Government House section, and the precedence list of who goes in to dinner in which order starts with the governor and his wife (no women governors yet) and descends through judges and politicians to city mayors.

Lillian's book was given new reprint life a year before the Royal Visit in 1954 of a young Queen Elizabeth and her husband Prince Philip. Mayors' wives bought it to bone up on how best to physically acknowledge their inferiority in the presence of majestic blow-ins.

"Learn to curtsey."

Only a handful of women have needed the advice on how to behave if they suddenly married into money (such as 19th-century stage performer Fannie Dango) or royalty (like the

The only known photo of Lillian Pyke, likely with her husband, Richard. She's probably wearing her engagement or wedding dress, about 1906.

Fannie Dango, from a family of Music Hall performing sisters that included Lydia Flopp, Adelaide Astor and skirt-dancer Letty Lind. She married a rich squatter in 1911 and travelled with silk sheets and servants thereafter.

concert violinist and model Patricia Shmith, who later became the Countess of Harwood). But thousands of Australians would be in the presence of the Royal Family on tour, and it was best to be prepared.

There was a huge boom in curtsey lessons in 1953, some run by charm school pioneer June Dally-Watkins and her former student, the Miss Australia pageant winner and model Pat Woodley.

In her 2015 book *Royal Visits to Australia*, Jane Connors reports that the curtsies at the 1954 Sydney ball were described in the snarky, republican *Bulletin* as a 'mass stagger'. Australia went doolally for the visit: the Queen waved away flies in 57 towns over 58 days; inspected an endless row of sheeps' arses in Wagga; ate Australia-shaped sandwiches with Vegemite borders at a reception in Rockhampton; and said hello to a bedridden woman in Hobart who was trundled four miles for the meeting. She, at least, didn't have to curtsey.

"Be gracious."

Many etiquette books talk about sympathy, tact and 'gracious-ness', repeating an illustrative story about an 'old lady of high rank', soothing the feelings of lowly folk by copying their gauche act of putting a hankie over their knees at the Palace, or chucking their tea leaves over their shoulder in a fancy room, or a senior soldier smoothly and silently putting an offered ice cube into a soup, instead of his drink, after a flustered young soldier did the same. It's a lovely thought.

But in practice, etiquette was used much more to keep people *out* than include them in society. A 1920s book by an anonymous 'Member of the Aristocracy' reveals a most ungracious trick snobby women employed – giving only two fingers in a limp, wet-fish handshake to 'people whom she does not care about'. The book adds that a lady may express her coolness by bowing instead of shaking hands. One can only imagine the hot bloom of mortification to be on the receiving end.

It only matters to 'correctly' pronounce Beauchamp as Beecham, Cholmondeley as Chumley (or Nigel as Niiiiiijel) so you can snub people if they don't know. It's like a secret code. One wonders if part of the code was being able not to laugh at the vision of every single governor and governor-general of Australia for years wearing a ceremonial hat that looked like a White Leghorn chook having a lie-down.

My own limp copy of Ward, Lock and Company's *Etiquette for Ladies*, 1930 edition, says, 'Sincerity, simplicity, courtesy and tact are the outstanding characteristics of good breeding and carry their own charm, alike in peer and peasant . . . throughout history there have been shrews and even vampires born in the purple (royalty or aristocracy).' Sadly, there was no more about the vampires.

'The purple' was a collective noun for the aristocracy, because when purple dye was invented, only rich people could afford it. Queen Elizabeth I de-mauved any upstarts by forbidding anyone but her rellies to wear it. Which seems *very* ungracious.

The etiquette-writing Lady Laura Troubridge (some of her work, left) was not the interesting lesbian sculptor Lady Una Troubridge (right), who hung out with dachshunds and Radclyffe Hall (not a building).

Reading a whole etiquette book creates the rare effect of being both terrified and stupefied. Intimidated by the impossibility of remembering it all – gloves and hat on, off, or a combination? How *can* I eat jelly and ice-cream with a fork? And bored to catatonia by the volume of rules listed by Lady

Troubridge's *Book of Etiquette*, designed for the sort of person whose entire life is leisure, punctuated by shooting things and going to fancy-dress parties at which you dress up as yourself.

"Don't eat."

Harold Nicolson wrote in *Good Behaviour* (1955) that his grandmother, as a girl in the Victorian era, was not allowed to eat cheese or red meat or 'rich', strongly flavoured foods. She said she had been told as a young woman that 'Brummell had broken off his engagement when he discovered his wife liked cabbage and that (Lord) Byron had mentioned it made him sick to see a woman eat'. Rich young women, he said, got maids to bring them secret food to their rooms. I hope the maids were able to get the occasional bite in, on the stairs.

According to a book of manners published under the imprimatur of The Ritz Hotel, it was not until the late 19th century, when the King's mistress and titled women ate in restaurants, that posh women were allowed to take their gloves off and eat in public.

These days, a romance novel isn't complete without a scene of a woman moaning involuntarily as she bites into something while a man finds this sexy, in full contravention of Lord Byron.

"Act feminine."

As you'll recall, 'feminine' has largely been defined as being quiet and obedient, keeping still and dressing in flounces. It's no wonder then, that a skilled woman in the act of impersonating a man (and vice versa) has always been entertaining.

Male impersonators were wildly popular in Music Hall and vaudeville acts from the 1850s to the early 20th century, partly

Performer Minnie Tittell Brune, doing manly lounging in 1893, before her wildly successful tours of Australia. Later, she became a nun. (State Library Victoria)

because the shock and transgression of them immediately seemed funny, or impressive. Part of the success was the idea that you 'couldn't tell', and part was due to songs and jokes sending up the swagger and behaviour of a certain type of man. It was a way for women to laugh at men, in their presence, something that wasn't safe almost anywhere else.

A hundred years after Music Hall's heyday, a new wave of female comedy performers emerged to send up blokey body language and behaviour. Decades before we used the shorthand terms mansplaining and manspreading, women in audiences immediately recognised the archetype: the loud, unsolicited expounding, the insulting stares, the supreme unearned confidence, the obliviousness to the thoughts and feelings of others, the taking up of extra space. All the things women have been forbidden to do for centuries. The results were uproarious.

In the 1850s, Lola Montez's satirical 'Hints To Gentlemen on the Art of Fascinating' was included at the back of her book for women called *The Arts of Beauty*: 'Always make yourself comfortable in the presence of a lady, which you may do by sitting on the outer edge of your chair and allowing your shoulders and body to fall backwards, while your legs are projecting forward into the middle of the room and thrown apart like the divergent prongs of an immense pitchfork. This in an elegant and tempting position'.

In 1981, pregnant with her third child, writer and performer Sue Ingleton performed as 'Bill Rawlings, the Pregnant Man': cocky, chippy, rocking on the balls of his feet, hand in pocket, the other one gesturing as he embarked on a monologue. Men in the audience made bets about whether the person on stage was really a woman. (A bloke claimed that he made $300 at one gig.)

I had a strong memory of Bill's up-on-his-toes physicality and country racecourse bookie-like costume. I thought I must be misremembering that he held a cigarette (he was pregnant after all) so I found Sue to ask her about the indelible character she invented more than 30 years ago. What was the key to doing him? '(As Bill) I was superior to every woman in the room. A patronising attitude, happy to be quite nice to women, too.'

Sue Ingleton as Bill Rawlings, 'The Pregnant Man', early 1980s.

'(Pregnancy) was all twice as important because it had happened to *him*,' she remembered. Bill hadn't tried to get pregnant: he talked about how he was going to hand over the kid to 'Right to Life Protestors' when it was born. He was incredulous about having to go and see a 'gynocolonist', 'It wasn't a doctor at all, it was a bloody woman!' He talked about being up on the table, legs apart in the stirrups: 'you've got nothing on . . . not once did she look at me!' Women in the audience *roared*.

Finally, I found a photo of Bill online. Bugger's holding a cigarette.

A little later in the 1980s four women in the comedy cabaret drag act The Natural Normans played cheesy male singers with stereotyped grown-up boy-band choreography, all slicked-back hair, pencil moustaches and goatees, sequined lapels, and a scrotum-first stance. Norman Denise Scott remembers, 'There was a lot of thrusting of pelvises, and willy adjusting (though I never did that), feet wide apart, swaggering, knowing nodding of heads. In many ways it was the massive ego of The Normans that made it a masculine vibe. I did nothing to hide the fact I had big boobs and long hair. We didn't change our voices to sound like blokes.'

The Natural Normans going wide in tuxedos: Lynda Gibson, Lynne McGranger and Sally-Anne Upton. Denise Scott and her bosoms were momentarily and uncharacteristically obscured. Sorry, Scotty. ABC TV's The Big Gig, c1990. (Photograph by Dr Peter Milne, courtesy M.33, Melbourne)

As with Bill Rawlings, some audience members were convinced the performers were men. They simply couldn't process the idea of women not behaving the way women were supposed to.

"Suffragettes were demure rich ladies in big, giant-arsed hats."

Well, actually (don't you hate that phrase?), the anti-alcohol Woman's Christian Temperance Union and its affiliate suffrist organisations were known to smash up bars and shout at politicians. Their polite requests, petitions and peaceful protests had been entirely ignored or ridiculed by politicians and the Press. The suffrists – activists for women's right to vote, re-dubbed with the diminutive 'suffragettes' to insult them – broke windows with toffee-cracking hammers, committed

'Tremble King Alcohol' – a Woman's Christian Temperance Union junior league badge threatens a liquid. (University of Melbourne Archives)

'Have a strawberry fizz, Dulcie, and don't mention our history of white supremacy.'
– 1950s Woman's Christian Temperance Union poster. (University of Melbourne Archives)

arson and criminal damage, threw stones at the British prime minister, were brutally force-fed and tortured during prison hunger strikes, and sexually assaulted by police and bystander men during riots.

Emily Wilding Davison, a militant member of the Women's Social and Political Union in England, disdained even the approved extreme tactics: she was killed in 1913 when she ran onto the Ascot racecourse track with a suffrist flag and was tumbled under the horses. Emily had earned a first-class degree at Oxford but was prevented from graduating because she was a woman.

The suffrist movement and the temperance activists understood that the fight for rights and change would require sacrifice and grit. What many of them didn't recognise was the ugliness of their white supremacist views. For others in the movement, it was the start of understanding that if feminism was to be real, it had to include all women.

A double-fox fur stole thinking seriously about biting someone. It has two expressions: one shocked and one mournful, c1930. (Museum of Applied Arts and Sciences)

"Get used to being in danger all the time."

A search of the Trove newspaper archives for the words girls and danger provides many matches: education; flannelette; hypnotism, 'trashy' novels, rape if they are allowed out in the evening (or stay in), 'green-sickness', hysteria, loose morals, mothers who allow small schoolgirls to wear knee-exposing dresses which would inflame men's desires and urges to attack, cocktails, men who are danglers (men who don't propose) or mashers (dandies), pin-up pictures of actors instead of missionaries, speaking to young men in public, and accidental bites from the teeth in a fox-fur stole which could be fatal.

A fox-fur stole is the entire taxidermied corpse of an animal worn as a scarf. It became emblematic of class respectability from the 1930s to the 1960s.

"You're safe at home."

It follows, of course, that a woman who does not behave by the rules – even if the rules are wrong or impossible to follow – may be punished by abuse, control and violence.

Under English law and the developed law in North America and other colonies, men were allowed to beat their wives, children, apprentices and animals, though causing death in this way was frowned upon. The required loyalty to a man by a wife or servant meant if they stole from or attacked their 'master' it carried a higher penalty than if they transgressed against a stranger.

The Women's Liberationists – 1970s feminists – set up the first 'women's refuges' (if you don't count medieval nunneries), launched publicity campaigns and lobbied for legal changes. Before then, partner abuse and violence were either jokes from

'The little girl should be taught never to be alone with a boy or a man without her mother's knowledge or consent.' – The Ladies' Handbook of Home Treatment *by Eulalia Richards*

'Women can be overwhelmed by the crisis but once it is over they start thinking, "Oh, I can't believe all these services are here for me".' – Family violence outreach worker, 21 Years of Women's Health in the West of Melbourne, 2009

vaudeville stages and early TV series, to newspaper cartoons not spoken of. 'Domestic violence' was considered a stigma on the person who was being brutalised, unacknowledged, and when injuries were too visible to be ignored, they were referred to in cryptic ways. 'I walked into a door' was a common euphemism. It was revolutionary to talk about it openly.

What is the lesson of thousands of reported assaults a day, and an average of one or more women killed each a week at the hands of her partner or ex-partner? It is this message: 'You're lucky if he is not beating you, and if he beats you, you're lucky not to be dead.' And, 'You don't matter enough for us to truly change this.'

In Australia, at least one woman a week is murdered by her partner, or ex-partner she tried to get away from, and most suburban courts have whole days each week devoted to partner abuse and violence cases and orders. Many women every day live with fear in controlling and coercive situations. We are warned that the statistical danger to us is highest when we try to leave to protect ourselves and our children. 'Why didn't she leave?' Because he threatened to kill her, her children and/or her pet, if she did. Women can literally be dead if they do, and damned if they don't.

Inquiry after inquiry has concluded that women need safer places to go, ways to force a partner to leave, better protection under the law, better police policies and conduct, and schools and public health campaigns need to concentrate on changing minds about attitudes on equality and the right of women to choose and run their own lives without fear.

Women and their allies continue to fight for better programs and support to make us safer.

A radical depiction of family violence to tell women they were not alone. More recently, women have asked that more positive images of women's survival and strength be used to illustrate articles about abuse and violence. – Colleen Jones, Witchworks Posters, Wollongong Women's Centre, early 1980s. (Museum of Applied Arts and Sciences)

"You're safe outside."

Men going home at night usually think only of how long it will take, and the best route. On every night-time journey, women calculate the risks in every car park, at every bus stop, on every street, that she will be attacked, raped or killed. Women take their high heels off, walk in the centre of the road, hold their keys pointy-side out in their hand as a weapon in car parks, and stay on the phone to a friend while walking from the bus to home. Women travelling for work don't head out after dinner to explore the neighbourhood and look at the stars on a balmy evening. Men go for a run blasting music into their ears and never look behind them. Women runners are routinely shouted at, propositioned and assaulted.

Men don't have to choose whether it's more dangerous to get out of a taxi earlier so a creepy driver doesn't know exactly where they live, or avoid the last bit of the journey on dark streets. Men are afraid if they sit in the back seat of a taxi they might be thought a snob. Women are afraid if they sit in the front seat of a taxi they'll be assaulted by the driver. Women are killed in their own home, in graveyards visiting the resting place of their relatives, in the street, on the stairs of their home, in public parks, by rivers, next to skyscrapers. We have absorbed the undeniable message: nowhere is safe. We are told

Indefensible advice from New Idea's 'agony aunt' Elizabeth Wyse to a woman whose husband hit her and her baby: 'Show your husband you love him, make home as happy as possible,' 1972. (Photo by David Johns)

Want to save my marriage

"OVER THE past few months my husband has hit me many times and hurt me far more than he knows. He works with his father and puts him first, before his family. He even hits our baby daughter for the slightest reason. I have been feeling so depressed lately I just don't know what to do. I am expecting our second child soon and love my husband in spite of everything and I do not want to make a mess of our marriage."

FIRST of all may I suggest that you do everything you can to avoid provoking this physical violence. I'm not saying you do, but simply asking, do you ever goad your husband? And are you tactful, no matter how boiling mad inside? If you still love him, I guess he also still loves you, and I don't think he really puts his father first. Don't look to him for emotional security. Look to yourself and your doctor. Have a good talk to him and ask him to help you cope in the months ahead. And show your husband you love him, make home as happy as possible, standing firm against the physical blows for yourself and your baby. Some things you can tolerate but others must not be tolerated. Remember, though, don't goad.

| 56 NEW IDEA, 29/1/72

by the police not to go out alone. We tell our daughters to stick together, not get too pissed. We're just used to making ourselves as small a target as possible, knowing that there's no such thing as us being no target at all.

Women have been warned against anything that might give her more independence: reading, exercise, education, and 'the streets'. Many girls and women were at risk at home, and Aboriginal girls and others were told they had been 'removed' or 'taken into care' due to alleged risks of the streets. Many were then routinely abused at orphanages, industrial schools, missions and 'girls' homes'.

An early Sydney newspaper, *The Australian Journal*, reported in 1848 that street-walking girls who had been written off as 'fallen' knew they could not expect help from the respectable colonists. They clubbed together to pay the rent of a girl who was sick: 'These outcasts, whose earnings were a crime, and whom men trampled upon as the worthless ones . . . were steady in their reckless kindness'.

"Women are fair game."

Women doing their job have been subject to harassment, insulting comments and stares, and were usually expected to be silent about it before the sentiments of the Time's Up campaign and #metoo movement. In 2019 the three main political parties all hit the news because of rape and assault claims about officials or former officials. In 2020, it happened again. Almost every time no action was taken, aside from somebody 'looking into it'. Women doing live news crosses have been slapped and had obscene insults yelled at them. The common link between all these women is not what they wore or whether the incidents went unpunished. The common thread is they didn't want it, they were subjected to it, and in the vast majority of cases, the perpetrators get away with it.

In 2020, many accusers spoke to journalists about how they had been sexually propositioned and touched by former High Court judge Dyson Heydon. The Chief Justice of the High Court, a woman, ordered an independent inquiry and created a pathway to report such behaviour. In reports of the accusations, it was always stated that Heydon had 'vehemently' or 'emphatically' denied it. Legal requirements aside, the women's actions are never accorded such qualifiers by journalists, such as 'bravely accused' or 'forcefully reported' but were most often termed 'claims', itself a word of diminishment, compared to 'reported', or 'said', or 'accused'.

Women in professional situations and representing their job are faced with a deluge of propositions and inappropriate comments about their bodies, appearance, and likelihood of interest in dating. Men approach women for sex on general social media using direct messages and professional job search websites. Women who meet men from dating apps have been stalked, assaulted and raped. Women have learned on public transport and at the pub to smile and say 'thanks, but I have a boyfriend' because saying just about anything else, including 'I'm not interested', can then result in a barrage of abuse or threats.

"Insults & attacks are rare."

One of the important realisations of the #metoo movement was the number of men shocked that just about every girl and woman had been subject to social media insults, public abuse, private threats, harassment, assault and rape. It's time for girls and women to share their stories, to tell friends, partners, brothers and sons: it is not a compliment to be propositioned, or complimented on your body, when you're just trying to go to work, come home safe from a night out, do your job. The new advice to women is radical compared to the silence of the past: call it out.

"Rape isn't real unless a man says so."

A 1655 English legal textbook called *The Country Justice* by Michael Dalton said that a woman could not conceive unless she consented to sex, making pregnancy a legal 'proof' that a rape had not occurred.

The rape of children is deemed by current Catholic hierarchy as not reportable to police if it is mentioned in a small cupboard in a Catholic church called a confessional.

Rape within marriage did not become a legally recognised crime in many countries until the late 20th century. It is still not a crime in many countries. Rape is not a crime in some places if a woman agrees to take monetary compensation.

In the 1600s, as noted by historian Patricia Crawford, it was believed that women would only conceive if they enjoyed the sex. This has been repurposed by some judges and religious extremists to advance the lie that women cannot be raped unless they are aroused, and can't become pregnant as the result of a rape. The attitudes are disproven, stupid and literally medieval.

"Rape is your fault."

Was she drunk? Was she out late? What was she wearing? Women have also been told – by generations of defence lawyers, and gossip, that what they wear can provoke assault and rape. A 2014 art exhibit by Jen Brockman and Dr Mary Wyandt-Hiebert called *What Were You Wearing?* displayed real outfits that were worn by women when they were attacked. They included long pants and a long-sleeved shirt, a two-piece swimsuit, a sari and a school uniform.

In 2015, after the killing of yet another woman by a stranger, a Victorian homicide squad chief advised the public, 'I suggest to people, particularly females, they shouldn't be alone in parks,' he said. 'I'm sorry to say that is the case.'

Minister for Women and Minister for Prevention of Family Violence Fiona Richardson acknowledged his intention was in the best interests of protecting women but reflected community reaction by saying it was time to focus on stopping offenders, not just asking women to stop going about their normal lives at work and exercising.

When a woman and her three children were burned to death in public by her estranged husband in Queensland in 2020, another police officer said police would keep an 'open mind' and investigate whether a 'husband was driven too far'. After an uproar, he immediately stepped aside from the investigation, saying in listening back to his comments, he was 'gutted' at their likely effect on people who had experienced family and partner violence, or deal with the consequences.

By 2019, Victoria Police Assistant Commissioner Luke Cornelius broke with tradition at a Press conference: he focused on perpetrators rather than advising women to curtail their movements. 'What is it in our community that allows some men to think that it's still OK to attack women or take from women what they want? Violence against women is

'The danger of short dresses . . . It is no wonder that little girls are so often in danger of being assaulted . . . It should cover the knees' – Adelaide Chronicle article, 1924. A response to the editor agreed: 'The beauty of face and form, coupled with helplessness and submission through fear, is what makes a child the prey of the passions of men.'

absolutely about men's behaviour . . . attitudes against women needed to change.'

In Australia, campaigns focus on not saying the names of perpetrators and using the names of women who have been killed. Jane Gilmore (@janetribune) uses Twitter to fix the thoughtless, anti-woman and anti-children headlines and reports of violence and rape with the hashtag #fixedit. 'Man had affair with student', for example, would become 'Man exploited and raped child'.

"'Girl' is an insult."

Insults used against men that accuse them of being womanly include, effeminate, sissy (originally 'sister'), doing something 'like a girl' or behaving 'like an old woman'. Though the etymology is complicated, slang words for women's genitals and coward, 'pussy', are the same.

Compliments never directed at men include: 'You're not just a pretty face', 'Not bad for a woman' and 'You don't throw like a girl'. There's no female equivalent of uxorious – meaning overly fond of one's wife, and no female version of overlord.

Slut was originally a name for a lowly female servant, and then it came to mean untidy and

I say, Sylvia's got the revolver again. British boarding schoolgirls in scrapes were the business of 'girls' own adventure' books for teens soon after World War II, Cole's Great Girls' Book, *1950. (National Library of Australia)*

50

slatternly. 'Broad' was originally used in America to mean prostitute, as in abroad and about on the streets, and then came to be a disrespectful word for women (and probably led to the Olympic broad jump becoming the long jump). It's such an old term now, it has lost much of its sting and has been reclaimed on our behalf, as has 'bitch', the name of a feminist media site and magazine.

Perhaps one of the most telling woman-only insults is, 'She's let herself go.' She's given up dressing to please others. She can't be bothered putting make-up on. She's no longer tightly wound and stitched in. She's not running her life according to the rules which don't apply to men. She's free.

Of course, if she *hasn't* let herself go, she's terribly vain and a figure of pity – mutton dressed as lamb. Wouldn't want you to think we nearly got away with something there.

'It's unladylike to show anger.' Well, if you can read this chapter and not feel righteous rage, you're not a lady – you're unconscious, sister.

INSULTS TO WOMEN BINGO CARD

Here are some words used specifically to insult, silence, classify or intimidate women over a few hundred years. Some have been reclaimed or worn as a badge of honour.

Airhead	Blowsy	Dollymop
Amazon	Bluestocking	Dowdy
Baby mama	Bossy	Doxy
Babylonian whore	Brazen	Dumb blonde
Bag	Breeder	Dragonlady
Baggage	Broad	Driggle-Draggle
Ball and chain	Bubbly	Fag-hag
Ballbreaker	Butch	Fallen
Banshee	Butterbody	Feisty
Barbie	Butterface	Female Humanoid
Barren	Cat	Organism (FHO)
Battle-axe	Chick	Females
Bit of muslin	Chippy	Feminazi
Bit of skirt	Chit	Femoid
Bit on the side	Cock tease	Filly
Bimbo	Cow	Fishwife
Bint	Cougar	Frigid
Bird	Crone	Frowzy
Bitch	Cunt	Frump
Blower	Daddy's girl	Fustilugs

Girl Friday
Girly
Gold digger
Gorgon
Gossip
Hag
Hairy-legged
Handmaiden
Harlot
Harpy
Harridan
Hellcat
Housewife
Hoyden
Hussy
Hysteric
Let herself go
Loose
Madam
Manly
Mannish
Man's woman
Mare
Matron
Mean girl
MILF
Minger

Missish
Mistress
Moll
Mouthy
Mrs Grundy
Mumsy
Muse
Mutton
Nag
No lady
Old bag
Old bat
Old bitty
Old chook
Old maid
Opinionated
Outspoken
Pert
Prawn

JAMES M. CAIN
Shameless
Original Title: The Root of His Evil
By the author of
"THE POSTMAN ALWAYS RINGS TWICE"
AVON BOOK · THIRTY FIVE CENTS

Prostitute
Queen bee
Rantipoll
Resting bitchface
Rumple
Sassy
Saucebox
Scarlet woman
Scold
Screaming sister
Sex kitten
Sheila
Shrew
Shrill
Skank
Slag
Slapper
Slattern
Sloven
Slut
Soccer mum
Spinster
Spitfire
Stacy
Strident
Strumpet
Succubus

Sugartits
Tart
Tattler
Temptress
Termagent
Thot
Tiger mum
Tomboy
Town bike
Tramp
Trollop
Varmity woman
Virago
Vivacious
Vixen
WAGs (Wives and
Girlfriends)
Wallflower
Wayward
Wench
Whore
Wifey
Wild woman
Witch
Woman
Women's libbers
Yummy Mummy

You will not BELIEVE where they want you to put this.
(*From* The Wife's Guide and Friend *medical catalogue, 1898, National Library of Australia*)

2

YOUR HEALTH IS HYSTERICAL

AS YOU WELL KNOW, it is a woman's duty to be healthy so that they can have more children, or be more attractive. We have been helped in our noble cause by doctors who burned vapours near our vulva to try to herd the uterus around the body, and more recently by models selling us 'wellness elixirs' that look and taste like grass clippings, and may have the same effect on your health as grass clippings, though are almost certainly not actually grass clippings, shout-out to the publisher's lawyer.

Women have traditionally been held responsible for the health of the family, even while being told that garlic in a sock might stop a cold (it doesn't). We've been told that our own health problems were a) imaginary or b) caused by our defective bodies, which are a factory-reject version of men's bodies.

There have been tremendous gains. Vaccinations. Antibiotics. Anaesthetic that doesn't accidentally kill people half the time. Obstetric knowledge. Women who would previously have been diagnosed with, say, hysteria or a 'wandering womb' are now far more likely to be diagnosed with hysteria *and* endometriosis.

When a new medication is invented and peer-reviewed and repeatable studies have cleared it, medical advice changes straight away. But what if the medication isn't properly tested on women? What if there's a cheaper, non-medical remedy that has as much of an effect? What if an implant device is marketed heavily to women's doctors, even while evidence shows that it causes damage?

Because so much information to women is handed down by their grandmothers and mothers, and swapped in comments online, often it takes much longer to change. People still advise homeopathic 'remedies' though not riding a penny farthing, despite both being from the same era. Penny farthings, given the right conditions, actually work, whereas homeopathy can't. (There are other dangers. Wait till you hear about getting bicycle face.)

"Your body is weird."

A lot of women's bodies don't behave themselves. Without medical help, millions of women will have period disorders, pain and gynaecological cancers, they'll die in childbirth or soon after from infections and injuries.

The reason for this, said medical men and philosophers for centuries, was not that doctors didn't know what to do about it. No, it was because women's bodies are just weird and inferior. Only men were smart and logical enough to understand science and reason, it was said, which was a bit rich since the science was often bonkers opinion and the 'reason' of 'learned philosophers' fell squarely under the heading of 'stuff I made up and wrote down while somebody else was doing my washing'.

The underlying tenets of medicine boiled down to this: women are naturally weak and unhealthy. This was later modified to include: okay, we need somebody to do all the heavy housework so let's say non-white women are much stronger, also, erk, stuff is coming out of vaginas, what IS that, probably a disease. Thank you, matron, I *shall* take a small sherry.

"Your uterus wanders around."

Women were told for centuries that their womb wanders around their body causing personality changes and physical ailments. Plato, the ludicrous clod, said the uterus was kind of an animal, that pootled about different parts of your body, which could cause suffocation. The 'cure' was usually said to be getting married, and/or pregnancy. The wandering womb theories are now such a well-known a blunder that it's a shorthand cliché for medical cluelessness and misogyny.

Hippocrates, a total fruitcake, wrote in 400 BC that for 'dislocation of the womb' a woman should eat as much garlic as she could, have her womb 'fumigated' – phoofing foul-smelling herbal vapours up her vagina (I'm guessing patchouli) to tell the uterus to get away from the liver – and use perfumed pessaries. If she got her period she should stop the pessaries. If she didn't, she had to 'drink four cantharid beetles with their legs, wings and heads removed, four dark peony seeds, cuttlefish eggs, and a little parsley seed in wine.' While other doctors said the womb was like a small animal wandering off, Hippocrates said it was because the womb had gone looking for semen, which is *quite* enough from him.

Anatomists doing dissections from the 1400s and 1500s realised it was physically impossible for a uterus to saunter off and lodge in your sternum, or elbow, because it's held in place by ligaments and other organs and *hasn't got any legs*. Never mind, said some doctors for centuries afterwards, the wandering womb theory seems right, let's just keep it anyway.

Early doctors blamed the uterus-on-the-lam for anaemia, 'hysteria', heavy periods, no periods, the lot. They were a lot like Gwyneth Paltrow, in their attraction to the steamed-vagina idea.

Prolapsus Pessaries
For Affording Support in Cases of Prolapsus
(Falling of the Womb).

Napier Stem Pessary.

A belt with a cup attachment worn in the vagina to hold back a uterine prolapse not caused by ski-jumping. From The Wife's Guide and Friend *catalogue, 1898. (National Library of Australia)*

Back then, some put animal or human poo in the vagina, or applied a red-hot poker to the cervix and leeches to the vulva to entice the uterus back into its proper position.

Without any evidence, by 1900, doctors were still saying that sport, exercise or dancing could cause a uterus to fall out. The true medical condition of prolapse – some of the uterus pushing its way down into the vaginal space – is associated with a history of pregnancy and childbirth, and post-menopausal hormonal changes, which can weaken pelvic floor muscles and ligaments. Doctors didn't tell women they could prevent prolapse by avoiding pregnancy.

The president of the International Ski Federation explained in 2005 that women were banned from competing because their 'uterus might burst upon landing'. He then explained that women weren't very good at ski-jumping. The first time women ski jumpers were allowed to compete in the Olympics was 2014. Men started in 1924 because they were much less bursty.

"You're hysterical."

Hysterical is still an insult almost exclusively thrown at women. The words hysteria and uterus both come from the Greek language. For hundreds of years until the mid-20th century, it was an official medical diagnosis treated with torturous, useless 'cures' and procedures.

Symptoms attributed to hysteria included sexual desire, numbness, evidence of demonic possession, melancholy, nerves, anxiety, mania, imagination and psychosis. Other hysterical manifestations are now recognised as tetanus, seizures, anaemia, and being furious.

The 1755 dictionary by Samuel Johnson defined 'hystericks' as 'fits of women, supposed to be to proceed from disorders of the womb', and quoted a doctor who thought uteruses farted: 'Many hysterical women are sensible of wind passing from the womb'.

HYSTERIA is a disease due to a deranged state of the nervous system, affecting women in easy circumstances and torpid habits. It differs from Epilepsy, there being no insensibility, the patient falling not heedlessly but in some comfortable place. Frequently the disease exists only in the mind of the patient. Occasionally terrible pain is complained of. The shin bones are supposed to be diseased, but on examination are found to be healthy and well. The best remedies are plenty of fresh air, good food, exercise, and a dose of Sal Volatile or Red Lavender during a fit.

This disease is much more frequent in single than married ladies. The bowels and menstrual functions should be carefully attended to and a cold or tepid bath taken every morning.

Faulding's Quinine and Iron Tonic may be given to brace up the system and improve the general health.

A definition in Faulding's Medical Dictionary, *1891. Apologies for the shadow from my phone camera, I think you'll find it was caused by my uterus. (National Library of Australia)*

Women diagnosed with hysteria in the 19th and early 20th century were told to submit to experimental, damaging, dangerous non-consensual surgeries: or they were not even asked for consent. Men with the same manic or florid mental symptoms were not diagnosed with hysteria, nor were testicles considered a cause.

Some women with mental illnesses were subjected to then-risky operations, including hysterectomies (the removal of the womb), oophorectomies (ovary removal) and clitoro-dectomies (yes). It took months for them to recover, if they didn't die of infection: and many did. As with the first decades of caesarean sections, and the cauterisation of cervixes: for the first few decades or even hundreds of years when they were performed, all women died, then most women died, then some women died. What no operations ever did was cure anyone of 'hysteria'.

Famous ye olde 20th-century psychologist, faffer and cigar-botherer, Dr Freud made up his own theories about hysteria, which he said was variously caused by past trauma, being jealous of penises, not enjoying sex enough and not being married enough.

'Whatever a superior group has will be used to justify its superiority, and whatever an inferior group has will be used to justify its plight.'
– Gloria Steinem, 1983

Eventually, 'hysterical' became an insult used to berate women who were angry or trying to be heard. You can still hear it on the odd current affairs panel show or when a man in parliament is trying to make a woman shut up.

"You're a walking reproductive health system."

Okay, sidebar: I don't like the phrases reproductive system or reproductive health because not every woman wants to use their organs to reproduce, or is able to, even if she does want to – and 'reproduce' is a way-weird word for having children, as if we were little clone-drones popping out versions of ourselves. So, saying 'reproductive organs' sounds a bit presumptuous.

As a separate issue this is as good a place as any to acknowledge that trans women (hello, and welcome!) do not have uteruses, and neither do some other women, due to medical quirkery. Calling uteruses, ovaries and the rest of the business 'women's organs' sounds like gender-based giant churchy keyboard instruments (pause for dramatic chord). Well, anyway, I'm going to try to avoid saying 'reproductive', but we're still visiting Uterus Land for a while, so pop the kettle on again.

"Your vagina is revolting."

Disenchanting words such as discharge and leucorrhoea have been used by doctors to describe the vagina's lubrications, which follow hormonal cycle variations and protect us from infection.

The vagina is a self-saucing pudding that never needs inside-cleaning or douchery. There's an infection that causes a different or smelly discharge, or you have an inelegantly named 'bacterial overgrowth' that can be caused by a fall in oestrogen levels after menopause: be off with ye to a doctor for medication.

I can't tell you how many girls are relieved to read in my *Girl Stuff* books that the 'white stuff' which can dry yellowy on their knickers is Totally Normal. Very few parents ever mention it in 'the period talk' or pass on info about what else vaginas get up to in the rest of a month.

From the late 1800s until the late 1920s, the *Wife's Guide and Friend*, and many other medical textbooks and home-health advice books, told women it was a disease and to squirt or pump water into their vaginas every day, or after a period. The usual cold (or hot) (or tepid) baths and poultices were also prescribed.

Normal vaginal fluid was said to be a symptom or cause of disease, including hysteria, 'uterine derangements', breathing problems and exhaustion. In the 1930s, Dr Thomas Faulker's perfectly frightful book for married women said it was caused by pinworms in the vagina, or by sexual excitement, corsets, sitting on cold ground, and abortion.

The mind boggles at how many girls were plagued with silent shame and worry about something normal that happens to everybody.

Companies selling 'panty pads' and 'feminine hygiene products' or insertable cleaning objects with slogans like 'freshness' play on fears that vaginas smell bad. Vaginal 'hygiene' products are douches and perfume sprays: they don't do anything useful and are a common cause of itches, rashes and allergic reactions on vulvas and in vaginas. Especially worrying are the squirters and douche products advertised and promoted for use after birth: they're a major infection risk until the cervix completely closes after birth, which can take about 6 weeks.

There is nothing that says exploito-misogyno-capitalism quite like selling women a cosmetic product that doesn't work, isn't needed, and may be harmful, for a part of their body that's invisible. I thought exfoliating 'butt-masks' took the biscuit, failing to anticipate one entrepreneur's 'anti-wrinkle' product for the *inside of the vagina*.

"Ancient wisdom is always best."

Herbal remedies and prayers – aka potions and spells – were women's first tools in the battle for their own and their family's health. Until relatively recent hygiene practices, vaccines and antibiotics and medical research, survival was largely down to luck. Women were the family or village apothecaries and midwives, who passed on knowledge. Without a written culture, Indigenous and colonial cultures across the world used 'word of mouth', song, rhyme, even stories and dance – now known to be the most efficient routes of knowledge that activate the right areas of the brain for memory.

Remedies were invented for everything from battle wounds to mental health issues, including 'melancholy water' and 'hysterick water'. Potions became cure-all 19th-century tonics and pills, and later morphed into the wholesale 20th-century prescriptions of anti-depressants, alcohol and amphetamines sold to women.

'Dalby's carminative (opium), hot baths and emetics to cause vomiting, doses of mercury and chalk.' – 'Remedies' used by my great-great-grandparents Horace and Sarah when their babies had croup or other illnesses, 1880s

Women used clay from the beach or a desert soak to stop blood flow from a wound, a senior midwife may have been able to 'turn' a baby in breech position before birth, a clove in a tooth-hole might check mild pain. They did their best, and, poor loves, their best was often terrible.

Almost every single remedy recipe or suggested treatment in housekeeping and home-medical books produced up until about the 1970s is useless, dangerous or damaging. Doctors wrestled the paying side of medicine from midwives and town herbalists and those who knew their barks and leaves, but their treatments were no more useful and often more dangerous, being more invasive and a lot more cutty. Medicines soon contained opium and distilled poisons such as mercury and arsenic.

Until relatively recently, in every society, sick people were treated at home by their mothers or wives, unless a doctor could be afforded to come to the house. Women were advised on how to do first aid for injuries, quarantine and treatments for infectious diseases. The 1950s *Household Encyclopaedia* edited by W. H. Steer says scalds should be covered with Vaseline or powdered starch and boric acid, and suggests puncturing blisters and giving the patient a drink of strong spirits. All wrong. Women were blamed for their children getting infectious diseases: a 'chill' caused shingles, they were scolded, even after its connection to chickenpox virus was discovered.

Medieval recipes, like modern DIY ones, rely on common ingredients for ordinary people, and flash-sounding ones for rich people. The reason garlic has been recommended for everything from whooping cough to vaginal thrush is because it's easy to get hold of, not because it works.

How's this for a medical recipe book title from the early 1600s? *The English Hus-wife Containing the Inward and Outward Virtues Which Ought To Be In A Complete Woman; As Her Skill In Physike, Cookery, Banqueting-Stuffe, Distillation, Perfumes, Wooll, Hemp, Flax, Dayries, Brewing, Baking, And All Other Things Belonging To An Houshauld* by Gervase Markham. (The only thing bigger than a medieval dude's book title was his ego.)

He told women to make medicines from 'the urine of a man child', 'new milk of a red cow', saffron (yellow) for jaundice (because 'like cures like', remember the homeopathy principle), and a specific flower for eye problems. Online forums still recommend tinctures of this plant for eye problems, unaware it was originally used only because each flower has a black spot in the middle that reminded people of the pupil of the eye.

Women were the first chemists, distilling and experimenting and passing on their research in recipes. Richer ones had servants to collect and buy things, and a kitchen where they could boil stuff up – 'fire burn and cauldron bubble', as *Macbeth*'s witches had it, busying themselves with fillet of a fenny snake and eye of newt. Which sounds as much like a recipe given to women of the day for a cough than it does for a curse.

Lucy Moore's wonderful book *Lady Fanshawe's Receipt Book* is all about Lady F's handwritten scrapbook of remedy and cooking recipes from the 1600s England. One of Lady Fanshawe's pals was the über-bonkers Sir Kenelm Digby, whose cure for wounds called for the weapon which caused it (say, a sword) to be treated with a poultice of various herbs, including moss from the skull of an unburied man, and perhaps some animal poo. The wound on the person was left alone. Sir Ken also explained that barnacles grew up to be seabirds and flew away. Genius.

Lady Fanshawe copied out his version of a cure-all medicine called Gascoigne powder, which required pulverised pearls, herbs, crab claws and bits of viper. The Countess of Kent, Elizabeth Grey, has one to cure 'French pox, Small Pox, Measles, Plague, Pestilence, malignant or scarlet fevers' and 'Melancholy' in her book of receipts which was printed in 1664, almost

15 years after her death as a 'manuall' of 'Rare Secrets in Physick and Chyrurgery'. It also had a recipe for lollies.

"Medical experts are men."

Women herbalists were forbidden to attend medical school, even if their family had the money to afford tuition. The doctors were killers spreading fatal post-birth infections by using unwashed hands between childbirth patients, and using poo in poultices and pessaries. The go-to treatments were mostly expulsive ones: blood-letting, causing diarrhoea or vomiting. Often, they kept doing this (sometimes simultaneously) until the patient miraculously came good or mercifully died.

Hundreds of years ago, surgeons were in the same union guilds as barbers and others who used scissors and shears for their work. Doctors took control away from midwives for attending to pregnant women and births with the help of lawmakers of their own class, and churches (which wanted more souls for the Church and suspected midwives of helping with terminations or registering babies with rival religions).

Lady Fanshawe's book had her mother's recipe to treat a bruise with wine and herbs. The tuberculosis medicine instructions underneath have been crossed out; perhaps it didn't work.
(Wellcome Library)

The assumption is baked into so many of us that doctors are men and women are nurses, that men should be in charge and women assistants. Women doctors and surgeons have run social media photo campaigns trying to combat the assumptions with the hashtag #WhataDoctorLooksLike.

Many medical terms that reflect the patriarchy are now being questioned or phased out. Do not, on any account, start me on marketing terms for the made-up

names of cosmetic surgery procedures that exploit the fears and repression of women: 'breast enhancement', 'hymen repair', 'vaginal rejuvenation' and the 'husband stitch'.

Other objectionable medical terms include the notion of 'non-compliant' patients, and conditions with names such as 'incompetent cervix' and 'failure to progress' in labour.

Also, doctors are now agreeing to use newer names for the parts of women that male doctors had rudely named after themselves: The Pouch of Douglas (recto vaginal space, though I *will* keep suggesting The Clutch Purse of Mavis), and Fallopian tubes (uterine tubes). Same goes for the different labour forceps named after men and the Pap 'smear' test (cervical screening test).

The Pap test was named for Dr Georgios Papanicolaou, which obscures the contributions of two women essential to cervical cancer research. Henrietta Lacks was an African-American cervical cancer patient in 1951 whose cells were taken and used without her permission as the basis of an 'immortal' cultured cell line used for biomedical research. Dr Papanicolaou's wife, Adromachi – Mary – subjected herself to daily vaginal and cervix swabbing *for 21 years* as part of 'his' research.

Technicians analyse early Pap tests at Melbourne's Royal Women's Hospital, 1959. From the top: Betty East, Ellen Rothbart, Pat Archer and Sandra Searle. (National Library of Australia)

Before the revolutionary HPV (Human Papillomavirus) vaccination, screening programs using Pap smear tests were the frontline in preventing the progression of cervical cancers, letting women know when they needed treatment and reducing death rate by 80 per cent. In countries where there is no organised screening service or routine HPV vaccination, the death rate of women from cervical cancer is still high.

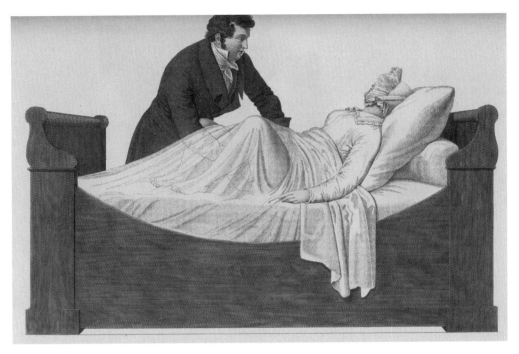

Well done for keeping your bonnet on, madam. In some parts of the world, male doctors are still not allowed to examine a woman. (Maygrier's obstetrics textbook, 1822.)

"Your doctor is in charge of you."

My nanna's generation used the startling phrase 'I'm under a doctor', to mean consulting a doctor and being told what to do. Doctors were seen as a kind of god, or all-seeing medical boss. It was considered such a big deal to get a second opinion in case it offended a doctor that the late 1920s edition of *Ward Locke's Etiquette for Ladies* provided delicately worded template letters to send to a doctor to let him know (it was almost always a him).

Women have felt dismissed and belittled by doctors for years. My mother, along with millions of other women around the world, was told by an obstetrician that her 'morning sickness' – pregnancy nausea – was her imagination; others were told it showed they unconsciously didn't want to be pregnant.

Do not hesitate to obtain skilled medical advice when in doubt regarding your health. Life and health are priceless treasures.

A patient in a squashed hat gives a well-deserved stink-eye to the medical patriarchy, The Ladies' Handbook of Home Treatment *by Eulalia Richards, 1956 edition.*

Now, we know for sure that it's related to levels of specific hormones in pregnancy.

Many women have learned not to trust doctors, due to personal philosophy, unconscionable behaviour from some pharmacological companies and a history of misogyny, racism and experimentation in the medical industry, and the dismissal of women's pain from individual doctors. (But apart from that they've been great.) New attitudes, and a welcome tsunami of women doctors joining the ranks, are changing things.

"Pick a side: science v. women's knowledge."

Sick of patronising doctors, 1970s-styled feminists schooled in books like *Our Bodies, Ourselves* by the Boston Women's Health Book Collective rejected male-dominated medicine and converted to hard-boiled 'natural' medicine. More recently, veteran collective members have taken the side of 'new age' and folk remedies against evidence-based science advocated by a new wave of women doctors and gynaecologists. There's no evidence that putting yoghurt in your vagina relieves thrush symptoms or that drinking cranberry juice for urinary tract infections is better than a placebo. Sadly, although the 'stand up for yourself and question everything' advice is still useful, putting garlic in your vagina isn't.

A history of women's health services in the west of Melbourne by Esther Singer in 2009 recalled decades of explaining to women they had a right to take control of and responsibility for their own health, to 'find doctors who listen', to know what to ask for, and to understand they had the right to say no.

"Your pain doesn't matter."

In the same way that doctors used to believe babies could not feel pain and did not need anaesthetic, women have been routinely advised that they are not feeling pain, they are imagining it, and assumed to need less painkillers than men. On average, women wait longer in hospital for pain relief than men, and are far less likely to be prescribed it in the same medical circumstances. Women's pain indicating a heart attack is far less diagnosed than men's. A reputable US study found women are seven times more likely to be discharged while suffering a heart attack because male symptoms are the standard to check for.

At the time of writing, peak organisations that list heart attack symptoms have different advice. An Australian one says the third 'key takeaway' is that women's heart attack symptoms can be breathlessness, nausea, and arm and jaw pain – with or without any experience of chest or heart pain. A US site adds that symptoms for women can include fatigue, cold sweats, as well as neck, back and stomach pain.

Many newer books by women have come out on the subject of their own pain and experiences with the medical profession, and how it accords with the way women have historically been treated by doctors. We are way behind on research into endometriosis, and auto-immune conditions, and multiple sclerosis, for example, because they were all dismissed as women's 'psychosomatic' or imagined illnesses.

I remember when I found out why my pain was called 'idiopathic', which sounded scary. It just means they don't know what causes it. (It was endometriosis.)

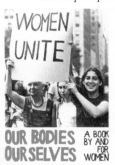

Philosophies in Our Bodies, Ourselves *still underpin some DIY feminist healthcare principles.*

'The Physicians' Health Study, which had recently concluded that taking a daily aspirin may reduce the risk of heart disease? Conducted on 22,071 men and zero women.' – Doing Harm: The Truth About How Bad Medicine and Lazy Science Leave Women Dismissed, Misdiagnosed and Sick by Maya Dusenbery, 2017

"Your research data isn't important."

Caroline Criado Perez first published her engaging, enraging book *Invisible Women: Exposing Data Bias in a World Designed for Men* in 2019. She asks why women experts are so often not quoted or interviewed, how can it be that everyday products such as medicines and seatbelts and Personal Protective Equipment (PPE) in hospitals are not only untested on women but can be extra dangerous for them. The default design is to suit men, from available medicines and the height of toilets to public transport design, standard office heating and working hours.

"If you're sick, it's your fault."

Women have always been told that their illnesses and troubles are self-inflicted. First, it was God's punishment for lasciviousness, and then more recently, it's the disproven 'wellness' idea that stress can cause cancer.

In the 1980s 'new age' writer Louise Hay claimed her cervical cancer was caused by her childhood sexual assault, and that she cured herself using her thoughts. Hay listed illnesses and their causes: pimples are caused by dislike of self; breast cancer by 'over-mothering' and being overbearing; ankle injuries happen due to 'inflexibility and guilt' and glaucoma is caused by 'stony unforgiveness'. Influencer Belle Gibson fraudulently claimed in 2014 that her cancer was caused by a vaccine and cured by food.

"One health book tells you everything."

From the late 19th century, countless thousands of books were published with instructions on housework and medical treatment. DIY home management books told in one volume how to make madeira cake, what to feed your chooks and the right deadly poisons to use when fumigating a sick person's room.

Household manuals were reprinted without much updating for decades, even after an author's death. *Mrs Beeton's Book of Household Management* (1861) was still recommending medieval-era treatments nearly 100 years later, including blood-letting.

Aside from the immortal exhortations to exercise and eat lots of vegetables and plain food (i.e. no foreign muck), most of the health advice was fairly bonkity. The new version of a health compendium is social media and online search engines. It's a boon if you need to find other people diagnosed with a rare condition, or to learn about your own health. But it can be an algorithm-led echo chamber of curated advice, dominated by anti-vaccination extremists or pharmaceutical company advertising, or ill-informed opinion. Just like the old days.

One such enduring classic, in print for 60 years until the mid-1960s, was the *Ladies' Handbook of Home Treatment* by the euphonious Dr Eulalia S. Richards.

After her divorce in the 1920s, she alone published her health manual for women. Subsequent editions seemed much more empathetic to the exhaustion of multiple childbirths. But there are few changes between the 1905 and 1965 editions. The multiple bees in Eulalia's bonnet became manifest: a continuing fondness for hot and cold compress treatments and white supremacy, a disdain for liquor and the children of alcoholics, and a baroque horror of masturbation.

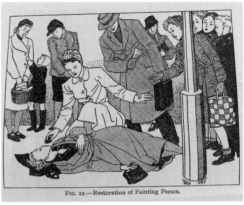

FIG. 22.—Restoration of Fainting Person.

'Stand back, I'm a fully-trained housewife with a vial of perfumed ammonia in my handbag'. (The Household Doctor *by S. King Hutton, c1938. National Library of Australia)*

A stoic with her feet into a kerosene tin of cold water, Ladies' Handbook of Home Treatment, *1912.*

By 1956 she had shuffled the section on sexually transmitted diseases further down the contents list, as antibiotics had made a dent in the terrible rates of damage due to syphilis and gonorrhea, including miscarriage and blind children. By the 1960s, an editor finally put their red pencil through her disapproval of too-tight corsets.

My still-sturdy 1912 copy of Eulalia's book is a thunking 6.5-cm thick with 1038 pages, and still has its pamphlet with 'Directions for Emergency Confinement' (childbirth) snugly tucked into an envelope slot at the back. Other editions were slimmed down to about 800 pages.

Unique for its time, the book showed detailed anatomical diagrams *of* women, *for* women, complete with pubic hair. It covered illnesses and problems in all parts of the body, including the vulva and vagina, womb, ovaries and related tubes, fertility and menopause. Readers were advised to get 'five or six feet of rubber tubing' and some Vaseline for douches and enemas. I wouldn't if I were you.

"One medicine cures everything."

Many of the tonics and pills sold to women in the 19th and 20th century were marketed as a cure for everything. Period pains, menstrual disorders, the effects of too much childbirth, exhaustion from 12- to 14-hour jobs at shops and factories, and life generally seeming awful. The cure-alls were recommended in pharmacies, from the Music Hall stage, Press and magazine ads and sponsored household encyclopaedias.

Long before the benzodrines and barbiturates of the 1950s and '60s, women mired in dull lives and drudgery were fobbed off with elixirs containing varying levels of narcotics and alcohol.

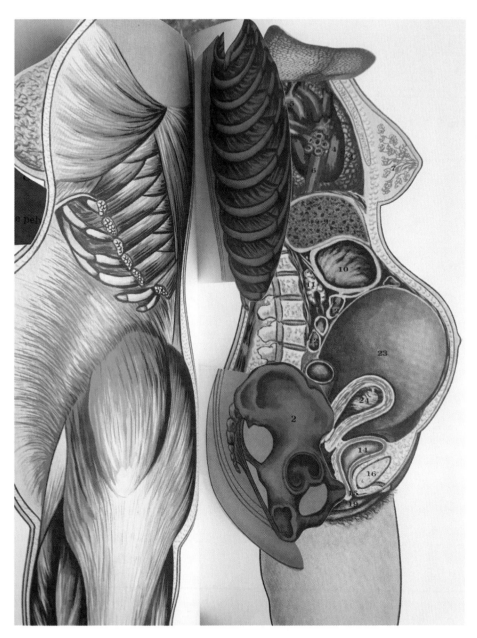

Anatomy diagram, complete with rare inclusion of pubic hair, from Eulalia's 1912 edition.

The 1880s book *Australian Housewives Manual, Comfortable Cookery etc. etc. etc.* (I do like the idea of putting three etceteras in your book title) was full of ads for them.

You could write away to Mr Terry for mesmerism lessons and tonics and herbal preparations for tired, listless women.

Marketing focused on testimonials, and their supposed use by royalty and celebrities of the day. Many medicines were flavoured to taste bitter, because if it tasted bad it must work. Others had memorable alliterative names such as bile beans and pink pills.

'Mrs Johnson's soothing syrup' contained chloroform and salt. Goulard's Solution included poisonous lead as well as mercury. The British Medical Association released an exposé in 1909 called *Secret Remedies: What They Cost and What They Contain*, which revealed most potions sold for several shillings cost less than a penny to make.

The ingredients of several 'cancer cures' and various 'reducing' lotions and tablets for dieters were mainly filler, like chalk, and flavouring. Pink Pills for Pale People contained iron sulphate, potassium carbonate salts, magnesia, liquorice, and sugar. Beecham's Pills were a mix of ginger, bitter aloes, and . . . soap. 'Cures' for alcoholism, sold under names such as Dispocure, Antidipso and The Teetolia Treatment, were usually a powdered sedative that, slipped into a drink, would at least put a raging husband to sleep.

"Have a cup of tea, a Bex & a good lie down."

When a politician told journalists in 2011 to 'have a cup of tea, a Bex and a long lie down', younger listeners were baffled. They didn't realise that almost everyone once knew this phrase, and it was used to advertise an all-pervasive product that killed women.

For more than 30 years Bex was advertised with testimonials: allegedly 'ordinary' people recommending it for headaches and 'nerve pain'. Like its rival 'Vincent's', it usually came as a 'headache powder', each individual dose wrapped in a folded piece of paper. It was also known as 'APC' – it combined aspirin, phenacetin and caffeine, each dose equal to a strong coffee. It was wildly addictive: women got withdrawal headaches when they wore off, so took another one, and so on, sometimes 30–40 doses every day. (That's not a misprint.)

Professor Priscilla Kincaid-Smith, a pathologist, medical science researcher and later a kidney specialist, confirmed in the 1960s that phenacetin was causing kidney damage and cancer, mostly in women. With the fresh eye of a newly arrived immigrant in the late 1950s, she was shocked by women's supermarket trolleys stacked high with boxes of Bex. Despite her qualifications, the professor was initially prevented from researching at a hospital or university because she was a married woman and supposed to be 'at home'.

Eventually she helped organise her specialist colleagues, who finally forced a ban in 1970. There was a sharp drop in kidney damage and cancer afterwards. On a plane in a first-class seat once, she overheard industry executives cursing her and planning to market Bex under another name in Malaysia instead.

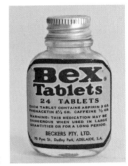

Bex, without the lie down. The year is unknown but given it contains the warning, probably the '60s or '70s.

'You can take Bex with perfect confidence because Bex contains no dangerous drugs.' – Bex newspaper ad, 1940s

'Although a lot of very talented women did medicine in Melbourne and topped their classes, all the women gave up medicine when they became married – often to less capable men – and the men continued to practise.' – Professor Kincaid-Smith, 1998 interview, Australian Academy of Science

"Hot & cold baths are medicine."

Like all clever influencers Mrs Caroline Smedley prescribed her product to women in good health as well as sick ones. My 1880s

THE WET PACK OR ENVELOPE

A patient undergoes a wet wrap ordeal in the dread chill of North England, Mrs Smedley's Ladies Manual of Practical Hydropathy, *c1880s.*

'Sea bathing or cold plunge baths, not unfrequently (sic) causes ovarian tumour or ovarian dropsy and is always hazardous to females especially, at all times and at all ages.' – Mrs Smedley's Ladies Manual of Practical Hydropathy for Female Diseases by Caroline Smedley, 1861

copy of *Mrs Smedley's Ladies Manual* prescribes a bewildering list of more than 200 elaborate variations of unpleasant fomentations of mustard and 'chillie paste', and baths and hosings for delirium tremens, baby's teething pain, hysteria, smallpox and having a period. Fatally, she advised women to use bread poultices and baths instead of going to see a doctor for breast tumours.

She recommended 200 baths of varying temperature and placement (some baths were just for one leg or arm). Hot and cold bath treatments were mainly based on the idea of doing things to the blood flow and temperature, and the accompanying douches and enemas were about expelling things from the body (going back to ideas of demons and impurities). Today, this has morphed into useless dieting 'de-toxes', 'cleanses' and the unsurprisingly less popular 'colonic irrigation'.

"To achieve 'wellness', you have to buy stuff."

'Wellness' was originally the idea of living to prevent illness, rather than just going to the doctor when illness or injury lobbed into your life. It started in the 1800s and went by different names, until by the early 21st century it had become a billion-dollar industry.

Wellness folk and celebrity spokesfaffers tell you everything has to be chemical free, although we all drink dihydrogen monoxide every day because that's another name for water, which is made of chemicals. And we all have small amounts of heavy metals in our bodies, and if we didn't, we'd be dead.

'Babies are born pre-polluted' warn the worry-mongers at the online store Goop, telling us to buy their organic products.

Well, yeah, babies are born with a huge bacterial load: that's how they get their immune systems working to help them stay alive.

A triple-shot immunisation that stimulates a baby's natural response to protect against measles, mumps and rubella is less of a challenge to a baby's immune system than it would get from playing with a dog or licking the floor.

In her 2005 book *The Wellness Zone, Your Guide to Optimal Health, Including Herbal Medicines and Ageless Remedies*, Dominique Finney lays out some of the key tenets of the genre. 'Wellness' means you feel healthier, and better able to deal with your illness or pain. The first and key advice is that you should choose an alternative to medical help. And of course, 'Let your food be your medicine.'

Many 'new age' and 'natural' health treatises hint or outright advise women not to go to doctors or psychologists and to trust their intuition, while recommending a complex series of supplements.

These days, anyone in a crop-top who can produce a guava smoothie is giving nutrition advice. Accredited Practising Dietitians – who have a university level approved science-based degree – are allowed to give individual nutrition advice, as well as general advice to the community. Anyone else can legally call themselves a nutritionist, who may hold a qualification of a three-year diploma or a short online course, or none at all: they're not allowed to give individual nutrition advice or advice on health problems, only general advice.

While the first 'influencers' may have been strong-willed local people interested in feeling powerful or being sure of themselves – fathers, husbands, and clergy, anyone with access to a platform and a printing press, they're now often models,

The poster reads:

Grow Your Own Grassroots Defiance Against the Capitalist Diet

VICTORY

A HEALTHY REVOLUTIONARY IS A STRONG REVOLUTIONARY

GROW VITAMINS AT YOUR KITCHEN DOOR

Feminist artist Frances (Budden) Phoenix redeployed World War II imagery and language for the Victory Poster, at Matilda Graphics, 1979. (Sydney University Art Collection, courtesy Sally Cantrill)

'footballer's wives' and celebrities leveraging their fame to spread their beliefs, often for more influence and cash. I beg your pardon, they are brand ambassadors for expensive, laxitiverous teas and other products. (Laxitiverous is not a word.)

'Wellness' concepts such as clean eating and green eating are often code for diets and diet supplements based on dysfunctional ideas of purity (clean eating), shame (secret eating) and virtue (being 'good' about eating), helped along by the fact that a lot of pre-packaged, mass-produced food isn't healthy. Various 'superfoods' and supplements come and go – vitamin D, ginseng, jojoba, chlorophyll, coconut oil, fish oil, olive leaf extract, gingko belohojoba (that's not right). Also in the came-and-went category are the miracle workings of such as 'anti-inflammatory', alkaline, anti-probiotic, paleo, intermittent fasting, and perennial marketing words such as 'anti-ageing', 'healing' and 'cleansing'.

There's lots of talk about getting rid of bloating when they mean having a flatter stomach. Trainers and bloggers talk about flattening the stomach and exercises to 'shape' the bottom.

Weight Watchers (rebranded as WW – Wellness that Works) and other calorie- and kilojoule-counting dieting companies and their apps are repackaged as 'health and lifestyle' products aimed at ever-younger markets. New words for diets have emerged as 'cleanses', 'anti-inflammatory regimes', 'making the body alkaline' and 'de-toxes', even though the ideas they're based on are medically wrong, or literally impossible. (If your body was alkaline, you'd be dead.) It's an echo of the Middle Ages idea that women's bodies are dirty or need to be purged.

The idea of 'wellness' is lovely, and eating mostly unprocessed fruit and vegetables is a great idea. But food, however organic or reduced-to-juice, is not medicine or magic. It's not a guaranteed protection for any individual person against getting sick, feeling tired, or having a difficult childbirth. Ill-fortune is random and bad things like cancer can and do happen to good, healthy people: and it's not because you did anything wrong or brought it on yourself.

"Women who believe in woo are stupid."

Woo (as in the ghost-like noise, *woooooo*) is the word used for unproven stuff like this, from TV show 'mediums' making a fortune to well-meaning earnest homeopaths whose medicines can't work.

Horoscopes, clairvoyants, fortune-telling, prayer, folk remedies, talismans, saints, rituals and spells are all things women have used when medicine failed

Your partner's having an affair with an actress. Or you are. How To Read Teacups *by Bushells Pty Ltd, 1950. (National Library of Australia)*

UNSETTLED CONDITIONS
These can be foretold by the first glance at the cup. If well covered with dots, streaks, etc., the consultant may well expect to be unsettled for quite a while; if a lot of dots appear at the end of a horizontal line, it is a fair indication that there will be slight trouble at the end of a journey.

ACTRESS
The figure of an active lady, one in a dancing or sprightly attitude, if on the side of the cup close to the handle, foretells that a single person should guard against jealous quarrels. A married person may look for temporary discord in domestic affairs. If in bottom circle of cup with many outlines that suggest people, much time will be spent in pleasing company.

them, or they couldn't afford it. Woo and 'wellness' practitioners listen to women, answer their questions and treat them as individuals. Woo tells a woman her life, her needs and her futures are important. Mainstream medicine needs to get better at those things too.

"Get health advice from celebrities."

It beats me how former sportswoman and model Lisa Curry-Kenny's company is allowed to sell herbal pills with labels that say 'Happy Weight', not to mention a herbal supplement called 'Happy Hormones', which has no effect on hormone levels. The website claims the supplement works not because it changes hormone levels but because its herbal ingredients cause the hypothalamic and pituitary glands in the brain to 'signal to the body to balance itself, and that's the secret'.

Testimonials on the company's website from 'ladies' (the company carefully does not call its customers patients) claim that the herbal pills cured their problems with sleep, hair loss, incontinence, premenstrual disorders, endometriosis, mood swings, teenage period problems, and menopausal symptoms. Each claim is stamped with a label saying 'verified'. I asked the company what verified means. It replied, '"Verified" means that the review has been posted by a customer who is really taking the product and not a fake person.'

In 2019 Curry-Kenny claimed medical hormonal treatment could 'dramatically' increase the risk of breast cancer. This is not true, and earned her a sharp rebuke from medical experts. 'A load of codswallop' was the memorable quote from a leading menopause specialist. (Women who've had breast cancer treatment are advised not to take oestrogen-based hormone medications, but that's a different matter.) Doctors were also shocked to find a non-medical person was advising women about hormone treatment on the company's website 'chat'.

The free marketing that has been given to former model Elle Macpherson's green powders is phenomenal. I don't know the exact ingredients and proportions of her desiccated dust, but I do know it doesn't give you cheekbones, alkalise your blood, or make you thinner. It might make your eyes water. From the price.

Macpherson has paid serious attention to marketing. The packaging is based on luxury-priced perfume bottles. Her product names contain Super (model, geddit) elixir (serum-ish but more magical) greens (clean & natural). The website says it has 'wholefoods, herbal extracts, vitamins, minerals and probiotics. Created by nutritionist Simone Laubscher' (not a medical doctor), it 'helps support overall gut health, provides immune support, enhances energy, and helps support the appearance of healthy skin, and stronger hair and nails.'

"If they're selling it, it must work."

Companies are far less likely to be in breach of health regulations when they use vague terms, such as 'supports' and 'the appearance of'. Billions of dollars' worth of stuff gets sold that doesn't do what its customers think it does.

If the government could put ten netball coaches in charge of the relevant regulatory agencies and give them another $100 million this would be sorted by Christmas, thank you.

'Beautiful bust' exercise with bikini and a raw chicken, Fabulous Feminique Program exercises book, 1970s.

"Exercise is a duty."

Advice for women to exercise began as a reaction against the enforced unhealthy lifestyles of idle girls, the daughters of the English empire and the United States.

Fit and strong women, we were told, would do better in childbirth (it's not always true), but more importantly, recover more quickly and be available for childcare, keeping house and whatever other womanly duties (ahem) were required. There's hardly any advice to women about exercise that doesn't at least mention its alleged effect on 'attractiveness'.

By the late 19th century physical culture for women had arrived with callisthenics and exercise classes, sometimes linked to the white supremacy idea of building a 'better race'.

Sedate walks were approved, strenuous or competitive exercise was discouraged. Strenuous meant horseriding with legs apart, wild dancing and anything that increased a woman's visibility or independence.

Annette Kellermann's diving instructions, from How to Swim, *1919. (National Library of Australia)*

The neck dive

"Jackknife" dive

The idea of women being in sport teams thundering about together and laughing loudly was enough to give doctors the vapours. Muscles were simply appalling unless they were invisible, round the middle and reserved for childbirth.

A few women rebelled against this: lady bicyclists, women who wore Grecian-statue style gowns and ponced about with small twirling batons, and Annette Kellermann. Annette was once a household name: first a vaudeville stage diver and champion swimmer and then a star of aquatic movies. I do bang on later about Annette being marketed as having the perfect figure, but for now, let's just give a sideways glance to the exercise advice in her 1918 book emblematic of the post-corset era advice to women, *Physical Beauty: How To Keep It*.

Annette rebelled against the prevailing medical view that 'your body is weird and periods mean you're sick' business. She acknowledged that there were 'troubles which may arise from the derangement of the sexual organs and functions'. But she

Diving feet first

The "Australian splosh"

believed women could keep themselves healthy by doing a lot of exercise.

She didn't consider women's health much in terms of diseases, germs, bad luck, misbehaving hormones and random malfunctioning of bits of bodies, and to be fair, a lot of that medical knowledge came after her time. Having a no-nonsense style is unfortunately no guarantee that you are not talking a load of nonsense.

"You'll get bicycle face."

Though the song went 'You'll look sweet, upon the seat of a bicycle built for two,' and the romantic ideal was a gentleman at the front of a tandem bicycle who decided where to go, women were quickly onto bicycles in the 1890s for fun and to get to work.

One doctor published a claim that a patient who had taken up 'striding' instead of doing girly steps had developed a 'bicycle face', a ghastly rictus of concentration and fear.

Given the state of the roads back then – no traffic control signals or signs, piles of horse shit, large holes and intermittent tree stumps, and much-reported cat-calls and heckling – most women on a bike probably did look a bit clenched.

Health benefits, newspapers wrote, were undeniable. But there were so many dangers: speed, independence, skill,

What a hoyden. From the National Police Gazette, *Boston, 1898.*

"CAN LIGHT MATCHES ON HER PANTS."
A CIGARETTE SMOKING BLOOMERITE AND "BIKER" WHO HAS STARTLED CHESHIRE, O.—"FOR ALL THE NEW VICES, CONSULT ME."

strength, muscles, women being able to escape, trousers and assertiveness. Cartoonists depicted bicycling women doing outrageous extra things like smoking and fighting rude men in the street.

"Exercise for women is dangerous."

Lots of doctors in the 19th and much of the 20th century said exercise was dangerous to women's health because muscles were unsightly or damaged the brain, activity and competition were 'unladylike', and women's bodies were too weak.

Meanwhile many of the 'weak' girls and women who worked in the doctors' own houses, and in nearby factories or fields did more heavy lifting, exertion and physical work in a day than these men ever did in a year. Much of the advice to exercise was for well-off girls allowed to piff about with nothing more than croquet and sauntering. It wouldn't do to acknowledge the mill-girls or the exhausted scullery maid, whose muscles had yet to unhinge her reason.

'Who wants a girl with biceps?' – Gordon Stables, advice columnist, *The Girl's Own Paper*, 1901, warning that fit, sporty girls were 'far indeed from beautiful'

' "The bicycle hand" is a thing of ugliness and a horror forever . . . it becomes flattened, bulges out at the sides, gets lumpy . . . the fingers all become crooked.' – Syndicated newspaper story, 1896

'Vulcana' was a Welsh vicar's daughter called Kate Roberts, who ran away from home aged 15 to become a strongwoman in a vaudeville act. She toured stages across the world lifting weights (including men sitting on chairs), and posed with new electric lights trained on her musculature. Reviewers conceded she was beautiful and strong but concluded that it was obviously abnormal. In a world where millions of strong and fit women lived, her training and artistry was presented as some sort of one-off weirdness.

ATLAS & VULCANA.

*A very unusual pose for a woman, even in a vaudeville postcard: strongwoman
Vulcana (and her husband), c1903. (State Library Victoria)*

"Only exercise to lose weight."

I'll just leave this here, shall I?

"Women shouldn't play sports."

The history of sport in many regional towns and suburbs is that women were 'associate members' or 'supporters' who washed the uniforms, ran the kiosk and were told to 'bring a plate' to fundraisers. Now that women are 'allowed' to do sport and exercise, they still fight for equal funding from councils, state and national governments, reporting and game coverage in the media and on streaming services.

Sportswomen have battled abusive coaches, dangerous training schedules, unhealthy imposed diet regimes and damage to bone density, abuse and threats from trolls given

Happy high school volleyball stars, Wangaratta, 1970s. (Bob Beel, State Library Victoria)

free reign by social media platforms, and the tenacious accusations that what they're doing isn't ladylike or as watchable as men's sport. Many countries' Olympic teams are nowhere near 50/50 mixed representation.

Australian Rules men's teams have been playing since 1859. The Australian Football League funded a women's league from 2016. Past players objected at 'men's competition money' being used for a women's league. It didn't occur to them that governments and councils had funded men's sports with women's taxes for more than a hundred years, or that women's unpaid labour had subsidised their entire sports career.

In 2020, the American women's soccer team lost a lawsuit against its governing body, which pays more money to male team players, even though the women's team wins way more matches.

"Periods prove women are toxic."

It's pretty gobsmacking the way men got to hijack available knowledge and assumptions on women's periods. Women's words for it or feelings about it were rarely recorded. Hundreds of years ago it was only officially mentionable by medical men who had already got it all wrong. Period blood was referred to as excrement, and periods as sickness, illness, and 'evacuations of the weaker sex'. Men just couldn't get over the idea that having periods might be normal, because they didn't have them.

Jane Sharp, author of *The Midwives Book* in 1671, thought periods were evidence that women's bodies were faulty, but perhaps this had less to do with assumptions of women's inferiority and more to do with her direct experience of so many things that could, and did, go wrong in pregnancy and childbirth.

Young women were diagnosed with green sickness (symptoms which now suggest anaemia, lack of nutrition, depression and boredom), said to be caused by a girl having no periods: the cure was marriage.

Heavy period bleeding and stopped periods were recognised problems. Having no periods was called mother-fits, which pretty much meant uterus tantrum. Treatments included bloodletting (opening a vein and draining some blood), smelling noxious fumes and induced vomiting, plus marriage for girls and sex for married women.

Aristotle, the perfect clod, thought menstrual blood was mixed with sperm to make a fetus, and the extra impure bits were sent out of the body (as a period). Annoyingly, his centuries-old views were republished and believed again in the 19th century.

Although early doctors recognised pre-menstrual symptoms and menopause symptoms, they weren't much interested. Women were told that heavy periods were caused by being excitable, having sex or approaching the menopause: the last one was true, but no useful help was offered. Instead, a laxative with some 12 drops of sulphuric acid before breakfast might be prescribed.

Women traditionally sought advice and knowledge from traditional herbalists and midwives on how to restore regular periods if they wanted to get pregnant: this was sometimes code for advice on using herbs to try to terminate a pregnancy. We were considered magic and dangerous for our ability to create life, and control our own bodies. Churches and doctors wanted the control for themselves.

"Periods are shameful."

People blow their nose in public and put the contents in their pocket and carry it about, but we're supposed to change a tampon in secret and hide blood stains. For centuries we've pretended we don't have periods. We used euphemisms like A visit from Fred and having the painters in and secret words in diaries to track our periods. Period apps now do this job, but less privately: some app-makers sell the data to marketing companies that target women who might be pregnant or trying to be pregnant. Some are owned by Catholic anti-abortion groups.

Periods are referred to as 'flowers' in the literature of different cultures, from English to Sanskrit. I don't know if this was due to the bloom of womanhood or the shape of a blood stain on a menstrual-rag pad.

Period product ads have been disguised for a long time, not mentioning what the products were for. Many people watching late-20th-century TV ads could be forgiven for deducing that tampons caused horseriding – it was a coded message that tampons reduced the risk of leaks. Later, the ads showed pads absorbing blue liquid because red was considered 'disgusting'.

Corset makers advertised belts, worn by women to suspend hammocky pads made of rags, using safety pins. It must have been an awful palaver dealing with changes and washing, and for 'theatrical' women who had to travel for work, and the servants, factory and rural workers who were on shift for 10–12 hours a day without access to running water even inside their homes.

The advice women gave to each other for dealing with normal or heavy periods, or the heavy bleeding associated with approaching menopause, is largely unrecorded. Periods were ignored by the Press and male historians.

"Periods are dirty."

The idea that women have periods to 'purge' themselves of toxins or impurities was official medical thought until the start of the 18th century, and socially the idea that it's unclean has clung on for dear life and been enshrined in the phrase 'menstrual hygiene'.

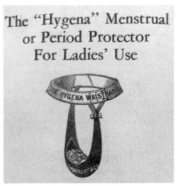

Rare illustration of rubber belt and contraption for periods. The hammock part contained wadded rags to absorb the blood. Wife's Guide and Friend catalogue, 1898. (National Library of Australia

By the 19th century, upper- and middle-class women were cast as delicate creatures with a dreadful monthly illness. Women should not have cold baths during periods. She shouldn't do any running, dancing, bicycle riding or use a sewing machine, or take exciting music lessons.

After each period ended, a woman should wash out her vagina with soapy douches, 'about two or three pints of water as hot as convenient', said *The Wife's Guide and Friend*, published from the late 1800s until almost 1930. This would 'induce the female organs to perform their duties in a perfectly natural manner'. Heaven knows what the duties were, light vaginal housework perhaps.

'The sanitary napkin should be attached to a suspender which passes over the shoulders.' – Ladies' Handbook of Home Treatment by Dr Eulalia Richards, 1905

In many countries, cultural teachings emphasise the time of a period as providing a welcome break from chores and recognition of and respect for its connection to being able to 'give life'. But in other places, because of these old prejudices and wrong ideas about periods, religious texts and cultural traditions have been interpreted to ban women from various areas and tasks while menstruating.

Ishwari Rajak wrote in her 2015 thesis, *She Got Her Period: Men's Knowledge and Perspectives on Menstruation*, about growing up in a Nepali community in which girls from the age of about 11 or 12 were sequestered in a room for the days of their period and were not allowed to see or hear any boys or

Advertising for menstrual products is no longer coy and baffling. (Moxie)

men, or help prepare food. They also celebrated their first-ever period with their family and friends.

For others, the experience is more difficult. Many girls who are sequestered, or have no period products, can't go to school. Although it's been illegal since 2005, some Nepali girls and women are locked in small sheds, where being in the home is considered to offend Hindu gods. Village women have died of cold or suffocated from fire-smoke in unventilated sheds.

Activists and aid agencies, like the Adara Group, are working to include positive school lessons for both boys and girls about periods, and focus on education and confidence as well as the provision of period products, formerly known as feminine hygiene products. (There's also important change underway from using the phrase menstrual hygiene to dignified menstruation.)

"Periods have terrifying magic powers."

Pliny the Elder, the revered philosopher and colossal fool, said that menstruating women cause fruit to fall out of trees, grass to die and wine to sour. Nothing, he reckoned, was more 'monstrous' than menstruating. (At least he was scared of us.) A menstruating woman who took her clothes off could control the weather and kill pests in crops.

The insightful feminist historian Patricia Crawford called out *The Lancet* medical journal for publishing a letter in 1974, asking 'Why does a menstruating woman cause flowers to wilt?'. Professor Crawford, who fought to be properly employed by universities as a married woman, submitted a groundbreaking article in the history journal *Past and Present* called 'Attitudes to Menstruation in 17th Century England', in 1981.

She laid out the nonsensical, accepted historical theories: women have too much blood in 'em, that they get out by breastfeeding (because they said breastmilk was white blood) or feeding a fetus in the womb or having a period. Any illness in a baby after its birth, including measles, was 'caused' by menstrual blood that touched it in the womb.

As she records in her 2004 book, *Blood, Bodies and Families in Early Modern England*, women were considered disgusting but dangerous and powerful. There was a common prohibition on sex during a period because of the damage it could do to a man. Professor Crawford unearthed 16th-century advice on how sex with a menstruating wife would cause a child to be leprous and detested, caused by 'malignant Female Filth'.

Menstrual blood was used in love spells, as contraception or fertility medicine, and to remove birthmarks. By the early 18th century, people were catching on that none of that worked. As a young woman in the 1980s, I was mortified when a restauranteur asked my male friends to tour the kitchen: I was not welcome in case I was menstruating, he said, because I would spoil the sauces.

Into the 19th century, rumour had it that period blood could excoriate a penis. In the 1500s, a writer said it would kill a husband with its poison (whoops). A man who touched menstrual blood should be put to death according to the Christian Bible's Leviticus section, which was written by some dude called The Priestly Source, or maybe Stephen King.

"Periods synch with the moon, & flatmates."

You know how we're all supposed to synchronise our periods with each other, or with the moon? Doesn't happen. Periods were assumed to be related to the phases of the moon, as both had average cycles of about 30 days and the words menses and menstruation come from the Latin for moon. The original 'study' on synched periods was unscientific and has been disproved by stacks of large studies since.

While many women have been told their periods should synchronise to the phases of the moon, or to the cycles of women they live with or friends, large studies show neither is true. One woo-ish website isn't taking this lying down and instructs us how to make our period cycles match the moon's, by using self life-assessment, and 'moon-bathing'. (It doesn't work.)

One thing's pretty certain, if men menstruated, decades ago, private companies and public places would have tampons and pads available free in every public or business toilet – the way toilet paper is. More recently, New Zealand and Victoria have led the way in public schools, and Scotland has made period products free.

"Your period pain is imaginary."

Painful periods, according to one old medical guide, happened to women who were 'of indolent habits and irritable constitutions'. You grumpy, lazy, crampy old bag. More commonly, we're told all period pain is normal and just to 'put up with it'.

Few women have been told that their uterus activates cramps to help the period blood on its way, using exactly the same muscles that are used in childbirth. Women can get really bad cramps and other dragging pain, but partly because it varies between women, and some doctors don't listen properly, the pain has been dismissed as unimportant. Unfortunately, our bodies are not 'designed' for anything. If they were, more of them would work better and we'd probably get our money back.

One of the most common reasons for period pain is a condition called endometriosis. After first asking for medical help for typical symptoms it takes an average of about seven years for a woman with 'endo' to get a diagnosis. Symptoms include severe pain during periods, heavy period bleeding, bowel problems and painful penetrative sex. The World Endometriosis Society, which represents peak organisations in many countries, estimates that 200 million women have endo.

Many women don't get better with medical or surgical treatment, which has flummoxed doctors. Doctors in the past suggested that the pain of endometriosis is phantom or psychological – echoes of the old diagnosis of hysteria.

"Older women are obsolete."

Well, this is going to be the subject of my whoooole next book, so for the moment I'll just leave you with this image of all of us being told what sort of medical information to expect as we get older:

A woman in 1850. She might be as old as 32. (Daguerreotype-maker Mathew Brady, Library of Congress)

An unnamed bride braces herself before her wedding in 1924.
The bridesmaids are in full horror of regret about their outfits.
(Spencer Shier, State Library Victoria)

3

FIND A MAN &
DO MARRIED SEX

WHEN I WAS A TEENAGER IN THE 1970S I worked in a second-hand book shop which ran a decent discount-for-exchange racket. Lots of elderly ladies (over 40, I tell you) would come in wheeling their vinyl upright shopping trolleys, dive down into them to get the books they'd bought last week, return them to the counter and go straight to the shelves with the Mills & Boon brand romance novels.

Each woman would take down a flimsy paperback at random, turn it to the back, open the back cover and look at the last page. Then she would either replace it on the shelf, or stack it on top of her trolley, ready to buy it. Curious, I asked a woman one day whether she was checking to see if it was a happy ending. 'Oh they're all happy endings, love,' she said. 'I'm just checking to see if I've read it before.' She held out the book. On the last, blank page, there was a column of neatly written names in Biro. 'See? There's me.' She pointed to her name, and put the book back on the shelf. All the books had lists of names at the back.

This was a clever system, because who could tell if you'd already read a Mills and Boon? They were so formulaic, the title, cover picture and blurb were all pretty indistinguishable. Reams of nurse-marries-doctor and governess-marries-widower, scads of the secretary-marries-boss, and oceans of Cinderellarian servant-marries-prince.

The writers had none of the wit of Georgette Heyer and Jane Austen, but they could write to a formula.

Defenceless, lowly woman is rescued from poverty, danger and loneliness by a rich, high-status man. Every main character was white. Often, she was 'a girl' and he was 'a man'. The women were sweet, kind and shy, and the men had hard, brooding eyes and a harsh nature masking a tragedy; he insulted her, but had melty eyes. In some books the eyes were known to change colour from page to page (more an editing glitch than a plot twist). Hers were green, usually, and she chewed her bottom lip a lot. His lips quirked, and on occasion his ardour hardened (though nothing else, only kissing allowed).

Decades later, digital books are a boon to Mills & Boon and other romance and erotica booksellers, bringing the privacy of e-readers and the immediacy of downloading. Mills & Boon now has sub-publishing 'labels' including themes of royal involvement, African-American writers, supernatural stories, historical settings, and other sub-genres. These days, erotic novels don't leave out the sex, but it's as unrealistic as servant-marries-prince, what with the multiple orgasms with no clitoral stimulation to speak of, and so forth.

"Fantasise about men who order you around."

There are some well-written erotic novels, but a digital dumpster fire now burns brightly of cheap, even free e-books, often full of cross-plagiarism. As soon as a writer invents a sub-genre (shape-shifting-man-into-wolf-or-bear-paranormal-romance, for example, or lost-in-a-snowstorm-rescued-by-mountain-man-with-mansiony-cabin), a hundred badly wrought copycats are uploaded. There are sub-genres of alphas, enemies, bullies, bosses, bikers, tattooists and billionaires (millionaires are so yesterday), LGBTQI+, reverse harem and 'doms' (short for Dominant).

The old idea of 'bodice ripping' has been replaced with 'alpha men'. The fantasy oxymoron of 'a welcome rape' in the books means a woman can enjoy sex without being slutty enough to ask for it. The new romance heroes are very tall men with unfeasible penises who growl and appreciate your skills and desire to open your own cupcake bakery and will protect you against harassers and stalker-exes, or they might be bossy billionaires who'll only pause from spanking sessions to supply an extensive wardrobe of designer clothes in exactly the right size.

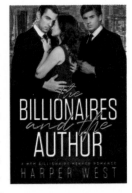

I am unacquainted with this phenomenon. (Guaranteed HEA and no cheating.)
(Kindle edition book cover)

Online bookstores now give women a detailed heads up in an advisory note before they buy and download a romance, to avoid unhappy customers. Potential Kindle readers of *Possessive Undercover Cop* by Flora Ferrari (sure you are) are told it's a 'standalone insta-love romance with an HEA, no cheating and no cliffhanger'. That means it's not part of a series, it gets to the action fast, it has a Happily-Ever-After ending, nobody has an affair or lies to their partner, and there's no ending that requires you to buy a sequel to find out what happens.

Readers are advised of 'dark romance' (which can include abuse and assault), 'power exchange' (women being ordered about and told when they can orgasm, etc) and general arse-covering 'If such material offends you, please do not read this book.' Sometimes, they even include a word count. *A Cowboy Billionaire Best Friend's Secret* by Hanna Hart is a fairly informative title and so is *Virgin for the Trillionaire* by Ruth Cardello.

Once an algorithm kicks in, you may find yourself advised to buy the same popular themes, which might be summed up as curvy, green-eyed, clumsy cupcake-bakery-owning nanny librarian abducted by a bossy billionaire bikie gang bodyguard with no manners called Blade, Lucas or Gavin who is secretly an alien invader spanking-enthusiast mechanic who wants to train her for anal sex using increasingly larger bedazzled butt-plugs with ponytails on them, who has brothers interested in a reverse-harem relationship, and who shape-shifts into a wolf or small-town handyman vampire cop because of his time as a Navy Seal.

There are glossaries available to explain acronyms like BBW (big beautiful woman: the heroine is not thin) and MFM (Ménage à trois with two men who have sex with a woman but not each other) and MMF (ménage à trois, bisexual). Googling a glossary can help you avoid books on themes that I can't even write here for fear you'll throw the book at a wall and scream your house down.

"You need a man. Go get one."

Mothers like Mrs Bennett in *Pride and Prejudice* knew that the best way to keep a daughter out of poverty and even the dreaded workhouses (where poor people were corralled to keep them off the streets) was to make sure they 'married well'.

In the early- to mid-1800s, English girls were encouraged to emigrate to the colonies to become servants and perhaps find a husband in the male-dominated colonies. Men had relatives in England choose and dispatch a servant or a wife, and in some cases, one and the same.

By the 1960s, pamphlets for migrants produced by the Australian government still assumed they were coming from Britain, though there was special

Bloody Judy. What is she playing at? How to Get Along with Boys from a Brenda Starr comic, c1940s–1950s. (State Library Victoria)

E - MIGRATION
or
A FLIGHT OF FAIR GAME

material for people coming from the Baltic states in the 1950s. Women migrants were being told that Australian frocks had gayer colours than England's, and frankly, so did the food. Would-be or newly arrived migrants were officially informed that Australian women wore hats more often, ate more meat and had more refrigerators (one each, I mean).

Servants and workhouse inmates in England watch fancy young women – the butterflies – flying to Tasmania to marry men waiting with nets and a clergyman. (E-Migration: A Flight of Fair Game, lithograph by Alfred Ducote, 1832, National Library of Australia)

"Play hard to get."

If boxes of matches had instructions as useless as the ones usually given for romance, every house in the world would have burned down. For a very long time we've been told women should feign disinterest for modesty's sake, and men are free to employ 'determined' stalker-tactics.

Women have been given lectures, books and newspaper columns of advice about how to get a husband. Social events such as harvest festivals, dowry ceremonies, fancy debutante balls and reality TV shows have been employed to reinforce the idea.

I no longer have the book *The Rules: Time-Tested Secrets of Capturing the Heart of Mr Right*, by Ellen Fein and Sherrie Schneider, because in 1996 I threw a copy of it over my shoulder on a TV show, and burned another one on hot barbecue coals just for fun: it was a dating book that was the forerunner of *He's Just Not That Into You* and other romance manuals.

Rules in *The Rules* include: Don't Talk to a Man First and Don't Talk Too Much, Don't Accept A Saturday Night Date After Wednesday, Don't Tell Him What To Do, Let Him Take the Lead, Be Honest But Mysterious, and Don't Live With A Man (before marriage), the disturbing Don't Discuss The Rules With Your Therapist and the fairytale promise Do The Rules And You'll Live Happily Ever After. (Of course, fairytales were originally ghastly fables: Red Riding Hood, Rapunzel, Sleeping Beauty and Cinderella included rape, dismemberment, canni-balism and oppressed women looking to escape.)

'We noticed that women who acted "hard to get" got their man, while women who were too available or eager got hurt,' the authors wrote. Had they had that thought years later, perhaps *The Rules* might just have been a tweet. One of the sequels, *The Rules For Marriage*, suggested in its intro that capturing a man wasn't enough, you had to 'keep him'. Sadly, and inconveniently, Fein filed for divorce during the publicity tour.

Rona Jaffe's 1958 novel, *The Best of Everything* (filmed with Joan Crawford in 1959), chronicled the underpaid, ambition-thwarted typists in a publishing firm dealing with timeless issues: being 'felt-up' by the publishing company managers; single mothers; abortion; and a woman desperate for romance who loses her mind and ends up a stalker.

Helen Gurley Brown's 1962 smash-hit advice book for the new generation of office 'girls' of America, *Sex and the Single Girl*, talked of a new kind of life – apartment living, a little independent income. Gurley Brown is fascinating because she patrolled the border between independence and the rules about being meek and ladylike – being attractive. Like comedian Joan Rivers, she personified an era when, often the smartest person in the room, she accepted she'd be judged on her appearance.

A single woman should employ style, follow fashion, cook well, get a good job, work hard, use her brains surreptitiously, 'work on' her face, not 'harbour an ounce of fat', make her apartment cool. 'Creep up on decorating as you would any new skill. Remember how long it took to learn shorthand?' Gurley Brown asked.

Though the aim is to find a husband who'll raise her standard of living and make her feel wanted, a 1960s unmarried life had its perks: 'A single woman never has to drudge. She can get her housework over within one good hour Saturday morning plus another hour to iron blouses and white collars.'

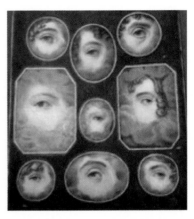

Eye portraits by Georgiana McCrae, 1880s. Set in a brooch or ring, they professed love of a secret person where a whole-face portrait would give the game away. (State Library Victoria)

'February thirteenth: Galentine's Day, is about celebrating Lady Friends! It's wonderful, and it should be a national holiday.' – Lesley Knope, Parks and Recreation television series, 2010

"It's a compliment."

'Negging' (from 'negative') is a promoted pick-up technique recommended to men trying to make women feel bad or off-balance while pretending to compliment them. It is a way of making someone feel dismissed and belittled. If a woman objects, she's told she's too sensitive, or it was just a joke, or just a helpful suggestion.

It's hard to learn that you don't deserve insults or being treated badly, especially when you're in the middle of it, or still reeling from the effects.

"Manipulate men."

From medieval exhortations against wheedling women, we 'progressed' to wink-nudge advice to women on how to manipulate men into marriage, and how to manage them by similar tactics, as wives. The idea was to pretend that men made all the decisions, to preserve their ego, but a clever woman could engineer such decisions from the background.

The 1955 copy of *How to Manage Men* in the National Library (which had been borrowed 25 times) advises women to play hard to get, on principle: 'Manage your lovers sensibly, keep them at an appropriate distance and they will probably always remember you as the unattainable and untarnished figure of womanhood, not the easily acquired and easily forgotten pieces of frippet in their chequered lives.' Frippet yourself, for heaven's sake.

Forbidden any actual power, women were told they could gain a few little advantages by manipulating men using deceit and ransomed sex. Two 1960s sit-coms exemplified the stereotype: a witch who's way smarter than her advertising executive husband (*Bewitched*) and a magical harem-genie of a hapless astronaut, who calls him 'master' (*I Dream of Jeannie*).

I've never suspected a literary hoax more than while reading the book sold for a shilling in 1885 called *Men & How to Manage*

Author Mary Hyde has a fag while her husband, Douglas Rose, does the dishes, which would have been an arresting image at the time, 1958. (Tony Marshall/ ANL/Shutterstock)

Them: A Book For Australian Wives and Mothers by An Old Housekeeper. If that book was written by a woman, I'm an otter.

'I propose to regard man as a plastic, invertebrate, manageable animal, indocile and intractable undoubtedly, seldom to be led, driven or persuaded, but usually to be cajoled and circumvented, and . . . reached through his stomach . . . she must be content to chuckle over it in secret. One look of triumph may undo the work of months,' the author claimed.

By the 1950s, there was plenty more. Mary Hyde's *How to Manage Men* advised (I'm paraphrasing) that if you can never get the education, advantages, employment, pay, prospects or entitlement of men, you'd have to fiddle round the edges to get anything. Women had to learn manipulation from birth, she said, then improve with experience, 'by trial and error . . . it depends to some extent on one's distribution of curves, a developed instinct, and a large degree of feline cunning.'

Hyde's book is pretty creepy, telling girls to practise by manipulating their fathers and making themselves, 'the most attractive child of all, excelling at lessons, games and behaviour.' Surviving stern, horrible fathers was good practice for handling difficult men later. 'Learn to accept men as they are, imperfect, childish, selfish and very ordinary. One day you'll find one who seems extraordinary to you,' she promised.

An incentive was being able to have some freedom first. 'The modern girl of today has a much fuller life. She can look forward to five, ten or fifteen years of happy spinsterhood (before marriage) . . . marriage is no longer the limit of their ambition . . . some women find fulfillment in a career.' Fancy that.

I suppose women in the past may as well have tried to manipulate men as they were blamed for everything anyway, controlling the weather with their menstrual blood and causing the fall of Sparta (said ludicrous Aristotle) and the French Revolution (bloody Schopenhauer). Dicky old Freud just said they were a 'retarding and restraining influence'.

"Do all the emotional labour."

Of all the countless studies and surveys about who does what in a heterosexual relationship or marriage, not one has found that men on average do more housework, or more emotional labour or more organising for a family. We're often told it's because women care more, have higher standards, or are better at organising.

It happens because most men don't pull an equal weight of unpaid work in relationships. It happens because men in power don't make funded childcare a priority, and when things are difficult it is usually women who do that work, because they earn less than their male partner or because they can't afford supportive childcare. They are forced to forgo experience, advancement and superannuation employer contributions.

Women tend to organise all the parent–teacher interviews, pack for, and plan the holidays, at which they also are still responsible for most of the meals. If you actually earn more or pay more than half for everything, don't mention it so you don't 'emasculate' him. Old excuses and old dynamics keep being recycled.

"There's no such thing as a lesbian."

For a long time the general public assumption was that lesbians and bisexual women didn't exist – straight men in charge never even considered the idea, and the women weren't telling.

In the 1830s white women were so outnumbered by white men in Melbourne that they had their pick of husbands. Quite the thing, then, at the time, for squatter-farmer couple Miss Caroline Newcombe and Miss Anne Drysdale to take up with each other and move to a farm in Geelong, where they designed and had built a house with one bedroom for themselves.

When Miss Drysdale died in the 1850s, Miss Newcombe had a gold brooch made using their combined hair, plaited in Knitting Nancy style, and gold symbols of devotion and love, including a lyre and roses.

Though people have said crossly since that they were Methodists, not lesbians, I think they could have been both. Whether or not they had any sex is none of my beeswax, but they loved each other and considered each other lifetime companions, so that will do.

In many countries, lesbians can legally marry, but elsewhere, being gay is still illegal and LGBTQI+ people are persecuted

The mourning brooch made from their hair to symbolise the love of Misses Newcombe and Drysdale, c1853.
(State Library Victoria)

Mr Perrin is young.
He's young.

Mrs Miller is married.
She's married.

Mr Bell is old.
He's old.

Miss Green is single.
She's single.

*Miss Green is single,
I tell you. SINGLE.
English lesson book for
migrants produced by the
Australian government,
early 1970s. (National
Library of Australia)*

and punished. In Burundi, girls and women wear a secret symbol on their clothes to connect with each other. In 2019, a story about the code from the BBC chose not to identify the symbol, to protect women from violence.

'There's no such thing as a lesbian' has been recycled against trans folk by many a church and state: 'First we'll say you don't exist, and when you prove you do, we'll be horrible to you'. (Church and State are no fun at parties.)

"A wedding dress says you're a virgin."

Lillian Pyke agreed with everyone in 1916 that the wedding dress must be white. This idea had been popularised by Queen Victoria in 1840, who asked that her guests not wear white, then wore it herself, with a train, lace and veil. Her biographer, Julia Baird, says that the choice was to best show off the lace over-flounce. Within a decade, women's magazines had re-purposed the intention as representing purity and innocence – code for virginity, and aligning with the idea that having sex made a woman dirty or stained.

Before then, most people got married in their best clothes, handmade or something they could recycle for later; mauve was popular. The Queen's proposal to Albert somehow didn't set the standard for women to propose in the same way.

"Take your husband's name."

A woman was elevated in society by her husband's status (but never as high as his). Even now, women who are medical doctors or professors often have their earned honorific ignored as they are demoted to 'Mrs' by travel agents and officials. Married women are often asked their 'maiden' name, meaning their young girl name.

An unmarried woman was pitied, her children labelled illegitimate, while a married woman gained more respectability. My daughter, born in 1998, was recorded with an asterisk in the family trees compiled by some relatives, because her parents were not married.

A man was a Mister regardless of his marriage, but women were either Miss or Mrs (with widows retaining their Mrs) publicly and in correspondence. Women were required by law, and then convention to 'take' their husband's name. For many women after marriage, their birth name disappeared. They were addressed in the form of 'Mrs Horace Goomball' thereafter. The non-explanatory all-purpose Ms was proposed as early as the 19th century, and women's fight to use their birth name if they wanted to, regardless of marriage status, gained supporters in the 20th century, especially through the lobbying of the Lucy Stone League.

Women are still commonly told by fiancés, in-laws and parents and friends that they must take their husband's name, or that it's legally required. There's a tenacious fear that children without their father's name might be shamed as 'illegitimate', or their mother considered improper. Following 20th-century pharmacy policy, many prescriptions for contraceptives are still dispensed with the honorific 'Mrs'.

My great grandmother, born Eva Irene Wills, known as

US illustrator Neysa McMein, one of the founding members of the Lucy Stone League, leads a suffrist parade in New York, early 1900s. Instead of a honeymoon, she went on holiday with her gay pals. (Bettmann Collection/Getty Images)

Rene or Nene, officially became Mrs Bertram Cooke. Her 1921 divorce was a mortifyingly scandalous affair that was reported in *The Brisbane Truth* but according to family lore, not in the Melbourne or Sydney editions due to bribes paid. When her husband's remarriage meant the two Mrs Cookes were confused in the society pages in about 1924, Nene sailed into the Melbourne office of the Registrar of Births, Deaths and Marriages in high dudgeon and a good hat and shouted at the registrar, on whom you should not have placed a wager.

Against regulations, he acquiesced and changed her own and her children's last names to Wills Cooke. 'No hyphen!' she insisted. She had re-bestowed her family name and kept the married one, and the 'Mrs' for respectability.

Slate website columnist Danny Lavery answered an anguished letter in 2020 from an imminent bride whose fiancé was insisting she at least hyphenate or entirely take his name. She didn't want to. The reply was to offer that, if he wants the names to match, 'He can take yours.'

"A wedding is the most important day of your life."

There were etiquette rules for who to invite and where they stand and sit, which kind of jewel to have in the engagement ring, how long before the wedding invitations should go out, how the bridegroom was to wear lavender gloves and a top hat (bring that back, I say).

Punch newspaper reported the 'many handsome presents' were displayed at my great grandmother's wedding in 1906: cheques, fish carvers, an unfeasible number of cruet sets (salt, pepper and vinegar shakes). Mr and Mrs Egbert Wills gave a silver coffee pot; Miss Violet Cooke ponied up a fancy silver bread board. I wish I'd met Miss Spooner, who gave 'a book of Tennyson's poems'.

Rules for the wedding day have remained largely unchanged except for wartime necessities: white dress, change name, father gives you to husband, promise to raise your children in the right religion and not behave like rutting beasts in the field (in the case of an eye-opening Baptist ceremony I once attended).

These days even a wife who wants all of these traditions doesn't want any of the old sexist assumptions that created them in the past. In some cases, the traditions survive just because they were done before, and are endlessly copied: arriving by horse and carriage is a notable one.

Detail of the board for the dice game 'Courtship and Marriage', c1905. You could land on 'Parents charmed, advance to proposal' or 'Jealousy, return to seaside'. (National Library of Australia)

"Your purpose is to be a wife."

Every woman's etiquette, guidance and medical book before the 1970s told her to be a wife. Everything was geared towards becoming a wife and fulfilling that role. Now that women have other ambitions and ideas for their life aside from subservient wifehood and motherhood, the wedding day itself has become far more the focus.

More than a hundred years ago, for a few decades, board games were distributed with popular Japanese girls magazines. The form of the games is hundreds of years old, called sugoroku, meaning double six, the highest possible dice score. Earlier games showed jobs from nannies to factory-hands, and encouraged girls to contribute to war work. All these girls' sugorokus, spanning decades, have a central image goal: to end up a wife and mother.

A 1910 sugoroku game emphasises fate and fortune in accepting one's role in life: the player chooses a corner to begin from, as a rich girl playing badminton, a maid starting a fire, a student or a factory worker. The dice determines your path: making silk flowers, putting on make-up, using an abacus to do accounts, an artist, a hairdresser, a washerwoman, giving birth, a telephone operator. The central panel shows a three-generation family group. The player wins by getting 'home' to a family, including a baby, other children, and several grandparents.

Specialist librarian and translator Rika Wright showed me a beautiful full-colour, double-page sugoroku game from 1926 at the National Library of Australia's Asian Reading Room by illustrator Sunakawa Seji and writer Ishiguru Royū. It came as a bonus with the 1926 New Year edition of a Japanese girls' magazine. It's not so much instructional, but advises girls of their possible choices.

As befitting the progressive 1920s, it shows a well-off girl going to the theatre, skiing in trousers, playing music, at an art gallery admiring the work of a 'genius girl sculptor', helping with the dishes, and listening to radio news.

"A wife is always inferior to a husband."

The internet is still chockers with recycled advice for traditional wives – especially those who are in religious communities of any sort, to 'submit' to their husband. This inability to accept the idea of an equal partner means wives are often isolated, ill-advised by

A Japanese sugoroku board game for girls, magazine supplement, 1926. (National Library of Australia)

clergy, and unable to find an escape route from abuse and control.

Some selectively quote the Bible or the Q'uran, while fancy-pants philosophy types have quoted the story of Xantippe, who was not sufficiently repressed by her insufferable slacker husband Socrates, who was decades older, didn't earn any money, used her family funds, hung out at exclusive men's clubs, said he loved another man, went on about women being inferior and chucked her and his child out of his condemned cell before his execution so he could have a philosophical discussion with some dudes. So if Xanthippe was a bit cranky-pants, and once threw a chamber pot's contents over him, she was entitled to it.

After that we had, oh, a few centuries or so of religious teachings and etiquette books telling women they were lower than their husbands.

"Being single is frightful."

When I visited an elderly lady called Joan on a research visit to an assisted living village a few years ago, we talked about how she was one of many widows there. She leaned towards me, and confided in a whisper, 'It's bliss not having to make anyone's dinner. A lot of ladies here are very relieved. Sometimes,' she paused, 'we'll just have a *biscuit*.'

"Virginity is important."

Chastity, or virginity, has been an obsession of religions and romance books. Girls are often told they are 'virgins' or 'no longer virgins', that virginity is a gift they give to a boy, or man, or husband. Very large studies show that by the age of 15, about half of girls will have had some kind of sex. When the unwitting parents of girls say, 'Save it for somebody special,' what those girls can hear is that they've already been ruined or changed; they're being told they're not special anymore.

There's no special state of virginity. Most girls who play sport or otherwise live a normal life have stretched their hymen. It doesn't break, or pop, or always bleed if a 'virgin' has penetrative sex for the first time, though a male expectation that it will has led to many women using sponges in the vagina or other means to produce expected blood at the right time. 'Virgins' may have had hundreds of orgasms, lots of anal sex, oral sex and seen all manner of degrading porn. Very slowly, feminists and others are trying to reinforce the idea that 'virgin' is not an ideal, or even a meaningful label.

"Sexual abstinence is moral."

Many religions teach 'abstinence', sometimes withholding sex education, or teaching lies such as 'abortion raises your chance of breast cancer' or 'condoms don't work'. Evangelical Christian girls in the US have used jewellery, such as an 'pledge' ring, signed certificates, and participated in ceremonies with their fathers to affirm their chastity. The correlation between religiosity and the rate of birth to teenage girls is high. There's evidence that by the end of their teens religious young people don't have less sex, but are less likely to use contraception or to choose pregnancy termination.

Abstinence books such as 2005's *Real Sex* by Lauren Winner have been taught in schools with slogans such as, 'Chastity is God's very best for us. God created sex for marriage and that is where it belongs . . .'

Large studies of pledgers in the early 2000s showed that,

on average, they broke their vow but held out an average of 18 months longer than non-pledgers. Because they didn't use contraception, they were more likely to get pregnant. More than half said the only sex that counted in abstinence was penis-in-vagina. Another study found the activity that delayed girls having sex the most was organised team sports, not church.

Elsewhere, there are activist groups lobbying for laws to protect girls from ritual and damage to their clitoris, labia and vaginal opening, known as female genital mutilation (FGM). The cultural excuse for the practice is that it represents, or actually removes the possibility for women to enjoy sex, and renders them more chaste. It is all part of the same abusive idea that women are some sort of sexual 'gift' to a husband.

"Sex education is always useful."

Except for how most of it has been bollocks. *China's First Modern Treatise on Sex Education* by Dr Chang Ching-sheng was translated in 1967, more than 40 years after its original, by Howard Levy. The author meant it to be scientific, despite its reliance on a 1926 write-in to a 'Peking' newspaper survey with sex questions on masturbation, menstruation and contraception: mostly responded to by young men. It makes several pronouncements and rules: 'After washing (your genitals) rub with a soft cloth until the flesh gets warm, and desist when you feel like you're generating electricity.'

And, 'Someone has discovered proof that when the sexual desires of certain women arise the muscles of their sex organs have an extremely strong power of suction.' Reeeeeally.

The information wasn't much better in the government-issued

1940s *Sex Instruction for The Adolescent Girl and The Young Woman: The Facts Without the Humbug*, 'Written by an Australian Author in Consultation with Medical and Clerical Authorities'. By this time, a big majority of citizens believed some sex education was a good thing.

The priorities of the day are imposed as if they are natural urges. Girls are told they may become more interested in house-work, as well as 'dancing with young men, to improving your appearance, to smartness in dress, to your future, indeed, to having a dream home of your own one day.'

The mating instinct leads to automatic sex between a 'man and wife' during which 'the penis of the husband is naturally inserted into and received by the vagina of his wife, impelled by the directive and momentarily all-powerful mating instinct of both persons.' May I just say, the uselessness of this as an instruction really beats the band.

This mating instinct, the book explains, shows how people are similar to fish and poinsettias.

In other news from the *Sex Instruction* book, girls are warned cruelly that they must be virgins or no man will want to marry her, as she is then 'anyone's toy' and told the lie that, 'Any man who has union with a woman can immediately tell if she is a virgin or not.'

The most famous sex advisor of the late 20th century was Dr Ruth Westheimer. Her 1983 book, *Dr Ruth's Guide to Good Sex*, sold many millions of copies. She'd been doing a phone-in radio show for three years so had the transcripts ready, and a following for her frank use of words for body parts, a matter-of-fact delivery in an instantly recognisable Eastern European accent. She worked on TV too; a tiny, forthright woman who'd been orphaned by the Holocaust, and earned a doctorate in education. She answered questions people were too scared to say out loud and discussed things they'd never heard of.

She was firmly non-judgemental, and talked about faked orgasms, myths of menstruation, how not to get pregnant, contraception ideas, guilt, and suggested, 'Maybe put a finger, or even a cucumber or a banana in the vagina...' (May I be candid: I think most people would advise against a banana.)

Her first edition came out when herpes was considered the most worrisome disease and before much useful information at all about the emerging AIDS pandemic. Of course she amended her later advice, but it's poignant to read that first edition, advising somebody, uselessly, how not to get 'Kaposi's sarcoma' – don't have sex with anyone 'promiscuous'.

It was the activism of gay men and lesbians in the later 1980s that compelled public health action on AIDS that would eventually save millions of lives, and help normalise public discussions about sex in many countries around the world.

You should have sex outside with high heels on near a sprinkler, judging by this photo in New 101 Kama Sutra Sex Positions, *1995. The book was sold inside a plastic bag. (National Library of Australia)*

Dr Ruth talked about the possibility of a 'G-spot' in the vagina that might afford a woman a non-clitoral orgasm, though more recent research from clitoral researcher and urologist Professor Helen O'Connell makes it clear that supposed spot is just the closest bit of the wall of the vagina to the other end of the clitoris. Dr Ruth went on to write more than 40 books and was still giving advice – about online dating – in 2018, when she was 90.

"Sex education is about how to please men."

The golden era of 1970s and 1980s women's magazine advice influenced by Helen Gurley Brown's *Cosmopolitan* magazine was often more of the 'how to give a blow job' school of thought. Meanwhile, *Dolly* magazine in Australia led the world in matter-of-fact sexual and anatomy advice from the 'Dolly Doctor' columnist.

More than 4000 girls responded to my survey in 2006 for the first edition of my book *Girl Stuff: Your Full-on Guide to the Teen Years*. Asked what they wanted to know about sex, few asked, 'How do I avoid getting pregnant?' or 'What about sexually transmitted diseases?' Instead, a huge number of girls asked a variation of 'How do I do it to make it seem to the guy like I know what I'm doing?'. While many teen boys are told by porn that anal sex makes women go wild with desire and gives them an orgasm (it doesn't), girls are often not advised of how much it will hurt, how it puts them at more risk of infections and that they don't have to do it. Anyway, that makes for some long conversations in your editor's office about 'How are we going to tackle anal sex?' that startles all the people passing in the corridor, I can tell you.

A three-dimensional model of the entire structure of the clitoris which, when worn as jewellery, causes some men to say the mini-Klingon warship around your neck isn't quite correct. (Created by Odile Fillod, photographer Marie Docher, 2010)

"Masturbation makes you craaaazy."

That 1920s Chinese sex education treatise claimed that masturbation caused TB and girls to 'lose their fragrance'. Australia's 1940s government-issue *Sex Instruction* book told girls, 'This act is most harmful and disgusting, and you must never allow yourself to do it ... rendering you unfit for marriage, or the enjoyment of the sex act, or the procreation of children.'

Masturbation was for a long time cited by all available doctors and advice authors as the 'sin of self-abuse', aka 'habitual pollutions', 'contaminations' and 'unnatural vice'. It was, they

'It's not fair, I think you're really mean ... you never make me scream.' – From the song 'Not Fair' by Lily Allen, from the album It's Not Me It's You, 2009

said, a direct cause of insanity for both sexes, and prostitution in women.

It was the cause of pale, listless women and all their illnesses, although that was also caused by tight-lacing, or being inferior, or opium, or arsenic beauty treatments, or exhaustion, or being a vampire.

The obsessively anti-sex campaigner, eugenicist, Seventh Day Adventist, vegetarian activist and 'sanitarium' (private hospital) owner Dr John Kellogg first marketed Cornflakes as a healthy food which would stave off the desires to masturbate.

Images of masturbation by women were long considered a titillation for men, and positive ideas about it being by women and for women were longer in . . . coming. In her 2003 thesis about 19th-century banger on-ers in fiction and medical texts about masturbation, *The Secret Vice*, Diane Mason, tells us that sex chronicler Nancy Friday described masturbation as a 'beauty treatment' and Betty Dodson said 'it's the way we learn to love ourselves and to build self-esteem'.

Sex educators suggest that masturbation is a way for girls to learn how they can feel during sexual activity. Woman-friendly sex toy online retailers have gone a long way to normalise it. Bzzzt.

"Contraception isn't a big deal."

Contraception has always mattered more to women than men, because 'left holding the baby' wasn't just a charming metaphor.

It's hard for us to imagine now that a woman without contraception could easily have eight or more pregnancies in 10–12 years. Her body was often damaged and she was exhausted by a life of pregnancy breastfeeding; back-breaking, soul-destroying, constant housework and a desperate need to feed and clothe children.

Male doctors and scientists in professions traditionally dictated who could get contraception, and how it was used. The Pill and the Women's Liberation movement in the 1970s made the biggest break with that past.

A Women's Lib booklet from about 1971, now held at the National Library, puts it starkly, 'The man simply cannot be trusted to be sufficiently careful about contraception, and his mistakes are your problem.' The booklet, subtitled *What Every Girl Should Know About Contraception*, was based on a South Australian Women's Liberation group, which was used as a template around the country. When more than 18,000 copies were distributed in Sydney, and some were found in school lockers, detectives from the New South Wales 'Abortion Squad' turned up to question the principals of girls' high schools. No charges ensued.

The copy in the National Library is not 'designed', and has no illustrations or graphics; it's just pages of plain copied typing, limp and worn, after being passed hand-to-hand to who knows how many women. It has done good service, and now spends most of its time having a good lie down in a darkened room.

Now we're used to searching any info on a computer, it's hard to imagine that this precious, grubby pamphlet would have been a revelation to women in their 20s or 30s, listing the contraceptive methods she could use, if she pretended she was married to get a prescription. A month's supply of the Pill was expensive, but you could manage it: $1.97. It revolutionised women's lives by giving them choices.

By the late 20th century, nine out of ten married couples in

'A woman needs a man like a fish needs a bicycle.' – Irina Dunn

Badge.
(State Library of Victoria)

Few things look more like actual doodles than contraceptive Inter-uterine devices (IUDs). (Museum of Applied Arts and Sciences)

Western countries took contraception, because they could. Left to her own (contraceptive) devices and methods, women overwhelmingly chose to have one to three children, a huge reduction from common families with eight to fifteen children.

The history of contraceptive methods is about beliefs and hope, mess and failure. It's about strange insertions, interference from sociopathic religious extremists, shameful white supremacist attitudes, blood poisoning from incompetent abortions on kitchen tables, sex strikes and all sorts of strange devices.

Going through the online catalogue at the Museum of Applied Arts and Sciences, noodling around looking at Gräfenberg rings, 75-year-old perished condoms, loopy IUDs and other contraceptive devices, I spent some time staring at a particularly confusing one before realising that I was staring at a vase that once belonged to 1930s aviatrix Nancy Bird Walton.

"Contraception was invented in 1967."

Ancient Jewish, Islamic, and Asian texts recommended all sorts of activity for women to allegedly expel semen after sex – including star-jumping. Contraceptive pessaries of the past include crocodile dung, honey, and ant-gum.

Chinese men were traditionally advised that they should stop their penis from ejaculating inside a vagina by 'gnashing the teeth a thousand times' and 'pausing nine times after every series of nine strokes'.

Coitus interruptus – withdrawing the penis from a vagina before ejaculation – was a popular attempt: *The Curious History of Contraception* by Shirley Green (1971) cites an estimation that this produces a pregnancy 18 times in every 100.

She goes on to say that 'coitus interruptus' (everything sounds politer in Latin) was widely recommended in India and the Islamic world. Christ had nothing to say about it, and St Paul had conniptions at the mere thought of sex – so no joy there.

The Greeks and Romans were said to be not so good at prevention but regular practitioners of abortion and infanticide. On every continent (maybe not Antarctica) people independently tried to invent contraception using long breastfeeding, abstinence and various attempts at barrier methods.

A pre-1920s book called *The Wife's Handbook: Radical Remedy in Social Science or Borning Better Babies Through Regulated Reproduction by Controlling Conception* went through dozens of editions, and advised, 'Want of restraint in speech and conduct, too great a love of fun and excitement or admiration, may lead a girl to do or say or allow things which are lowering . . . I appeal to you as women. For the sake of the Empire, for the sake of future men and women of the Empire, above all for the sake of the children, do all in your power to make our country purer and cleaner.' This was all coded advice for women to refuse any sex before marriage, and thereby cut down on cases of syphilis and gonorrhea.

Women have always tried to control their own fertility: to avoid pregnancy, to try to save their own health, to try to save their own lives. Women from Ireland to Ghana and the Americas have used herbs, amulets and other tokens, often worn as jewellery, and attempts at pregnancy termination, as well as cultural rules about abstinence and extended breastfeeding to try to 'space' their children.

The 1981 book *Abstinence as a Method of Birth Control*, by Israel O. Orubuloye, used information about Yoruba women living in Nigeria, drawing on joint research since 1972 by the Australian National University and the University of Ibadan. Hundreds of women in two large village areas talked about the traditional advice to use abstinence and breastfeeding to put three years between each childbirth if they could manage it. (Breastfeeding can lessen the chance of pregnancy for some women, but it isn't a reliable contraception method compared to medical methods.)

'Abstinence is the most important single factor in the containment of fertility in Yoruba society', he reported. It always gives my heart a lift when I see research that tries hard to listen to women. It paints a bigger picture to know that grandmas usually came to stay for three months after a birth, to help. Most grandmas were women over 45 who'd had decided at the arrival of their first grandchild and subsequent responsibilities to give up having sex themselves.

Most women in the study had heard of charms and medicines from native doctors to use as contraception, but didn't use them. They knew about condoms, but didn't have a means to buy them.

Yoruba women living in larger cities were far more likely to have access to contraception other than abstinence but still commonly practised abstinence for up to nine months after the birth. Abstinence was recommended by older women to younger ones, most often a joint decision within marriages and accepted by men and women as the usual way, not as a hardship.

The 'word-of-mouth' advice on contraception is strong across cultures and down generations. A study into the emergency contraceptive knowledge of young Nigerian women university students in 2005, led by obstetrician and gynaecologist Dr Chris Akani, found results that mirror many of the ineffective methods which have also been rumoured around the world, including douches of Coca-Cola or alcohol, herbal preparations, laxatives and drinking gin, and more particular to African countries, the popularity of various quinine preparations, with many dangerous side effects, or taking large doses of antacids, 'a dose of salts'. None of these methods is effective contraception.

"Family planning should be racist."

Campaigners for women's rights and access to contraception were often born of the suffrist and women's rights movements and women doctors who'd seen the misery of unrelenting fertility. But most of the well-known ones, including Marie Stopes and Margaret Sanger, were also big fans of shameful hardcore white supremacist eugenics, called 'race hygiene'. Exhausted women injured by too many childbirths weren't good at keeping the white race strong, the argument went.

There were many persistent lies of early colonial Australia used against Aboriginal women. One was that Indigenous women and women with darker skin were able to do more physical work, and had an 'easier' time giving birth and recovering. Another lie was that Aboriginal women practised regular infanticide and cannibalism to space their babies out more. The truth was that the miscarriages and stillbirths caused to Aboriginal women by the illnesses and malnutrition inflicted by the 'settlers' went unaddressed, and often unremarked by the colonisers.

Dr. Patterson's Inflated Rim Pessary

Three Sizes—Small, Medium and Large.

Feminine Sheath or Capote Anglaise

One Size Only.

Contraceptives (not hats). From The Wife's Guide and Friend, *1898. (National Library of Australia)*

Lots of historical white supremacist contraceptive information is kept at the National Library, and in its ephemera collection of pamphlets there's a 1930s booklet, *Sex In Life: Young Women* by Violet Swaisland, published by the 'Racial Hygiene Association of NSW'.

There's a set of detailed instructions from the same era in a booklet called *Equipping A Birth Control Clinic* by the contraception pioneer Marie Stopes. Some of the advice is kind and thoughtful: have a waiting room properly warmed by a guarded fire, with childcare, 'someone to mind the little ones while the mother is in the clinic being fitted and advised'.

But how might a mother with dark skin have felt, passing such a 'cheerful' institution with its bunch of flowers and white-painted rooms, needing information about family planning, all withheld from her?

Many of Stopes's books were published by the 'Mothers' Clinic for Constructive Birth Control and Racial Progress'; her 1919 book *Wise Parenthood* is 'dedicated to all who wish to see our race grow in strength and beauty'. The contraceptive pessaries her clinics sold had the brand-name 'Pro-race'.

The global women's health organisation that bears Marie Stopes's name now stands against her racist attitudes; it began in 1975 after taking over a mothers' clinic and now operates in 37 countries. More than 30 million women are using contraception it provided them.

"Men should control contraception."

When a family company which sold medical devices including trusses and contraceptives published its 1898 catalogue wrapped in a booklet called *The Wife's Guide and Friend* by

'Dr S. Warren', a meddling Melbourne cop took it to court on obscenity charges.

The notorious Detective Macmanamny (I haven't fallen on the keyboard, that was really his name) was variously described by the ever-undaunted *Truth* newspaper of the day as a bounder, an orangutan, a maker-upper of confessions, and a man with fancy possessions unexplained by a police wage. A frothing prosecutor told the court that it was all right to have contraceptive information in a book for 'medical men and experts; but this is a popular work, which any young girl may easily get hold of and read'. Quite right, imagine if she ever found out she had a vagina.

In any case, the magistrate wasn't playing, and dismissed the charges. The company kept publishing the catalogue until the 1920s, though I don't know that there ever was a real Dr Warren.

The booklet contained illustrations of contraceptives, such as re-usable pink rubber condoms and black rubber bowler-hattish diaphragms ('With constant use one will last a year'), and fountainous douche equipment, with 'lengths of drab India rubber hose' and bulbs; sponges and tablets made of quinine, and a solid gold spring-shaped metal IUD. It also sold sanitary pads, lozenges to protect against diphtheria and measles (which of course didn't work) and DIY childbirth kits.

Many other contraception campaigners tangled with the law: Margaret Sanger was arrested in 1916 for opening a 'family planning clinic' in Brooklyn, New York. And many campaigners had their books banned.

Shameful eugenicist Margaret Sanger looking very pleased with herself after being released from jail. (New Haven Historical Society)

"The 'morning-after pill' is an abortion pill."

No, it isn't. The morning-after pill prevents pregnancy, it's not a medical termination. Journalists, anti-contraception and abortion campaigners and even lawmakers consistently get them mixed up. (I've done it myself.)

"Condoms are awfully modern."

Casanova, the scrofulous root-rat, was said to use a sheepskin condom in the 1700s, and since then they've become far more effective, much healthier, way thinner and part of a multi-billion-dollar industry and front line against sexually transmitted diseases.

I still remember a rousing argument I had on late-night radio with a venerable male commentator during the publicity tour for my 1988 book *The Modern Girl's Guide to Safe Sex*, during the emerging AIDS pandemic, who was very cross at the idea that men would need to, or would voluntarily wear condoms for sex. At least he was better than the Sydney radio host who asked me sneeringly if I'd had all the diseases mentioned in the book. Readers, let us draw a veil.

Pissed? Stoned? Horny? A condom packet design suggested the reasons you might need a condom, possibly 1980s. (National Library of Australia)

"The Pill is a miracle & marvellous for all."

The availability of the contraceptive Pill changed the course of women's history. For the first time, women had a way to control their own fertility, mostly in the Western world, although they initially had to pretend they were married.

Early versions of the Pill, 60 years ago, had much higher hormone levels with more side effects. Modern pills are far more sophisticated and well 'tolerated' by millions of women. While millions take it for contraception, other millions take it for hormonal symptoms and to control misbehaving periods.

Pill-makers originally advised to stop the Pill for seven days, which produced a bleed that 'feels' and looks like a period, because they thought women would want periods. There's no health reason for this, so these days many girls and women take the Pill to skip having periods altogether, as do some trans men.

There's been a scandalous lack of interest in the medical profession to do large studies on how the Pill might affect brain chemistry, mood, and other things that women have a right to know if they're paying for it. If men took the Pill, you can bet we would know more about what else it might do besides preventing pregnancy.

One of the questions women could have asked doctors was, 'Why are you such a patriarchal arse?'; health pamphlet, c1970. (Museum of Applied Arts and Sciences)

"The Pill is terrible & makes you have sex with the wrong person."

Many naturopaths say the Pill is bad for women because it isn't natural. Some use phrases to describe the Pill, such as 'Pill steroids' and 'forced Pill bleeds'. Many 'natural' health advocates oppose hormonal medication on various grounds, saying it suppresses libido, causes women to choose the wrong partners. So far no studies support the claim that being on the Pill can delay fertility and the libido thing is hard to study because of so many variables (is your partner bad at it; have you got a good book to read?).

Some studies claim that the Pill makes women choose unmanly men or experience the smell of sweaty T-shirts differently which interferes with their choice of 'mate' (I know, euw). I've waded through a lot of them and will never get those hours back. They provide fleeting clickbait with headlines like, 'Unsexy guys annoy fertile girlfriends'. A cognitive neuroscientist consulted for this book reckons the findings in such studies often are used to bolster the researcher's own theories. Meta-analysts have disagreed about whether they show anything at all.

"Trust your body."

A common slogan women hear is to reject hormone medication as 'unnatural' and to 'trust their body'. This can often make women feel their body is defective, even less womanly, and that it's their own fault if they have a hormone-related medical condition. In fact, hormone misbehaviour and its related symptoms and conditions are incredibly common – and for many women, it can mean lifelong difficulty. For many, hormone medication will be an almost miraculous help, while others struggle to find useful treatment.

"'Natural' contraception is a thing."

Abstaining from sex for some time during a menstrual cycle has been used as a birth control method for aaages: centuries. The main problem with it is that it's extremely unreliable.

After ovulation was studied in the 1930s, it made for better calculations of the likely fertile and infertile times of a woman's menstrual cycle. Abstaining from sex for the likely 'fertile' days was known as the 'Calendar Method' in 1934, and was promoted by the Catholic church as the 'Rhythm Method', or the 'Billings Method'. It was especially prized by the church because it didn't work. Midwives in the 1950s nodded to each other in the break room, having a fag, saying, 'another Billings baby' about recent arrivals.

Despite the repackaging of 'natural fertility' with vaginal thermometers and phone apps to predict or identify the time of ovulation, it still relies on hope and the ability to 'not have sex' at the indicated times. Condoms and hormonal methods still have a much higher rate of reliability.

In 2019, a podcaster called Bria Badu tweeted a list of recommended herbal and plant 'alternative natural contraception', some of which, said doctors and botanists, can cause liver damage and other side effects, including possible death. None of them work (including figs and ginger, which is not contraception: it's a dessert).

Marketing material for the 'Rythmeter' calendar-calculator, which came with 20 years of blank menstrual calendars (and probably children), 1960s. (National Library of Australia)

"Contraception is a sin."

Women carried the terrible burden of being disallowed the right to contraception by religious leaders. Married women had to keep producing children endlessly, through injury and exhaustion, depression or poverty – or else they'd go to Hell. This was reaffirmed by the leader of Catholics in Australia, Cardinal Gilroy, at a 1968 Press conference. Gilroy was flanked by flunky priests and a Catholic doctor.

Despite there being two women reporters and the women of Australia involved, Gilroy stood up and began, 'Good afternoon, gentlemen,' before continuing to condemn Catholic women to lives of uncontrolled fertility which was already causing drudgery, exhaustion, medical injury, and even death. If women found the edict difficult, he said, they should pray.

Worldwide, hundreds of priests rebelled, and millions of women would ignore the reaffirmed rules.

Cardinal Gilroy wrote extensively of the evils of contraception, directing Catholic pharmacists not to sell contraceptives, effectively banning them in some suburbs and country towns, a situation which continues in some places. He described birth control as evil, lamenting that it had prevented more extensive 'white occupation' of Australia.

Five years before this Press Conference, Gilroy sent accused paedophile priest Denis Daly to WA, to avoid him being charged by police. Nobody knows how many others he moved. Gilroy was subsequently knighted and made Australian of the Year.

"Abortion has always been considered murder."

Abortion used to be legal and okay with most of the men who ran churches and called themselves philosophers as long as it took place before 'the quickening', the first time a woman felt her baby move in her womb. This also left it up to the woman to identify and make decisions for herself. It was usually a matter of when a fetus was considered to develop a soul. Aristotle, that insufferable tool, said it took 40 days for a male fetus and 90 days for a female one.

Theologians argued about whether women should be punished for any abortion, whether it was okay if her life was threatened, and whether she was a murderer. Women might be forgiven for wondering which rule was which, when. Catholic canon law has prohibited or restricted and allowed abortion at various times.

In 1930, the Pope (the global head of the Catholic church) reaffirmed that a mother should die before a fetus, even if the fetus couldn't live after the woman died. In 1999 another Pope said God could forgive an abortion, and yet another one said in 2015 priests could decide not to excommunicate a woman for it.

In 2019, a newer Pope said a woman who needed an abortion for medical reasons was the same as hiring a hit-man. He announced this wearing a dress and slippers standing next to a man dressed in a 16th-century striped full-body costume with puffed-sleeves and a giant feather on his head, holding a spear.

"Abortion is a new phenomenon."

Instructions for causing a 'miscarriage' by Emperor Shen Nung 2737–2696 BC were quoted well into the 16th century AD. For hundreds of years European midwives used herbal recipes.

Lots of ads in the 19th century had coded messages about 'regularity' and 'stoppages', which I thought were about constipation until I saw a lecture by researcher and author Robyn Annear, who explained they were code for 'bringing on a period' – in other words, end a pregnancy. Of course, the 'cures' no more caused pregnancy termination than they fixed 'bad legs', nervousness or anything else claimed, but who would be game to complain about that?

Gideon Haigh's book about the history of illegal abortion in Australia was called *The Racket* because it was a crime for decades, but corruption and religion combined to perpetuate its great danger to desperate women who were exploited. Most police turned a blind eye while women were damaged or killed by 'backyard' abortionists. Prosecutions were rare, unless a woman died. Whole hospital wards in Australia were dedicated to women suffering from resulting lacerations and sepsis.

Most women in the 19th and 20th century who died from post-attempted abortion tried to do it themselves using unravelled wire – a metal clothes hanger symbol came to be a silent slogan for the right to a safe surgical operation), or injuring themselves somehow, including throwing themselves downstairs. At a time when very few women knew how to swim, many threw themselves into rivers and drowned.

Writer Kate Jennings was good and furious at her left-wing male colleagues by the time her words were included in a Women's Liberation pamphlet distributed at a 1970s anti-Vietnam war protest: 'How many of you . . . who can see women can't get abortions . . . would get off your fat piggy arses and protest against the killing and victimisation of women in your own country? Go check the figures, how many Australian men have died in Vietnam and how many women have died from backyard abortions.'

Nobody knows how many girls and women died of abortions and attempted terminations before it became legal in

'Women are often blamed by conservatives for high abortion rates. The truth is that women do not "want" abortions, they need them.'
– A History of Contraception by Angus McLaren, 1990

some circumstances. A common estimate of illegal abortions each year in Australia was about 100,000. The ABC reported that by 2017 the estimated yearly rate of modern, far safer surgical abortions is believed to have fallen to below 65,000, as contraception use has risen.

Anti-abortion activists call themselves 'pro-life', while advocates for legal abortion called themselves 'pro-choice'. Some say if you oppose safe abortions, you are arguing for forced birth.

Recognised elements of partner abuse and coercive control include preventing women from taking contraception or choosing a pregnancy termination, and in some cases includes forced termination, under threat. Independent counsellors and doctors will talk to women about all their available options with an unwanted pregnancy. Church groups and anti-abortion extremists have set up 'Pregnancy Advice' phone lines and services and advertised themselves with similar names to independent services. In the last five years I have seen these advertised online, and in uni student orientation information, as independent services.

The right to terminate a pregnancy is one of those still denied many women in the world, and where the legal right has been won, it's constantly under challenge by churches and their government allies.

Badges, c1970s.
(State Library of Victoria)

"Abortions are dangerous."

The medication that causes the termination of a known pregnancy is commonly taken a few weeks into a pregnancy, up to 14 weeks. It's often known as RU-486, or a specific course-combo of two medications: mifepristone and misoprostol. It has to be prescribed by a doctor, but can be taken at home in private. Both medications are known to be very safe, and statistically much safer for women than childbirth.

"Abortions always make women feel depressed & regretful"

Large-scale studies show that the vast majority of women don't regret their terminations. Some will, of course, just as some women will at times regret having children, though there is a much bigger taboo against saying so. Feelings are necessarily complicated about such things.

I'm sorry that I was pregnant at the wrong time, as a younger woman, but I don't regret the termination. I think it allowed me to be a better mum when the right time came.

Some of writer Glen Tomasetti's lyrics for her blues song 'The Punishment of Eve', about unwanted pregnancy and abortion, 1969, found among Dr Bertram Wainer's papers. (National Library of Australia)

"Abortion is selfish."

Abortion is often portrayed as a 'lifestyle choice'. Many women want a pregnancy termination because they want to able to be a better mother to the children they already have, or may have in the future. They have pregnancy terminations so they can be a good mother to the children they already have. And they have terminations for medical reasons that are complex, and often very difficult to cope with.

The swinging modern world said to me,
'Time for everybody to take their liberty,
Love affairs? Just as many as you will,
Have no worries – simply take the pill.'

At last that old man world said to me,
'Oh what a pleasure you will be!'
And I beguiling and beguiled.
Yielded to persuasion, now I am with child.

Society in general, said to me,
'An unmarried mother you're gonna be,
You must have the baby and when you go.
O't by, will we make it hard for you!'

"No might mean yes."

In his 1992 judgement in a marital rape case, South Australian Supreme Court judge Derek Bollen felt secure in using the phrase 'rougher than usual handling' for what he described as permissible conduct from a husband 'persuading' his wife to give a 'reluctant consent'. The 'sex' involved in the case was a violent assault, including with a bottle, to which a man had pleaded guilty. Bollen told the jury some women fabricate rape accusations: 'It is a very easy allegation to make.'

There's any amount of that sort of vile palaver in our recent history, so it's good to know that sexual rights advocates are pushing education and the legal recognition of clear, verbal and enthusiastic consent before sex.

Though conservative commentators have said that a clear question-and-answer system would be a romance-killer, erotic novelists would disagree with the unsexiness of 'yes, yes, yes' or 'please, please, do it.' A *Rad Sex & Consent 'Zine'* was published in 2014 by Melbourne Uni's 'Student Union Wom*n's, Queer, Indigenous, Creative Arts and Disabilities Departments, the Monash Students' Association Wom*n's and Queer Departments, and the La Trobe Student Union Women's and Queer Departments. (Under the circumstances I hesitate to say 'mouthful'.)

Consent, the zine says, 'is conditional, situational, should be freely given and understood that it can be retracted at any time.' Author Cinnamon wrote: 'Fucking becomes a privilege enjoyed by those who society deems fuckable, and for everyone else – get fucked.'

The advice continued, 'You are allowed to ask for sex. Politely, clearly and before any other sexual advances are made, it is okay to express an interest in having sex with someone you like . . . make it clear . . . that you will respect whatever answer they give. No means NO. If they tell you they are not interested, you don't ask again. You don't pressure them, judge them. Or treat them unkindly.

'You have the right to say no. Saying no does not make you a bad person. Saying no should not end a friendship . . . It is ok to say no within a consensual relationship.

'It's okay to change your mind. A yes is not a green light for all things sexual . . . consenting to sex doesn't encompass every foreseeable act.'

"You're a slut."

The word 'reputation' when applied in a certain tone of voice to a woman is often enough to carry the implication that the reputation is not professional, it's sexual, and it's bad. A woman or a girl who had sex was disparaged as 'easy' or a 'slut'. The phrase 'town bike' was employed to shame a girl, but not a guy, who'd had sex with more than one person.

The accusation of being no longer a virgin was sometimes levelled at a girl who said 'no' as revenge, or to 'ruin her reputation', so she may as well say 'yes'. A reputation was considered indelible, and even referred to as a 'stain'.

Lady Pennington wrote *An Unfortunate Mother's Advice to Her Absent Daughters*, a 1760s manual for the daughters she was prevented from seeing ever again after a divorce. Her advice was clear – a blameless life was not enough; it also had to be seen to be blameless. And once a woman had even been seen flirting, the assumption would be that she had 'committed adultery'. (One always 'commits' adultery in the same way as murder.)

Lady Pennington confides that although she was a virgin on her wedding day, her 'great gaiety of temper' made a bad impression and she was done for in Society. She would, I imagine, feel for the girls whose private photos have been used against them in messages and on social media.

Centuries ago, teenage girls were told they were mad sex maniacs who need to be given sex or they go bonkers and waste away with 'chlorosis', aka greensickness said to be common in unmarried women.

According to the 1930s sex education guide *The Book of Nature: A Complete Marriage Guide for Men and Women* by Dr Thomas Faulkner, 'nymphomania' in women is caused by 'masturbation, exciting diet, and indolent and voluptuous life... or forced abstinence.' The treatments included an unstimulating diet, stitz (salt) baths, a vegetarian diet, not drinking tea, a cold douche up at least two apertures of the undercarriage, sticking your head in ice water, a wet bandage and a change of scenery.

'There are so many evils attending the loss of virtue in women, and so greatly are minds of that sex depraved when they have deviated from the path of rectitude, that [it] destroys almost every public virtue of the men.' – The History of Women, From the Earliest Antiquity, To the Present Time by William Alexander, 1796

"You're frigid."

A girl or a woman who said no to sex was liable to be variously described as a cocktease or frigid rather than discerning.

I was accused of being a 'frigid slut' by a shouty boy in the schoolyard when I was 12. It was a bit confusing until I realised he may as well have said 'Fat penis poo' – he was simply parroting accusing words that were supposed to upset girls.

"Inject your G-spot."

The G-spot is NOT a thing. It is just the point on your vaginal wall which is closest to the other end of the nerve system that underlies your clitoris. In other words, it isn't a magic button – it's just a next-door neighbour. The clitoris is somewhat like an iceberg in that most of it is invisible, but it's not usually a danger to shipping.

While reporters gleefully re-gargled the claims of the man who patented the name he used for the 'O shot' injection, gynaecologist and author Dr Jen Gunter pointed out that the 'Medical School, Birmingham' he claimed to have attended was not an accredited medical school.

Hundreds of thousands of dollars were spent on similar injections by women who were underwhelmed and unaffected by any results. There is no evidence that it's safe, and none whatsoever that show the procedure makes it easier to orgasm.

We are still being told to do things to ourselves which almost certainly don't work and which are ludicrously expensive, and possibly very harmful. Men are rarely told to graft on bulbous tentacle shapes onto the base of their penis designed to stimulate the clitoris. All right, I might have had a bad dream.

"Burn the inside of your vagina with a laser."

Some profiteering gynaecologists around the world have hired devices and are pushing a procedure to post-menopausal women called 'vaginal rejuvenation', aka other silly phrases such as the 'Mona Lisa smile'.

The laser machines cause low-grade burns inside the vagina. It's claimed without evidence that the recovery will 'rejuvenate' the vagina and make it more moist and tighter. There will be more on this in my next book, in which I shall go off like a box of fireworks.

"Women who don't want sex should be fixed."

I shall also lay aside until my next book the fact that not all women have a fall in libido in peri-menopause or after menopause. Women are routinely told to undergo expensive, unproven procedures or take medication to 'cure' their lack of libido. The partners of menopausal women are not instructed to take medicine to diminish their sex drive, or urged by doctors to scour their penises until they wilt.

"Decent women have no sexual feelings."

Oh, do shut up. This was the claim of the 19th-century galoot and anti-masturbation obsessive Dr William Acton, who added that if women did want sex, that was caused by periods or nymphomania.

In 1867 the New Orleans Medical Society Journal warned that women could get sexually excited by rhythmical use of the sewing machine foot treadle. For heaven's sake don't tell them about leaning against a washing machine.

Poor old Lady Pennington, who felt she was hurled out of Society due to flirting, never knew that one day a lady's insatiable desires would be considered fun or that one day hence it would be possible for a woman, perhaps without carefully reading the dimensions or prevaricating over a colour chart, to arrange to have delivered to her home a crimson dildo as long as her forearm that revolves to a precise, robotic rhythm, and can be operated by remote control. Now *that* would have set tongues a-wagging in the drawing room.

I just thought I'd end on a positive note after all those bastard priests. And bastard vagina-laserers. You're most welcome.

A model in a hostess apron and pearls brandishes a snapper in an ad for Terylene fabric, 1950s.
(Helmut Newton, State Library Victoria)

4

DO ALL THE HOUSEWORK

EVERY GIRL OUGHT TO WEAR AN APRON ALL DAY, advised *The Girl's Own Paper* magazine in the 1880s: It 'at once stamps her character as careful, economical and exquisitely tidy'. *Girl's Own* also made the arresting claim that Eve in the Bible wore an apron. (That was a *leaf*, ladies.)

In the 1600s rich women wore aprons as a sort of fashionable lady uniform; Queen Anne had one with gold lace and spangles, not that she ever did the washing up, I bet.

Working women have worn some form of overalls, often with trousers, for farm and factory work. In the 1950s, we were advised to have working aprons or pinnies (short for pinafores) that covered our chests for everyday use that could become stained and worn, but also a pretty, flounced hostess apron to pop on for visitors or the husband. Hostess aprons were basically a performance, a pretty costume to hide the real work.

Mrs Lance Rawson, the first celebrity advisor to Australian colonial women, told them to make their own heavy aprons. They should be sewn from hessian or calico bags, with separate pull-on over-sleeves, and needed to be high-cut and waterproof lined for wash-day: 'Anyone who has seen Madame Weigel's patterns will know the pinafore I mean . . . mine lasted over 18 months'. (Mrs Rawson's heavy washing would have been done by enslaved Aboriginal and Vanuatuan women paid nothing or a pittance; more of Australia's dirty housework secrets a little later.)

John Clarke testing his incidental apron in a costume try-on for The Brush Off. *(Courtesy Kitty Stuckey)*

When writer-actor John Clarke asked costumier Kitty Stuckey to find a suitable apron (but no shoes) for his scene as a character in the 2004 TV-movie of Shane Moloney's *The Brush Off*, it might have seemed incongruous. The character who was going to wear the apron was a powerful political advisor.

As I watched the short scene go to air, I realised it was the first time I'd ever seen a male character on TV series wear an apron that wasn't a joke, or to indicate an oppressed husband. *This* apron was quietly subversive: it said that it was normal and practical for a bloke, as well as a woman, to be cleaning up the kitchen, looking after kids, and doing his other work at the same time.

"Housework is a woman's duty."

What are we to make of the fact that, in Britain, homely means lovely and cosy, and in the US, it means not pretty enough?

As women in the paid workforce are discriminated against, sexually harassed, traditionally paid less (especially as nurses, teachers and childcare workers), women at home are assumed to be non-intellectual, uninteresting, doing work that is supposedly revered but is unpaid and not counted in the economy, despite being worth billions. Stereotypes cast the 'working woman' as selfish and ambitious, and the 'housewife' as a saintly, dutiful, worthless drudge.

This ignores the fact that it isn't always a choice, and that the same women will perform both roles at some time in her life, and often years of doing both simultaneously. The false war between women who 'work' and women who 'stay at home' is just another way of saying, if you're a woman, you're doing it wrong.

Women forced out of paid jobs when men came home from WWII were cross for the rest of their lives. Women were sacked from public service jobs as soon as they married. Married women were barred from job interviews. And then in the 1960s and '70s a big shift happened again among women rebelling against rules to confine them to their home after they were married.

They'd dutifully produced a baby boom and the kids were at school – now what? Why shouldn't they control their own fertility, and *choose* to study or work? Why couldn't they be recognised for their artistic work? Why couldn't they write a book instead of typing up their husband's? 'Housewives' were unhappy, and the widespread prescription of addictive antidepressants wasn't helping. Many women were understandably thrilled at the idea of 'Women's Liberation'.

Various possible apronry suggested by The Girl's Own Paper, *1881. (Courtesy Ruth Jones)*

The life of a fulltime housewife was relatively new in history. Women had been villagers, field workers, factory or domestic service workers. The Industrial Revolution and rise of a middle class, plus returned soldiers wanting all the jobs, condemned housewives to work alone. What's more, they had to fit into the role of lady of the house – but without the servants that traditionally came with it.

A 'lady' kept her house by managing her staff, and doing industrious decorative sewing and ordering the family's clothes, furniture, and meals from somebody else. In contrast, a housewife was expected to do all the chores herself: sew clothes, shop and cook, clean. It never ended: the ghastly prospect of years of pregnancy, breastfeeding and nappies, and lone housework, responsible for organising every doctor's appointment, every outfit, supervise homework and the family's health, all day, every day, including family holidays, for the rest of her life, must have seemed overwhelming.

Beautifying her home must have been an act of bravery, as well as industry. A housewife's decorative crafts and art and knowledge, the beautiful things she made were often dismissed as duties, or 'hobbies'. Women did the dull cooking and sewing, not like the men who vacuumed up only for accolades, were home-sewers but never fashion designers, cooks not chefs and dabblers not genius painters. The extraordinary decoration, design and engineering done by women went mostly unrecognised: except, of course, by other women.

My mum left a country high school early to get a job, moving into low-level typist pools and office chores in the city. When I was a teenager, she went 'back to school', earning a Year 12 qualification for 'mature-age students'. Others were against it: she needed to keep up the house and might neglect the children. She went ahead, with only slightly less sheet-washing discernible, still responsible for everything else. With the self-centredness of youth I had no idea how hard it was for her. We passed Year 12 in the same year and she went on to become an art teacher.

Although the earworm 1970s TV ad announced that mothers 'oughta be congratulated', they rarely were, except in the ad, for serving the right margarine. 'Housewife' became an insulting word; the job still exists on some official forms as 'home duties'. The old image of a dull and dowdy housewife is now being replaced with idleness, conspicuous facial cosmetic procedures, and vulgarity, a legacy of *The Real Housewives* TV show franchise.

"Housework has always been the same."

What housework used to mean for most women, and still involves for millions around the world, is an unimaginable amount of work, much of it outside the home (fetching and carrying heavy water, tending to animals and crops or garden) and work inside the home without any machinery or 'labour-saving device' for cooking or cleaning. The very indispensability of it – to keep yourself and your family alive – meant planning, execution, mad skills, and doing it over and over again forever.

To imagine the lives of women only a few generations back, we have to remember there were no shops to buy clothes, or any food that comes in packets, or ready-made furniture. No beauty aids or medicines for sale. Everything you or your family ate, wore, lay down on or owned had to be made from scratch. Everything was DIY: shoes, soap, lunch, a house. And after the sun went down, all you had to work by was a candle you'd made yourself from animal fat.

Clothes used to be made by women using their hands and rudimentary wooden devices to spin raw sheeps' wool or the fibres of the phooffy part of the cotton plant into long twisted strands that were woven or knitted until wooden looms came along, and then the steam-driven machines that women tended in the factories.

The resultant lengths of fabric would be hand-sewn into clothes, until affordable sewing machines were invented. In the Pacific, without fibres, Islander women would pound plants to make bark cloth. Other Indigenous people would use skins and handmade string and carved fasteners.

Everything available to eat was grown, harvested, cooked, and preserved for the winter if you were to survive it. Water had to be fetched from a river or village well (bonus points for having access to one that didn't spread typhoid), in a wooden bucket somebody had to construct, later boiled on an open fire, then clothes washed in that with homemade soap, and somehow dried in winter. To get milk, you had to keep a cow alive, milk it with your hands and try not to die from bacteria or tuberculosis in the milk before pasteurisation was invented.

Women were told, as soon as they were old enough to understand, that they would do this work. They learned from their mothers how to forage, plant, cut meat, cook the meals, and clean using ashes, sand, brick dust and brooms made of twigs.

Tasked with housework, women have only had machines and devices for the last two generations or so: a fridge in nearly every home, washing machines that soak, wash, squeeze, spin, and dry clothes, stove tops that don't need a chimney, enclosed ovens with a regulated measurable temperature, electric heaters, vacuum cleaners, ready-made clothes brought from shops. My nanna, on a farm, started her life without any of these. I have all of them.

"Women are the best at housework."

'Darling, you're so much better at cleaning the toilet. And the only one who notices it gets dirty, or cares. So, it totally makes sense that you would always be the one who cleans it.' Before this sort of nonsense, we were told that it was our religious duty to be the servants of our father and husband.

In the 1950s, author Mary Hyde listed the daily duties of a housewife, broken into hours from 7.30 am. Chores included: make breakfasts, see husband off without fuss, wash up breakfast dishes, tidy kitchen, make beds, clean bath and sinks, go shopping for food, thoroughly clean a different room every day, dust and tidy the others, polish some floors; an hour off to lunch and do mending or polishing silver. Then a free afternoon. Make dinner, and spend the evening 'amusing your husband'.

Generations of mothers and grandmothers would have been scandalised *speechless* at the idea of an afternoon off. 'The devil makes work for idle hands', they said, which means that if you weren't sewing, cooking, preserving, gardening, making something or cleaning something, you might dash off and rob a bank or worship Mr Beelzebub.

As women like my mum emerged from working or farm class to the lower middle class, they were given extra work to do like the dinner parties that used to be carried out by servants. Working hours and public infrastructure were arranged to suit commuting men, irrelevant to school hours and holidays, and the public transport needs of women. We were out of sight and out of mind.

"Women are the worst housekeepers."

There's a long tradition of men like 'Old Housekeeper', with their newspaper columns or books about how hopeless women are at their job of wife and mother, ranging from the 'not thrifty enough' to accusing mothers of murder when their kids get sick (because illness is caused by being dressed badly by your mother). Their idiosyncratic demands were many:

do pretty sewing to draw attention to your 'plump white hands', and make sure the soup is less than 180 degrees Fahrenheit.

In his 1885 edition of *Men & How to Manage Them: A Book For Australian Wives and Mothers* by 'An Old Housekeeper', women were told to change wash-day to later in the week, not to brush a man's hat and clothes because they were bad at it, and to only ask for things of a husband after dinner, and to overhaul their dreadful overspending habits. They ignored him.

One thunderer to a Balmain newspaper in the 1880s plunged mansplaining to new depths saying women should be good at 'bakeology, boilology, stitchology, makeology and mendology' but were 'too much averse to working, and too extravagant in all their tastes'.

One reader of *The Domestic Blunders of Women* column by A Mere Man, wrote to complain, 'You are a ruse to excite female readers.' Another said, 'Mere Man has mistaken his own saving and lifestyle for everyone else', but my favourite was, 'I wish when you wrote that article about women that someone had strangled you . . . PS I'm so mad I could chew his skin.'

"Being a repressed housewife is back in fashion."

New 'trad wife' blogs and 'surrendered wife' social media accounts promote the subservience of women to husbands, a movement with links to both evangelical Christian churches and white supremacy groups, who are recycling the old idea of women being responsible for creating new white children. Ugh.

"Housework is now shared equally with men."

Author Caroline Davidson reminds us that women, traditionally, have worked 365 days a year – often more hours on holidays such as Sundays and Christmas, to plan, make food for others, and clean up. A survey of 1250 urban English wives in 1934 recorded that most of them worked 12–14 hours on their feet.

Modern married men on average do more housework than their grandfathers, who did virtually none. But we also know women, even if they have a paid job as well, still consistently do more hours than men do. It's a rare man who does his half share: in households that can afford it, instead, a cleaner is hired. In households that can't afford it, even if the woman is in a paid job and a man is at home retired or unemployed, women overwhelmingly just do much more. It's still assumed to be women's work.

"Every woman needs a household guide."

The boom in 19th-century publishing replaced in-person instruction for many women. Smaller recipe and stain-removal hint books were sold by churches and charities. Others were stout all-in-one household encyclopaedias for the newly married, or women in colonial outposts: comprehensive manuals for housework, family medical care, etiquette and all manner of 'how-to's.

'Never argue with a man about chores. It kills eroticism. Hire an impecunious college student to swab out your place twice a week, and explode a few champagne corks. Marriage is supposed to be fun.'
– E. Jean Carroll's advice to a woman whose husband does no work in the home, *Elle* magazine, 2019

William Whatley's 1619 advice book to wives (and husbands) was called *A Bride-Bush. Or, A Direction For Married Persons: Plainely Describing The Duties Common To Both, And Peculiar To Each Of Them. By Performing Of Which, Marriage Shall Prooue A Great Helpe To Such, As Now For Want Of Performing Them, Doe Finde It A Little Hell.* Mostly, it tells women to stay home. *A Bride Bush* is full of the usual nonsense about being temperate, untired, diligent, witty, non-gossipy (etceteraarrgghh). But thanks, Bill, for introducing us to the words firefanged (burnt), loblolly (gruel) and splatted (split open).

Every household manual is emblematic of its era. The 1940s Australian editions of the *Book of Good Housekeeping* have a whole chapter on domestic hot water systems and boilers, and another on gas, oil and electric lighting. We ought to have a dressing table – a primping station for hair 'dressing', putting on make-up, jewellery and perfume. A hangover from a lady's home, it was a low place to sit while a standing servant did her hair.

The ethos of keeping and recycling everything is in favour again, but books used to have instructions on how to mend everything from a hole in the elbow of your jumper to one in a metal bucket, or a tear in the carpet, and a recipe for DIY coal briquettes. Everything should be spot-cleaned rather than thrown away, generations of different radio talk-back advisors and bestselling authors matched every possible stain – ink, lipstick, blood – to a substance that might 'get it out': metho, turps, peroxide, bicarb soda. Now people are far more likely to Google it.

A Country Women's Association book recently repackaged decades-old frugal hints as recycling and enviro-friendly household hacks.

In 2006, Victoria Heywood's book title *Household Hints: The Easy Way to a Clean, Clutter-free Home* foreshadowed the later bestselling spiritual minimalist aesthetic of *The Life-Changing Magic of Tidying Up* by Marie Kondo, in which she asked those overburdened by possessions to hold each one and ask if it sparked joy. If it did not, it was to be thanked for its service, and banished. This led to some inevitable jokes about husbands.

Some things don't change, but morph. The late radio handy-hints maven Martha Gardener, aka Kathleen Worrall, hosted a decades-long radio show, *Can I Help You?* She self-published *Everyone's Household Help* book in 1982 when in her late 70s. Martha advised how to clean Laminex, piano keys, furs and net curtains but became a household name for her DIY wool mix recipe – you can still buy a licensed commercial version, Martha's Wool Mix.

After a company sale and name change and to remove the possibility of any further royalty claims, since 2005 the wool wash labels say only 'Martha's' (although the Gardner name lingers on in some supermarket websites). Martha's middle-aged label photo is now an anonymous young model, fading into the background.

"Do what Mrs Beeton's book says."

The best-known household compendium is *Mrs Beeton's Book of Household Management* – the instruction manual for women first published in 1861. It made men rich for decades after she died (her husband sold the rights). Much of the book was a bit bonkers-aspirational, what with its advice to choose footmen not just because they were handsome, and how many

'I don't get very much help from my husband, I don't think many women (do) . . . his job is putting out the garbage can.' – Homemaker and factory worker in Martha Ansara's documentary film, Don't Be Too Polite, Girls, 1975

Marbled Jelly.

Blanc-Mange.

Trifle.

Almond Puddings.

Rout Cakes.

Jam Pudding.

Tartlets.

Mince Pies.

Vanilla Cream.

Apple Marmalade Tart

Cherry Tart.

Pear & Apple Dumplings.

Dessert Biscuits.

Charlotte Russe.

Gingerbread Pudding.

Milk Pudding

A bewildering array of desserts, to be precisely laid out by your servants. Mrs Beeton's Book of Household Management, late 19th century edition.

of them were needed to carry a picnic. But the cooking recipes were very useful, with weekly plans for the fashionable glop and flesh of the day: 'plain dinners' full of boiled-to-death vegetables, stodge puddings and curried fowl, which I am determined to use as an insult one day. You . . . you . . . *curried fowl.*

Mrs Beeton's blithe book lied to the women who were struggling in never-ending drudgery and loneliness. It set absurd standards of cleanliness, thriftiness and lists of tasks only achievable by having a squad, if not an army, of servants. Mrs Beeton assumed you had several, and that your servants' children 'have no other prospect' but to grow up and become servants themselves. It's clear from her expectations and descriptions that the work of maids was endless, thankless and injurious.

Beeton's book airily proceeds to assume you have a garden from which to cut flowers for the table every day, and the ability to decide whether to display French-style food (serve-yourself on the table) or à la Russe (servants filling your plate on the sideboard and then presenting it to you).

Our duty – imposed by God – is to be our husband's servant, bear children, raise them and do all the housework. Mrs Beeton (or her later editors, as the Royal 'We' is employed) trilled, 'We assert, and with reverence, that it should not be possible to over-rate the value of one, who, by patience, energy and self-sacrifice, succeeds in making all around her content and comfortable . . . they are helpmeets to their husbands . . .'

A maid is used to illustrate the first letter of the preface in Mrs Beeton's Book of Household Management, *1861.*

Top 10 handy hints from 19th-century ladies' manuals

1. Eat flying foxes for breakfast even though they smell disgusting.
2. Temper shows as plainly on the face as disease.
3. Throw a sick person's poo out their window and burn it there.
4. Have a nap between 1.30 and 2.30 then a cold bath.
5. The seaside cures whooping cough.
6. If you want to taxidermy a fish, consult a textbook.
7. Paint your chilblains with lead paint.
8. If somebody has convulsions, give them an enema.
9. Wallpaper a room with newspaper pictures of the Sudan war.
10. Choose a cow with a powerful looking udder.

A palm-sized scrapbook pasted with newspaper clippings of household hints with a handwritten concertina-index, 2017.
(Courtesy Lyndal Thorne)

"Cleanliness is next to Godliness."

Well, move it away then. There were of course, good reasons for basic hygiene, discovered to be relevant to health and disease control somewhere between The Plague and working out that soap could kill the germs on thoroughly washed hands.

The standards of clean and tidy that women have been held to are preposterous, achieved only through hard, boring work, relieved only by the

Flies have DIRTY feet

THAT CARRY GERMS AND SPREAD DISEASE

Keep homes and yards clean

AUTHORISED BY HON. C.A.KELLY M.L.A MINISTER FOR HEALTH

Guard against flies looking weirdly at you. Government health poster, 1940s. (National Library of Australia)

visible triumph of spotlessness the precise second before everything gets dirty again.

"Cleaning is trivial & also life-saving."

Cleaning as done by women is literally considered worthless, in economic terms, by governments, but at the same time we were told in official public health advice that the fate of lives depended on a high standard of cleaning.

Housekeeping manuals banged on about the link between dirt and disease; one in the 1940s told women it was their 'cleanliness' that had caused the average age of death to fall (to 50–60 years old). We were told if we didn't clean properly our children would die.

From the 1800s, public hygiene activists produced thrilling pamphlets called things like, *Under the Floor* and *A Bad Smell* and the even more arresting, *What Kills Our Babies*. In the 21st century, antibacterial sprays are still marketed using similar fears.

Women were told to combat germs and flies with scrubbing and handmade crocheted lids for milk jugs, wiping dust, and putting rubbish outside, as other dangers were imposed by things women couldn't control: infectious diseases, sewer systems, mining pollution and industrial poisoning.

Meanwhile, the products women were told to use were often more dangerous than not cleaning at all. The nasty chemicals in printing ink meant you could use sheets of newspaper to clean windows; baths were wiped with kerosene and a variety of other frighty substances were recommended for decades despite, in many cases, their noxious vapours, carcinogens, and dangerous corrosives. If they came home from school with nits, my nanna shampooed her three daughters' hair – Wanda, Linda, and Glenda – in sheep dip, full of spectacularly toxic, now-banned organo-chlorines.

"Housewives must be humble."

Self-published household hints author Marjorie Bligh built the biggest career she could as a 'housewife' in a small Tasmanian town in the 1960s and 1970s. If Marjorie was unsung, she was going to damn well sing herself.

Winner of hundreds of first prizes for her entries in cooking and handcrafts at the Campbell Town Agricultural Show, she had her own books printed, solicited testimonials, and signed every copy by hand. She hand-corrected a typo in hundreds of copies. The books were largely the print version of her scrapbooks; a book might have more than 3000 snippets, clippings from newspapers and magazines, a minestrone of quotes, housework hacks, sayings and mottos, scraps of poetry, gardening tips, pasted greeting cards.

She was a stranger to copyright. Thousands of items from newspapers and

Freaky 'Destroy That Dangerous Dummy' hygiene campaign poster, from the Maternal and Baby Welfare Division of NSW, 1930s. (National Library of Australia)

MARJORIE BLACKWELL "AT HOME"
1965

Marjorie Blackwell, later Cooper, later Bligh, on her book cover in the 1960s.

'I can go to my grave and say I've never been idle.' – Marjorie Bligh

Marjorie.

magazines were sifted through Marjorie's rubber-gloved hands and then published under her own name. There are occasional rare exceptions: Mrs J. Shackcloth's Savoury Mince, and Ethel Webster's Little Meringues.

One of her books was *Homely Hints on Everything*, so I felt a kinship with Marjorie; my own first book was *The Modern Girl's Guide to Everything*, though it had a lot more about condoms in it.

In a small Tasmanian town, I met Marjorie once, in her home museum stacked ceiling-high with shelves of her bottle and doll collection, and all the things she'd made, including a hat crocheted over the shape of a square plastic ice-cream tub using strips of plastic bread-bags. Well, I thought it was a hat, but it turned out it was a basket. She levelled a hard stare at me and said sharply, 'Is that your fiancé?' gesturing to the man with me. Reader, he wasn't.

Marjorie's staple recipes were the British empire stodge of the time, perhaps 'jazzed up' into the 1950s and '60s with pineapple rings which seemed to shoot out of Queensland in a never-ending barrage of cans.

Needs must, and Marjorie included budget Tasmanian meal possibilities, including rabbit stuffed with muttonbird, and an arresting recipe for wattlebirds on toast. This calls for the plucked bodies of birds to be grilled for hours on a wire rack sitting in an electric frypan, and then laid, in rows, on the toast. The recipe seems to create more questions than it answers. Were you supposed to eat the claws? How many dead birds per slice of toast? Did people do this in front of their budgies?

"Be fanatically frugal."

Marjorie Bligh represented generations of frugal 'housewives', horrified at the idea of being idle, and economical by necessity. Even if they were sitting down, women like Marjorie and my nanna had busy hands. They were embroidering a doily, or crocheting old Christmas cards together through homemade perforations to make a knitting basket. They sewed themselves dancing frocks, soaked the labels off jars, grew whole gardens from cuttings and seeds. I've looked at hand-embroidered tablecloths being sold for $5 in op shops and wondered about a woman, decades ago, who spent months of her life making it.

The pretty things they made were a defiance against harshness, a proud way of displaying skill, a form of work that was also about beautification, a way to use up hours when 'pastimes' were necessary instead of 'time-savers'. They were domestic economists in practice: buying in bulk when they could, cutting the family's hair with the aid of an upturned pudding bowl; they grew and preserved fruit and vegetables arranged neatly in Fowlers Vacola jars.

Crafts were made of the everyday items of the time: corks, pipe-cleaners, rags. I shall never varnish dried gourds for a table decoration, but if I did want to, Marjorie tells me how. (I suspect that when my mother realised that she was gluing orange lentils in neat rows onto empty food tins that she had covered in linen fabric to make 'pencil holders', it directly caused her to buy a copy of *The Female Eunuch* and become a mature-aged student.)

Some of Marjorie's frugal hints are still a bit startling: vinegar and water as a sunscreen; animal fat run-off from cooked meat for a hand moisturiser; treacle and sulphur as a

'Where the wife is quiet and good humoured, clean and tidy in her habits, and a good manager, the husband will . . . generally prefer [home] to the harvests of vice, and public-houses.' – The Cleanest Cottage, or The Influence of Home, Marianne Parrott, 1848

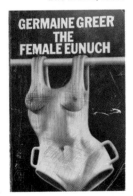

My mum's seventh reprint paperback copy of The Female Eunuch, *complete with her absentminded Biro doodles, 1972.*

Food science and cooking classes at Emily McPherson College of Domestic Economy in 1907, the 1920s and date unknown. (State Library Victoria)

pimple cure; wet bicarb soda as an underarm deodorant; butter as a make-up remover. But I keep a toothbrush amongst my cleaning supplies because Marjorie was right about it being 'unbeatable' as a crevice cleaner.

For a brief period in the 20th century, schools of domestic science and economy in special institutions elevated the role of housework to a learned, qualified one – but only taught it to girls and young women. Schools made desultory attempts to teach cooking and sewing, almost always to girls. When feminists pushed for all students to be taught these subjects, they were scrapped.

And so, generations of young men and women now leave school without knowing important things about food safety, budgeting, or how to make and alter clothes, or cook a few good meals. In time, this led directly to a travestational rise in the use of pesto from a jar.

The burden of frugality in the house has always fallen on women; either as a matter of pride and necessity, especially acute during rationing in times of war ('make do and mend') and economic downturn. Life has been transformed for so many: for us, buying a pair of socks is easier and cheaper than taking the time to darn. Hidden costs remain in the conditions of the workers where the socks are made and the damage caused by 'fast fashion' to the environment.

I wouldn't know a sprat from a smelt let alone a bloater, but generations of women have known which fish was cheapest, and consulted diagrams on which were the best budget cuts of meat (animal heads, offal and feet) and what to do with it. Old recipe books are full of instructions to 'scoop out the brains' or 'pull the skin from the tongue'.

When the Emily McPherson College of Domestic Economy was officially opened by the Duchess of York (later the Queen Mother) in 1927 it gave her an honorary diploma, which she had the grace to say she wasn't worthy of. She probably didn't know 101 ways with mince.

For that grand opening the streets were thronged with girls and young women: factory workers, schoolkids, uni students, nurses, Girl Guides and other groups. For decades, 'Emily Mac' turned out instruction books and thousands of accomplished students in domestic science; in 1952 the staff had more than 30 women and one man (tailoring), including many Mrses as well as Misses. All that respect and pride, all that women's tradition, and its extraordinary library and archives was later subsumed or given away by the Royal Melbourne Institute of Technology – its award-winning, purpose-built Beaux-Arts building is now the 'Graduate School of Business.'

Miss Eddie and Miss Chisolm, teachers at 'Emily Mac', 1930s. Please note Miss Eddie's hankie in cardie pocket. (State Library Victoria)

Make your brother's suit into a lady-outfit while he's in the tank corps. New Clothes for Old *booklet, which came with a letter from the prime minister, 1947. (National Library of Australia)*

"Take days to do the laundry."

Few people have written a book with a more patronising title, *Simple Rules for the Guidance of Persons in Humble Life,* than the insufferable Lady Eliza Darling, in 1837. She was the wealthy wife of the military governor of the NSW colony, himself considered to be one of the more towering arseholes in Australian history.

Lady Eliza's servants were no doubt required to follow the endless pages of laundry instructions in her book. The business of laundry, all done by hand in scalding water with corrosive soaps, took days. Washerwomen, aka laundresses, had to wash

by hand their employers' nappies and menstrual rags, sheets, blankets, and clothes. It was the hardest of labours, done by the 'lowest' servants, girls and women, underfed and badly clothed, in freezing or stiflingly hot conditions.

We think of the phrase 'wet blanket' now as somebody being unsupportive of an idea. It comes from the fact that a wet blanket was known to be so heavy – perhaps 20 kilos – if it was placed on anything, that thing would be thoroughly repressed and squashed.

First, often on Sunday, the 'day of rest', came the collection and sorting and recording in a book; the counting in and out the number of every item to be washed. Laundry was precious. The theft of laundry, even a hankie, was a common crime punished by transportation to Australia a few years earlier. The same theft was punished by flogging in the colony.

A lot of wood was be chopped the day before, ready to use in the morning to boil water in giant tubs called coppers. Lady Eliza's book lists the tasks for wash-day itself: hand-fetch the water in barrels or buckets to fill the giant heavy pots. This might be done at a river, or creek, or a nearby outdoor pump. A servant would then take the pile of clothes with any buttons, and tassels and coloured ribbons and lace collars, and snip them off, ready to be sewn back on after the washing, so they wouldn't 'run' in the wash and weren't damaged by chemicals or crushed in the mangle.

All of a household's washing – piles and piles of towels, sheets, clothes, blankets, menstrual rags and nappies – would be soaked, boiled or simmered in big pots over the wood-fires. Laundresses pushed it under the water again and again with poles that had little feet on them, and scrubbed the clothes against giant cheese-grater-like washboards, using bristle or wire brushes and caustic lime that stripped the skin.

Water would have to be tipped out or drained and refilled at least twice for rinsing, as stipulated by Lady Eliza (and all the other employers). Then each white item in a load of washing had to be turned inside out to be

· C'WOOD. OPEN AIR WASH·HOUSE. · TYPICAL OF THOUSANDS ·

Kids with their mum doing the washing in their Collingwood backyard, c1935. (Oswald Barnett, State Library Victoria)

'blued' – an extra wash stage into which was stirred little muslin bags full of 'blue' – originally crushed lapis lazuli stones and baking soda, then Prussian blue mineral salts. This effectively dyed everything white with a slight pale blue tinge so it looked brighter than clothes that had been yellowed with time.

After the rinsing, a laundress would then re-immerse everything that required an application of starch of an even consistency to every centimetre of the fabric: tablecloths, shirts, dresses, caps and aprons. Starch was homemade with cornflour, or other plant flour, and boiling water, to make a wobbly jelly-like, gluey coating that makes fabric stiff. It had to be applied to still-wet but not saturated fabric.

Until the spin cycles of washing machines in the second half of the 20th century, wet items were threaded and rolled between two heavy, horizontal marble or wooden rollers on a device called a mangle. Often there was one servant to thread clothes in, and one to turn a heavy wheel to turn and compress the rollers. A mangle was used to squeeze water out of laundry before it was

A three-roller mangle, which was in use in 1880. Items were folded and forced through between the rollers as a laundress turned the wheel. (Museums Victoria)

hung up, and also after drying and a spritz of water, as a form of ironing. Eliza bloody Darling required both, on each item.

Hardly anyone under the age of 70 knows what a mangle is. These days phrases like 'put through the wringer' and 'I mangled it' have lost their original meaning for a new generation untutored in mangling ways.

Clothes were hung in the sun, or in a drying room or shed, on lengths of washing lines or 'clothes horses'. Heavy metal irons heated to precise temperatures on woodstove hotplates were used to iron the laundry, often on large, purpose-built tabletops with drawers underneath for under-blankets. If the irons were too cool they didn't do the job, and if too hot they would burn the clothes and the servant would be punished.

The business of a household wash used to take two full days of 12 hours or longer. Drying took as long as the weather allowed, and ironing and folding was another day's work. A newspaperman advised around 1900 that it took two washerwomen four full days a week to do his household's washing and ironing. A correspondent to a newspaper in the 1890s calculated that two women in her home washed, wrung, dried, mangled, starched and ironed about 400 articles of clothing and household linen each week.

Doing the laundry resulted in steam scalds, fire burns, skin- and eye-damage from ammonia or other caustic chemicals, and freezing wet clothes worn all day in winter, repetition and load injuries and exhaustion. Scalpings and amputations were common, when women's and children's hair or hands were caught in a mangle. Absurd standards of cleanliness and work 'safety' were laid down by people who never had to do the work.

There are few more piteous sentences than this one in an

1895 news report about the death of an anonymous woman from a 'backyard abortion', also known as an 'illegal operation': 'The deceased was about 24 years of age and from the appearance of her hands it is believed that she was a laundress.'

"Make the disadvantaged girls do the laundry."

Convict women in Australia were 'sent to the tubs' as extra punishment. The tradition of making female prisoners do heavy laundry was maintained in Australia, allowing the famously gruesome god-no-not-my-hand-in-the-ironing-press-Bea assaults depicted in the 1970s TV show *Prisoner* and its remake *Wentworth* in 2018.

For decades, vulnerable girls and women were sent by magistrates and police to church laundries, where they worked for years, unpaid and trapped, doing housework for the institution and washing for commercial customers.

The other categories of imprisoned and enslaved women forced to do heavy laundry in Australia's history were the Aboriginal and Torres Strait Islander girls taken from their parents, or who grew up on, and were forced to work at church missions, 'training schools', government-sanctioned 'girls' homes' and industrial schools.

Every laundry run by the state or churches in our history was a crime scene: using indentured and enslaved labour, with girls emotionally and physically abused. An extra layer of judgement and atonement was spelled out: 'fallen', 'dirty' girls and women 'stained' by a pregnancy would be forced to clean things, make them white, as penance.

Laundresses were on their own, barred from joining a union. Governments, courts and churches conspired to exempt laundries from safety and wage laws. The British House of Lords exempted convent laundresses from safety and pay requirements in 1907.

The full bench of the NSW Industrial Court of Australia ruled against the Laundry Employees' Board in 1919, effectively ruling that the absurdly named Sisters of the Good Samaritan convent could enslave women.

In many of the Catholic convent laundries across the world even chatting or singing was forbidden, to prevent friendships. Common work hours were 8–8.30 until 6pm, with Sundays off still requiring sewing and other tasks. Girls were beaten, babies were taken from them and buried illegally. Survivors remember similar things: heads being shaved, daily assault; the bitter, bone-deep cold of winter, being given a new religious name to erase their identity, being frightened of their first period, which arrived without warning, and never explained.

"Wash-day is the same for everyone."

Though wash-day meant drudgery for so many, women have found joy in the camaraderie and the pride in a job well done and the gorgeous smell of sun-dried laundry. (In 2020, a report led by Italian-Danish scientist Silvia Pugliese identified the oxidised compounds and molecular behaviours that produced the singular smell of fabric dried in the sun.) Wash-day can evoke many different kinds of memories, and tell different stories, for women.

Nukgal Wurra woman Wanda Gibson,

Join the army . . . and wash 12,500 articles a week at an Australian army base hospital in North Australia, c1943. (State Library Victoria)

166

an artist from Hope Vale in far north Queensland, designed a printed fabric for the Magpie Goose fashion company called 'Family Washing', inspired by memories of the beach holiday she and her family had once a year, taking two days to walk to the beach from a Lutheran mission. As a child, Wanda was a 'domestic' worker for the mission after school.

'We only got two weeks holiday from mission life. When we had to do our washing, we'd roll a 44-gallon drum down to the creek, boil water in the drum, hang it up, and wait for it to dry! I drew the style of dresses the Lutheran Church used to give us for Christmas ... we were allowed only 3 dresses and undies. One to wash. One to wear. And the other one is spare.'

'Family Washing' print by Hope Vale Arts and Cultural Centre artist Wanda Gibson modelled by Samara Billy. (Photo by Helen Orr, courtesy Magpie Goose)

"Iron everything."

When I read Beatrix Potter's *The Tale of Mrs Tiggy-winkle* to my daughter in the early 2000s, we were mystified as to what the dear old hedgehog could be doing, 'goffering a pinny'. It means, it turns out, using a metal tube to iron little crimped pleats into frills, like the ones traditionally around the edge of an apron. In the book's illustrations, Mrs Tiggy-winkle is wearing the uniform of a laundress. Mrs Tiggy-winkle was doing the washing of all the other animals.

Newspaper articles instructed home laundresses to have several irons of different sizes, which you had to clean by scrubbing

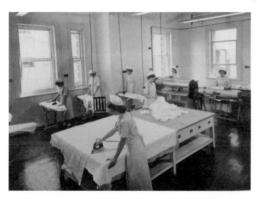

The photographer must have been expected in the ironing room at the Emily McPherson College of Domestic Economy: just look at all those starched caps on straight.
(State Library Victoria)

with powdered brick held with a pinch of brown paper to protect your hand.

Everything used to be ironed in houses where there were servants. Heavy felt 'underblankets' were hauled out of drawers and smoothed over large tables for the ironing. As servants disappeared, and housework became DIY for almost everyone, and standards changed, women did less ironing. Many of us do none at all.

An early memory of mine from the late 1960s is watching my nanna heating her clean black iron on top of a wood-fired stove and then ironing a frock on the kitchen table, through a clean cloth. Later she moved into town, and always thought electric irons were the bee's knees. She would be delighted at the way my iron squirts steam when you press a button.

My mum used an electric steam iron to teach me the right order for ironing a shirt: collar first, then sleeves and cuffs, back, then the fronts. She showed me how to use a tea towel underneath the iron so a pleated school skirt wouldn't go shiny. I recently discovered that my daughter, in her 20s, did not even know how to release the catch to set up the ironing board. A momentary frisson of horror immediately bloomed into relief.

"Boil all the food for several hours."

Early on, most cooking advice to women was about what piece of meat or vegetables to boil, or the ingredients of a boiled potion. You had a choice: boil the hell out of something or boil the hell out of it not so much. Women began to use their own experience and handy hints from each other to use pots with lids as little ovens, and judge the temperature or cooking times using the colour of coals, the sound of a fire, sound, by touch, the colour of the food in the oven or the pots they were in.

Before reliable temperature indicators on gas stoves from the 1920s and '30s, women had to judge an oven's temperature as slack, gas mark 3, slow, fast, hot or moderate by the colour of a piece of paper in the oven or timing how long it took for a pan to become hot, the feel of the heat on their face when they opened the oven, or their hand protected by a cloth on the metal handle.

Billions of women still cook on open fires and rudimentary stoves, including but not limited to Africa, India, Nepal, China, and South America. The dangers of these cooking fires (smoke inhalation, burn and explosion injuries) and the hours taken to tend them, hold women and children back from school and enterprise. The Clean Cooking Alliance, under the umbrella of the United Nations, estimates that women do 11–14 hours of work a day (men do 10 hours) because of extra work getting water and running stoves.

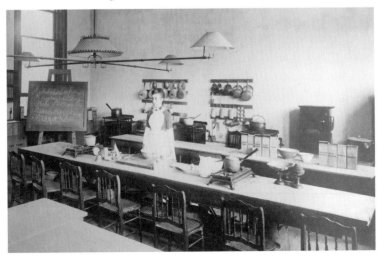

The least relaxed kitchen photograph in history, Sydney Technical College, 1889. (Charles Bayliss, National Library of Australia)

Two of Mrs Lance Rawson's bestsellers, 1890 and 1907. (National Museum of Australia)

'If you always keep several rounds of sponge cake . . . in a tightly closed cake tin, you will never be short of either cakes for tea or Sunday night's supper.' – New Standard Cookery, edited by Elizabeth Craig, 1933

"Australian cuisine wasn't."

Well, now they often are, and modern cookbooks reflect personalities, family heritage and the cleverness of publishers. But until the last few decades, most cookbooks were a *mélange* (or a blancmange) of the plagiarised, pinched and purloined.

Like most early colonial advice to women by men, the first Australian cookbook (by Edward Abbott) nicked recipes from other people. Plagiarism meant that old attitudes and ideas perpetuated for longer, and English ideas were transported to Australia where, like a boatload of convicts, they didn't belong. Abbott recommended recipes that others considered best left alone, for wombat, echidna, emu, 'Slippery Bob' – battered kangaroo brains fried in emu fat, and boiled maidenhair fern.

A later bestseller, *Kingswood Cookery*, was by the famously neat head-kitchen teacher at the Sydney Technical College at the time, Harriet Wicken. In 1898 the *Brisbane Times* reviewed not just the book but its light and sturdy spine, just the thing for years of sticky, floury abuse while propped open on home kitchen benches.

'Pioneer' housewives were encouraged to develop an Australian cuisine: tons of mutton; eventually, feral rabbits and any vegetables they could keep alive. The new Australian woman accepted little to no advice from Aboriginal women aside from expert knowledge of seasons affecting wildlife and fish availability. Thousands of years of knowledge about tubers, grains, salad greens, nutrition, taste and herbal knowledge was unsought, and actively scorned, as the 'pioneer women' brushed the weevils off their flour, and sweatily over-cooked roasts on a broiling Christmas Day.

Australia's first published female cookbook author was

Mrs Lance Rawson – aka Wilhelmina, or Mina – who began her guidebook career in 1894 with *The Antipodean Cookery Book and Kitchen Companion* and then followed up with *The Queensland Cookery Book*, and *Australian Poultry Book* and the *Australian Enquiry Book of Household and General Information*.

She advises the affianced to ask for things before the marriage: she boasts that she asked for a stove and a mangle instead of a piano, but 'got all three'. She breezes on to explain how to get the most out of a 'killing day' on a cattle or sheep station: harvest as much meat as possible by salting offal, making pickled cheeks, beef tea, fried liver and cooked cow heel. She tells where to saw through a calf skull, and claims that steak and salted animal brains 'make a nice breakfast dish'. 'Comfort baking' it ain't.

Chong Pik-Chu, a student at Emily McPherson College of Domestic Economy who looks like she's just been told to put boiled eggs and tinned pineapple together in a salad, 1955. (State Library of Victoria)

Colonial women were encouraged to grow lettuce, beetroot, endive, celery, tomatoes, radishes, onions and cucumber: I can't imagine how often these needed to be watered in outback far north Queensland with carried water. In one of her books she talks of wooden barrels being rolled up from the river – and I'll bet you a hundred guineas Mrs Rawson never did that herself.

Decades were wasted boiling hideous stodge before some Australian-born cooks, such as recipe book queen Margaret Fulton, embraced new ideas and cultural knowledge. Women with proud

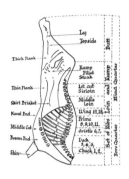

Diagram showing cuts of meat, including The Butt. (National Museum of Australia)

heritages taught new generations new cooking, including Sri Lankan-born Charmaine Solomon and third generation Chinese-Australian Kylie Kwong.

"Sew all your family's clothes."

Women helped develop all the extra skills and techniques to dye cloth different colours, print and decorate cloth, and use complex weaving techniques to make everything from delicate lace to heavy protective tweeds in complicated patterns.

They used fabric engineering techniques – darts, puffed sleeves and curved seams to make fabric follow, accentuate, or minimise the lines of the body. Sheets were turned – when they became thin in the middle, they were cut down a central line, each half flipped, and the former edges sewn up as a middle seam.

Mending and making sensible things, and decorative sewing, embroidery and other crafts that made things more beautiful, were both seen as an extension of duty. Women took pride in plain sewing and fancywork.

Paper patterns and home sewing machines revolutionised women's sewing abilities and saved time. Almost every home had one. Fabric shops (drapers) were in every shopping street, and pattern makers, including Madame Weigel, Enid Gilchrist, Butterick and Vogue, were household names. In only a generation or so we have flipped on sewing: most houses now *don't* have a sewing machine.

"Women's crafts are silly fripperies."

Shall we leave aside how women have been refused art training and exhibition opportunities for centuries, cast only as muses and too often have been unrecognised as painters, sculptors or photographers themselves, rarely called a genius even if their work is ground-breaking and brilliant? And how the ways in which those who did manage to make a life as an artist were disparaged and overlooked, unlike many of their pervy and pedestrian male colleagues? How they've been largely unsupported by public and private galleries, and presumed to be hobbyists and less important? How Aboriginal and Torres Strait Islander women's stories and dances and, later, paintings, were automatically considered lesser by a repressive society which forbade its practice? Oh all right, just for the moment, then.

A very rare early colonial artefact shows the decorative sewing made by Aboriginal girls under the 'tutelage' of the niece of the commandant of troops at the Swan River settlement near Perth, some time before 1848. A little, faded quilt is rolled with padding onto a sturdy cardboard tube suspended in a box at the National Library of Australia. Librarian Catriona Anderson and I unrolled it, very slowly and carefully, in 2019.

No. 3.

From the McCabe Dressmaking Academy booklet, 1930. (National Library of Australia)

The quilt made by Aboriginal children in Sunday school at the Swan River military settlement, WA, before 1848. Each square is about 4.5 cm wide. (National Library of Australia)

So many very tiny hand-stitches. Each one standing for a story we don't know. The quilt, about 1 metre by 1.4 metres, was sent to England, then donated to the Commonwealth Library in London in 1959, from whence it was dispatched to the National Library in Canberra with a note apologising that the 'strange relic' wasn't a find of much value. It's one of the most moving things I have ever seen.

"Only rich women are allowed to do fancy, decorative crafts."

Great Aunty Hebe in fancy dress, 1920s. In 1948 she judged 79 sponge cakes, 64 plates of scones, 85 fruit cakes, 54 handmade dresses and 11 tray cloths at the Melbourne Show. (National Library of Australia)

Nene doing sewing, 1938. (National Library of Australia)

In 1882 Lady Wolverton announced a needlework guild that would make useful items for the poor, instead of decorative antimacassars (which were doilies to protect armchairs from men's hair oil). But in general, women's satisfaction and joy in making pretty things prevailed, along with the need to make sensible things.

State libraries are full of women's scrapbooks of faded, pressed seaweeds. In London, a 19th-century woman saved fish bones for years and exhibited them, made into floral sculptures.

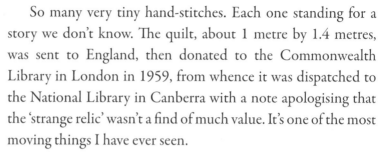

Annoyed by the male domination of exhibitions and agricultural shows, posh ladies and farming women alike lobbied their husbands to include women's work sections, from Mackay to Hobart. There were prizes for the 'best' article in scores of categories, ranging from fruitcake and marmalade to smocking on a doll's dress and landscape painting in oils.

By 1905, Lady Northcote, the wife of the Governor of Victoria, hosted a prestigious women's work extravaganza display at the Exhibition Buildings in Victoria, with commemorative books and prizes galore. Over the next 60 years, women stitched thousands of doilies and embroidering kits. By the 2010s, social media photo platforms led an embroidery revival from accounts like @badasscrossstitch, with needlework feminist mottos.

My great-grandmother Nene, pronounced Nee-Nee, a wealthy woman with nowhere else for her industriousness, skill or creativity to go, made a specialty of the decorative arts, entering every single category of the Royal Melbourne Show, including embroidery, pokerwork (burning an artistic image into wood with a poker) and barbola work, making frames and objects from a kind of hardening plasticine, at least until, in 1938, she won the Women's Work overall prize.

Mrs. Wills Cooke adds the finishing touches to her Christmas cakes.

My great-grandmother Nene in twinset and pearls with 16 Christmas cakes she made one year in the mid-1950s. (Newspaper clipping, courtesy Terry Wills Cooke)

She was known for her kindness but also for getting her own way. One family story about Nene is the time the woman next door wouldn't share a sewing pattern, so she kidnapped the toddler, whisking him out of his clothes, gave him a biscuit and took a pattern off his overalls, then dressed him again and shoved him back through the hedge. Nene and her sister, Hebe, didn't do any of their own heavy housework. Their cookery and craft were literally for show.

Among novelties (left) was a series of quaintly-dressed eggs which won for Mrs. R. Wills-Cooke a first prize.

The costumes Nene made for boiled eggs. The one on the right is a dead ringer for my grandfather's third wife. Royal Agricultural Show entry, 1930s. (National Library of Australia)

"Servants should be exploited & brutalised."

It is hard not to get indignant and exhausted just reading the list of things servants were expected to do. From ladies' maids who had to lace up their employer's corsets and the impossible task of cleaning mud from satin shoes, to the 'maids of all work' taking their employer's excrement in chamber pots down flights of stairs to empty them, doing all the heavy laundry and scullery scrubbing during 12–14 hour days. (Live-in servants and many other servants across the world still work similar hours.)

Servants were also supposed to be as invisible as possible – and inaudible. A governess who once worked for my great-great-grandmother wrote to her that her next employer was enraged by the rubbing sound of a maid's corset when she waited at the table. Mrs Beeton warned housemaids against having creaking boots or having to be asked for something; they should anticipate people's wants by handing them things without being asked for them.

The lowliest maid was a 'maid of all work', otherwise known as a slavey, slavvy or tweeny because she had to work between all departments of housekeeping and the kitchen. In the 19th and early 20th century she worked longer hours than almost any other servant, usually from at least 6.30 am to after 11 pm.

In his 1908 book, *Women of England*, Bartlett Burleigh James says house servants used to be men, especially in the share-houses of religious men (okay, monasteries), where the only women were employed in their traditional trade of beer brewing. In the times of Queen Elizabeth I, he says, servants were so lowly and unprovided for, they were expected to sleep where they dropped in the kitchen or in corridors of the house.

The more equal and shared jobs women used to have were swept away by the factories, sewing 'sweat-shops' and the mines of the Industrial Revolution, and in floated a 19th-century cartoonist's idea – men looked ridiculous for doing 'women's work', or wearing women's clothes.

"Servants are lazy & impertinent."

Employers of servants were described as master and mistress, the same words that were used for being in charge of a dog. 'The servant problem' was raised in Australian newspapers almost from the first convict ship arrival.

Remember Lady Eliza Darling, the colonial military governor's wife, who wrote the very rude book called *Simple Rules for the Guidance of Persons in Humble Life: More Particularly for Young Girls Going Out to Service* in 1837? She told servant girls they were 'obliged by gospel' – commanded by God – to obey their employer. If they quit they were likely to become sex workers, and they weren't allowed to want any fun or a nice bit of ribbon.

Darling's requirement in 1837 for every fireplace was that ashes be removed, the walls and floor of fireplace and all fire implements (like the poker) be scrubbed clean with soap and water carried in a bucket, the grate scoured with wire bristles and polished with brick dust, and then re-painted with black lead paint: all that, every day. Sweep carpets daily using damp tea leaves laid out, swept and then carried away; clean windows; dust and polish furniture; clean and polish the coal container; scrub the floor; set the tables; clear the dishes – pages and pages of it. In any idle moments (no chance of that, surely) servants should do needlework, she wrote.

Housework took a toll with exhaustion, falls, burns, lifting injuries, repetition strains, skin damage from chemicals, and inflammation injuries – one was called 'housemaid's knee'.

Some employers didn't bother learning their maids' own names, calling them Abigail, Bridget or Mary-Ann. The job description used in newspaper ads was often for a Bridget, not a

'Beware of giving way to the love of dress, of company and of amusements . . . have no visitors, not even your own relations . . . avoid all loose, improper companions.' – Eliza Darling, 1837

'The grounds on which a hired servant may be dismissed are: incompetence, habitual negligence, wilful disobedience, gross moral misconduct, dishonesty, drunkenness, permanent disability from illness.' – The Book of Good Housekeeping, 1948

'I should like fresh air once or twice a week.' – A seamstress on why she won't work as a housemaid, *Camperdown Chronicle*, 1889

maid. After World War I there was a steady decline in live-in servants with the rise of other opportunities. Newspaper columns heaved with complaints that servant girls would rather have the free night-times of schoolmistresses, factory girls, shopgirls, barmaids and seamstresses. The idea of women wanting their own time off was mocked as 'herculean independence'.

A note for Aboriginal & Torres Strait Islander readers

The following section includes photos of Aboriginal people who have died, and accounts of murder and cruelty perpetrated by white colonists. Aboriginal and Torres Strait Islander people may not want to read this, or the references to the history of brutality in the 'domestic service' industry, or the inclusion of hurtful language from primary documents, personal and official, all of which they already know.

I'm sorry I wasn't able to include the names of Aboriginal people in the captions of the historical pictures that appear; I couldn't find descendants that could identify them. The Aboriginal organisations and people who helped and advised me are listed in the Acknowledgements; any new information would be gratefully received.

Aboriginal and Torres Strait Islander women have their own recorded memories, writings, and recordings of their experiences and the legacy of the forced 'domestic service' industry. Those eloquent stories belong rightly to them.

"White Australian women are worth more than Aboriginal & Torres Strait Islander women."

This is one of the most fundamental and enduring lies of Australia. White and Black women have been given different, untruthful advice. Aboriginal and Torres Strait Islander women were told that they had no right to their own children, or their own bodies, or lives, or effective legal protection, or to their continuing culture established over tens of thousands of years.

White women were advised that Indigenous women were entitled only to a life of 'domestic service' and that white women were entitled to enslave them to do it. Advice to Australian women is a cloth still woven tight with the threads of ugly white supremacy and thousands of crimes, inventions, and hypocrisies of all kinds.

As part of the research for this book, I was grateful to be in Canberra for a three-month fellowship to work in the National Library. My uncle Terry had catalogued and donated many documents there of my family's history, including evidence of my great-great-great-great-grandmother Sarah's instructions for the first 'pre-nup' in Australia.

So, one afternoon in the library I ordered up some of the family scrapbooks and papers to be delivered to me the hushed Reading Room. There were so many, packed in pale-grey archive boxes, that they came stacked on a two-decker wheeled trolley. I trundled it over to one of the long, laminate desks under the supervision of the librarians' desk.

I opened a brittle, neat 1890s family album of photos with copperplate captions written underneath. Here were the descendants of that great-great-great-great-grandma Sarah and

her convict husband Edward, who'd arrived in the dying months of the 1700s. They prospered, hard-working chancers who took every advantage on offer: they had the first crack at the earliest Sydney boom times, land grants and other political favours. A small part of their income came from the vile Tasmanian seal industry with its reliance on the catastrophic rape and enslavement of Aboriginal women. (Turns out the 'elephant oil' in their import-export ledgers meant elephant seal oil.)

By the 1890s Sarah and Edward's grandchildren, now adults with their own children, were struggling to profit from a sheep station called Cullinlaringo, in the Central Queensland Highlands area. The album has posed portraits of girls in their sweet, ruffled, perfectly ironed pinafores, the daughters of my great-great-grandma, also called Sarah, and her husband Horace Wills. There was Ethel, Ida, Hebe and Eva Irene (that's my great-grandmother Nene, she of the egg costumes).

Aboriginal women who worked in the house, and families at the camp on Cullinlaringo station, described in captions as 'Blacks', 1890s. 'Kittie the tracker', second from left (facing page). (National Library of Australia)

As I turned the stiff cardboard pages speckled with pale-brown age-spots, pictures slid about, unmoored from their cardboard corner-mounts. I suddenly saw something I didn't expect. I turned back, went forward again.

Here were photographs of Aboriginal girls and women, in what looked like cast-off frocks, and some family groups with men: the station 'servants'. These, I realised, were people 'employed' by my ancestors – but hey, let's be frank about the realities of the time, shall we? Without choice or protection, they were enslaved. Only one of these women had her name recorded in a caption: Kittie, the tracker. The women and girls in the photos share a dignified countenance and a direct gaze.

If these people were all local Kairi (also known as Gayiri) people, it means they were survivors or orphans of a recent frontier war that had killed hundreds of their people. An early battle in 1861 was a rout, a devastating ambush of white invaders by Aboriginal people armed with fighting sticks and small axes. Startled out of a midday snooze in his tent, my great-great-great-grandfather Horatio Wills was killed in a notorious massacre along with his employees and their families – 19 white men, women, children and babies, as he arrived to 'settle' Kairi land with a mob of 10,000 sheep. Estimates vary of how many Aboriginal men, women, children and babies were killed in reprisal murders by white settlers and the dreaded 'Native Police': probably between 200 and 300.

My family felt proud of the enterprising, bold spirit of our ancestors – especially Horatio. 'We' had arrived on a convict ship, married into the Redferns, tangled with the printer of the first Sydney newspaper, served afternoon tea to the Macquaries, trekked for months to establish sprawling new farms in Victoria and Queensland, imported the first wool press.

Horatio's eldest son, my great-great-uncle Tom Wills, later became one of Australia's first sporting stars, the co-inventor of Australian Rules football, who managed an Aboriginal cricket team, the first Australian team to tour England. We weren't to speak of Tom 'living in sin', or his death by suicide with a pair of scissors, while in the grip of delirium tremens. 'He died, dear,' was how Nene put it, if anyone asked about Tom. (For god's sake don't mention the convict forebear. He wasn't, and if he was, he was almost certainly related to a . . . Lord, I think you'll find.)

The Cullinlaringo-Wills massacre became shorthand across Australia for an outrage. It cemented among colonists the fear of Aboriginal people and the acceptability of shooting them on sight, especially in the separate colony of Queensland, where historian Henry Reynolds estimates that tens of thousands of Aboriginal people were murdered. The Wills family retained

My great-great-grandmother Sarah's palm-sized gun, which she wore tied to her apron strings in the late 1800s. A tiny bullet is wrapped in tissue paper at the bottom of the holster. (National Library of Australia)

Hebe and Nene

Housemaids - Cullinlaringo

a ghastly cachet of celebrity. Decades later, Nene's wedding announcement said the family was 'late of Cullinlaringo' and family death notices continued to refer to it well into the mid-20th century.

Letters in the massacre's aftermath show that Wills family members, including Tom, approved of reprisals against Aboriginal people at the time. My great-great-grandmother Sarah, in charge of 'house servants' at Cullinlaringo in the 1890s, routinely kept a miniature working pistol tied to her apron strings 'to shoot Blacks' in case of insurrection or attack.

Her daughter Nene was born in the 1880s, her hair and frock styles later set by the fashions of the 1930s. I met her in

Great-aunty Hebe and great-grandma Nene, in starched pinnies with lace collars. And 'housemaids', 1890s, whose names were not recorded. (National Library of Australia)

the 1960s, when I was a little girl. I remember a rare visit to her house, with its unfamiliar silence, ticking clocks, doilies, swagged curtains, gilt-framed paintings and a table display of bristlingly marzipanned Christmas cakes decorated with cornucopias of walnuts, violently red and green glacé cherries, and Bertie Beetle chocolates in iridescent foil wrappers (we never got our hands on one). She was formal, and keen on respectability, but generous and jolly. She was kind to my mother, a country girl from another world. I still have six delicate teacups and saucers with little gold gilt dots in the pattern, that once belonged to her.

I had been holding two pieces of information in my adult brain without connecting them. Nene had lived on a sheep station in the late 1800s. Aboriginal people were enslaved on cattle and sheep stations in the late 1800s. In my white-Australian blindness, I never put the two together and saw the inevitable truth, until I saw that family album. My great-grandmother grew up in a house with enslaved Aboriginal girls.

Hebe and Nene grew up into lives of comfort, filling their days with afternoon teas and card games, tootling around in big cars and industriously preparing prize-winning cooking and sewing entries for the Melbourne Show. But what became of those 'servant' girls in the photographs from Cullinlaringo? What had life been like for them – lugging and fetching and carrying and cleaning and starching and ironing? What happened to them when the Wills family sold out during the 1890s Depression and came south? Not many opportunities for show prizes, I imagine.

"Plucky pioneer women did all the housework."

Remember the first woman to publish a cookbook in Australia, Wilhelmina, Mrs Lance Rawson? She wrote about her quintessential, plucky pioneer outback Queensland wife-life of hoisting her skirts to work from first light, sewing long into the night by mutton-fat candle to beautify her dear little homestead. Her newspaper reminiscences and books were published from the 1860s to the 1920s: *The Australian Enquiry Book of Household and General Information: A Practical Guide for the Cottage Villa and Bush Home* was a hit in the 1890s.

And there *was* hard work to be done on those farms and stations: birthing and burying babies; heaving and scrubbing wet sheets, blankets and nappies for virtual handwashing;

Detail of a poster carrying the false promise of equal social and legal rights to Aboriginal women in the colonies. ('Governor Davey's Proclamation to the Aborigines, 1816', lithograph, National Library of Australia)

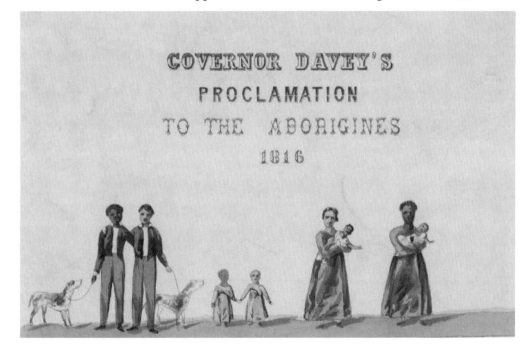

hand-sewing all the clothes; fetching water; killing, preserving and skinning animals; bottling fruit and vegetables; making cushions out of animal feed bags and furniture out of kerosene tins; raising up orchards out of the dirt; scratch-planting and tending crops; chopping wood; devising recipes for emu stew; and being 'alone' as husbands went out mustering or droving.

But Mrs Rawson was also emblematic of the dirty secret of 'pioneering women'. Their real story is chronicled in diaries, letters, official government reports and newspaper articles of the time – later expunged from white conversations, text books and country town museums. The early white women of Australia weren't alone in the outback at all. Mrs Rawson and her pioneer sisters enslaved and exploited Aboriginal women and children, and Pacific Islander women, and forced them to do the dirtiest, hardest work.

Mrs Rawson's books barely mention Aboriginal people, aside from co-opting their advice on using ashes and eucalyptus leaves on a wound, and the right season for oysters and crabs. She had no respect or curiosity for anything else they knew, although her life was entangled with theirs from the beginning: first as part of the frontier wars, and then as an exploiter. Mrs Rawson cheerfully wrote in her own words how she participated in brutalities and was a zealous cheerleader for 'slavery'.

In a 1901 letter to a newspaper, she furiously demanded that the 'slave trade' continue in Queensland because otherwise white people would have to do the work. She wanted to prevent 'the enslaving of the (white) wives and children of every man'. If white women had to do the work expected of Black people, she advised, it would 'ruin their looks' and make them give birth to 'idiot children'. (By 1926 she added a new spin, saying, 'There

"Mrs Lance Rawson",
prototype pioneer woman
and slavery advocate, and
her daughter Winifred.
(State Library of
Queensland)

was no slavery', though the 'boys worked under compulsion, with overseers.')

Mina Rawson wrote jaunty accounts designed to show her own derring-do, of shooting at and dragging bound Aboriginal people through the bush from her horse. She asked the government to imprison 'mixed race' Aboriginal girls in 'concentration camps' (a term she learned from the Boer War) from whence they could be sent out as domestic labour.

White women in my family were told that 'Blacks' might murder them. White people didn't bother telling Aboriginal women they would be raped, murdered and enslaved. They just did it.

"Aboriginal women must do 'domestic work'."

Colonial society assigned Aboriginal women at the bottom of an assumed hierarchy. The State told lies *to* Aboriginal women, but also lied *about* them to white women. An Aboriginal girl enslaved on a station farmhouse or in town was 'fair game' because her life as an Aboriginal woman was deemed worthless. To excuse her rape and brutalisation by white people, it was said she would otherwise be owned by 'brute' Aboriginal men. (I've recently heard supposedly progressive commentators talk about 'our' Aboriginal people, and 'their women'. It's a telling phrase.)

Aboriginal women, the Press and official reports told us, didn't feel maternal love like white mothers. In the 1920s, the barkingly deluded self-styled white-saviour-maniac Daisy Bates informed her South Australian newspaper column readers that Aboriginal women routinely ate their own babies. On the other side of the continent, Mrs Rawson explained to her readers that the Aboriginal laundresses of Maryborough had been properly whipped by white policeman each night to force them to swim to an island in the river to sleep, because otherwise they might break into houses and eat white babies.

First-person diaries, newspaper columns and letters show that Aboriginal 'servants' were treated as trade animals, by which I mean livestock rather than pets. They were never referred to as ladies, and virtually never as women. They were, hideously, called 'house blacks' and 'gins'. The 'n' word was routinely used. Aboriginal people were called stupid and lazy, and it was normal for white people to beat their 'servants' with pieces of wood or whips. White people treated serious injury to black people as a joke, and met their death with a shrug. It was said that Aboriginal people 'didn't feel pain'.

Mrs Rawson wrote of an injury that caused a girl's bloodied broken nose as 'one of the funniest things anyone could imagine', and when another girl's foot was severed by a shark, she wrote, 'I must admit that she became very thin and worn looking, but I doubt if that was through pain.' My own great-great-grandfather Horace, in an aside during one of his tenderly romantic letters to his wife, Sarah, tells how he paid an 'ugly old gin' a handkerchief to dig a bullet out from behind her ear with a knife where she was shot by a native tracker. He wanted it as a souvenir.

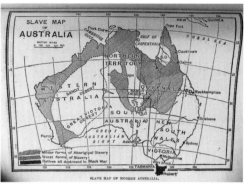

I took this dodgy photo of a page at the back of a book called The Black Police *by A. J. Vogan, published in 1890. (National Library of Australia)*

If I'm to be proud that my ancestors imported the first wool press, I must surely also acknowledge and feel profoundly ashamed of their depravity. My family participated in and benefitted from the smashing of Aboriginal families. The very least that I owe is to look at it clear-eyed, admit Australia's extensive history of enslavement and its terrible legacy, and recognise that my own advantages have been built on it. I am so sorry.

For generations, white Australian women were told they could have an Aboriginal girl as a 'servant' just by asking for one. Aboriginal children were given to station wives as the spoils after Native Police murdered the children's parents and other relatives; later the children were assigned by government departments. The enslavement and exploitation of Aboriginal, Torres Strait and Pacific Islander people in Australia morphed into an official system that destroyed families, stole children and forced them into indentured child labour at missions and

'All the (Aboriginal) woman bin washin' clothes, cleanin', caryin' water, waterin' garden. White lady never do nothin'. Big Queen.' – Maggie Ross, Aranda woman, quoted in White Aprons, Black Hands: Aboriginal Women Domestic Servants in Queensland by Jackie Huggins, 1995

children's 'homes'. In many Aboriginal families, generations of mothers became 'domestic servants'.

Women in 'domestic service' were told in different ways that their endless labour was worth next to nothing: they were not paid, their wages were withheld and stolen, or they were given an insulting pittance and rations of flour and tea, tobacco, old clothes, and perhaps a cast-off dress – many, cruelly, made of nasty, irritating fabrics including hessian.

Outsiders were often shocked. Visiting writers to Australia, including Anthony Trollope and A. J. Vogan, recorded what they saw as an unseemly enslaving of Aboriginal women and children, sometimes from birth, and the shocking indifference to humanity of the white women in charge.

"Aboriginal girls were looked after."

The fiction of well-intentioned missions and schools helping and protecting girls and women has been exposed in hundreds of official documents from the 1800s up to the *Bringing Them Home Report* of the *1997 Royal Commission, Inquiry into the Separation of Aboriginal and Torres Strait Islander Children From Their Families,* and beyond. For decades Australian women were told to buy church charity cookbooks to fund missions charged with educating girls in dainty tasks. Instead, mission girls and 'inmates' of infamous state institutions, such as Cootamundra and Parramatta 'homes', suffered years of forced labour, emotional cruelty, food deprivation and assault. (Some women later remembered a few experiences with fondness, but overall, the stories are horrifying.)

Countless little girls were sent by government officials to live in homes and farms far away, to work for white people,

'I used to wait on 'em hand and foot. Wait on 'em like a slave. They had a little bell to ring, for me to go in and clear off the table . . . couldn't eat with them, not in those days. That was slavery days.' – Mary Griffith, quoted in *'That Was Slavery Days': Aboriginal Domestic Servants in New South Wales in the Twentieth Century* by Inara Walden.

unprotected from rape and other brutality. Many girls – in some places, most – were returned to missions pregnant. Official reports described this as inconvenient. Other girls and women worked for decades, into the 1980s, as their promised wages were stolen by employers and the government. Tens of millions of dollars have been repaid to Aboriginal people in recent years. Other legal cases are still being finalised.

Aboriginal girls were deliberately denied any education but housework, listening to bits of the Bible, and the rudimentary maths and literacy needed to be a maid. Many state schools and nursing schools barred them into the latter half of the 20th century. Mrs Garnett, the superintendent's wife at Point Pearce Mission in South Australia told a Royal Commission in 1913 that girls from the age of 8 were sent away to be servants. Training them in cookery and dressmaking skills was a waste of time, 'because there is such a demand for them as raw material. They can all wash dishes and scrub floors.'

Aboriginal women continue to tell their own stories in oral histories, many held at the National Library, and in books, plays, songs, documentaries and other films (many available on the NITV channel). Moving memoirs have been collected all over the country, some in the anthology *Hibiscus and Ti-Tree Women in Queensland* and *Take This Child* by Darwin's Barbara Cummings. Other ladies have told their memories of domestic work to a wider audience through authors Christobel Mattingley, Francesca Merlan and Jackie Huggins – her mum's story of being sent out as a servant at age 13 is told in *Auntie Rita*. Memories of girlhood servitude include eating scraps, sleeping in sheds, scrubbing endless laundry, being beaten for not scouring saucepans perfectly, digging fence post holes and laying railway lines.

"Aboriginal women have lost their culture."

They have not. Tenacious Aboriginal and Torres Strait Islander women from hundreds of original language groups and communities across the country continue to share and instil advice and cultural knowledge. They did it through official, sustained attempted genocide and brutality, and continue to do it in the face of enduring racism.

From the Kimberley to the Central Desert to Tasmania, on scattered islands and in towns and cities, Aboriginal and Torres Strait Islander women entrust their continuing culture to their daughters, nieces and grand-daughters: ancient and contemporary versions of language, law, lore, complex kinship systems and points of view. They use different languages, dances, stories, visual art, music and song, comedy, films and documentaries. They share old information, such as how to

cultivate seasonal lily roots in a billabong, and new knowledge, from insightful PhD dissertations and research in science and medicine.

June Oscar, the Aboriginal and Torres Strait Islander Social Justice Commissioner of the Australian Human Rights Commission, released the *Wiyi Yani U Thangani (Women's Voices) report*, available on the commission's website, written after consultations with hundreds of Indigenous women all over Australia, with a message.

'Read this report,' she said. 'And listen to their voices.'

Yolngu artist Dr Banduk Marika's 1987 linocut of the two Wagilag Sisters and the freshwater python passing on knowledge of creation stories, cultural and kinship rules, the important roles of women, and the belonging to and ownership of the land. (Wawulak Wulay Ga Wititji, Art Gallery of NSW)

Nursing graduates in frankly indefensible starched bed-pan shaped hats that evolved from nun's veils, Wangaratta, 1970. (Bob Beel, State Library Victoria)

5

WORK HARDER, GET PAID LESS

WOMEN HAVE DONE EVERY JOB MEN CAN DO (with the possible exception of *Puppetry of the Penis* and frankly we can do without). And yet each one of those women is presented as an exceptional sort of rare woman, a novelty, a 'one-off'. Each 'trailblazer' had to re-blaze the same paths over and over again, as their way was barred, forbidden or covered up by men and laws and conventions. When others tried to follow, the earlier pioneers were forgotten, ignored, their record obliterated or their existence denied.

So the history of women's careers is partly a rolling series of cover-ups and sneers designed to discourage the rest of us. There's been a suppression of what women have achieved, while stories in the Press presented anyone in a non-traditional career as singular, and perhaps disreputable. We were forbidden from universities, then ridiculed once we were allowed in. We were herded into lesser-paying jobs by lack of opportunities, discrimination in hiring, rules that banished women from any career in public service from the day they married, and barriers to management or board positions. Meanwhile, the union movement still fights for factory workers, hospitality and caring professionals and others working split shifts, and long shifts.

We're still told that so many jobs are not for women, even though we can and do cave dive, fly combat aircraft, dig holes for thousands of miles of fences, help muster tens of thousands of sheep from horseback or helicopter, command naval ships, run multi-billion-dollar companies, start entrepreneurial businesses in the middle of Africa, calculate the trajectories for moon landings, climb up the top of skyscrapers in New York City, get a toddler to stop melting down, change ballistic-green poo nappies, shoot arrows into tiny targets, and wirewalk in circuses. And STILL we put 'woman' in front of any job they do because it's still, literally, remarkable. We say woman surgeon, woman astronaut, woman firefighter, because it's still unusual enough, it's still hard to get there, and every one who does has stories of dismissal, harassment and injustice because they're women.

Women who researched, analysed, concluded, wrote, typed and edited books and studies have had their names left off them. For more than 150 years women who were scientists, astronauts, researchers, mathematicians, doctors and inventors had their names left off research and discovery papers, patents and awards lists – often seen as second-class citizens to their husbands or team members.

To know what women have achieved, and could have achieved were they not restrained and discriminated against and snookered and stymied, is to see the world differently.

It's not that men sit around in a cabal plotting to take away our rights (except when they do). Mostly, they don't think about our inclusion at all. Lists of 'Best all-time album' and 'Top 100 sci-fi novels' are produced without a single woman on them. Imagine doing that on purpose. Imagine not noticing.

Autobiographies of famous and powerful men tend to nod only at sainted mothers, efficient secretaries and wives – they're devoid of women as colleagues, role-models, equals, friends. Most men might want better things for their daughters but rarely concern themselves with the needs and equality of women in their own workplace, unless they're forced to.

Historian Geoffrey Blainey once wrote movingly of the waste of young men in World War I. 'Perhaps the most drastic effect of the war on Australia would never be enumerated: it was the loss of all those talented people who would have become prime ministers and premiers, judges, divines, engineers, teachers, doctors, poets, inventors and farmers, the mayors of towns and leaders of trade unions, and the fathers of another generation of Australians.'

Without taking away from the tragedy of war, we can also think of the billions of women, in every generation throughout all of history, that were robbed of their chance to be anything they wanted to be and everything they could have been. Our progress is at once immense, and not enough.

My nanna refused to teach her daughters how to milk a cow because she didn't want them to be stuck on a farm. My mother wouldn't let me learn typing in case I was trapped into being an office pool secretary like her. I didn't go to university, and I wanted my daughter to have that chance.

Several girls came dressed as scholars to the 1887 Children's Fancy Dress Ball in Adelaide, including Bella McFarlane. (State Library of South Australia)

"You don't need an education."

Few women had an education; they were much more likely to be taught only enough literacy to read some of the Bible, if they were Christian. Until the late 20th century in 'developed' countries, women were unlikely to be taught anything more than housework skills; and if they were well-off, a few more refined pursuits such as decorative sewing, painting and accompanying oneself on the harpsichord.

For centuries, girls were denied education in anything but

Zelda D'Aprano protesting the Arbitration Court's rejection of equal pay for women, who were paid 75 per cent of men's salaries for the same job. Women protestors refused to pay more than 75 per cent of their tram fare, 1969.

housework and religion, on the grounds that they were 'inferior' and had to do all the housework and all the childbirth. By 1900, only the reasons had changed.

In the 2014 book *Picturing Women's Health*, an essay by historian Professor Hilary Marland explains how education was still withheld from girls around 1900 on the basis that it was unhealthy. Doctors said education caused general wiltiness and ruined a girl for her future duty of childbirth.

About 10 years later, a creep calling himself Dr Maloney was lecturing in Melbourne, claiming that an education for a girl caused the ruin of her 'girlhood and prettiness'; confusion about classical facts; physical and mental breakdown; the wearing of spectacles and listlessness. He added that it was all right to teach them how to swim.

When the rules were changed, allowing women to be accepted to university and trade schools, they often faced sexual harassment and assault, the open hostility of teaching staff, and the scornful accusation that they were trying to find a husband.

"You don't deserve equal pay, so there."

That, seriously, used to be the whole argument. Then it was said to be because women didn't need to support a family as a husband did. (Widows and single mothers aside, where they belonged.) Then other reasons were added: women didn't know how to ask for pay rises, women preferred to be in lower-paid sorts of jobs which coincidentally were lower-paid because women did them, then because they chose to leave jobs at a lower level because they wanted to have children, but then when they didn't and asked for affordable childcare . . . you get the picture. Women still don't get equal pay, mostly because . . . they're women.

"Women should have lower-status jobs."
Utter nonsense, of course.

"White women & rich women are more delicate."
FFS.

"Men are better workers than women."
In the 1970s, orchestras had a tiny proportion of women players. This changed when the convention was adopted for 'blind' auditions: to have a player audition behind a screen. The proportion of women employed rose to about 50 per cent.

Labour market researchers and academics say a similar phenomenon works against women and people of colour in getting job interviews unless names, gender and race are removed from resumés while qualifications and experience are retained.

Massed women workers, including pregnant ones at the front, at a fruit canning factory near Cape Town, South Africa, early 1920s. (George Bell, State Library Victoria)

"Women can't do 'men's jobs'."

In his 1796 book, *The History of Women, From the Earliest Antiquity, to the Present Time*, William Alexander told of Greenland's women who commanded ships, South Sea Islanders and Greek women who were deep-sea divers, and women who fought in armies. Then he went off on weird tangents about men's strength and women's beauty I shan't bore you with, so here's a photo of Violet Kelly, instead.

Australian exhibition whip-cracker and global sensation Violet Kelly. Here nudged out by manspreading of husband, Jack Kelly, 1890s. (State Library Victoria)

There's archaeological proof that centuries ago and ever since, all over the world, women have been hunters and warriors. Before the Industrial Revolution women were mercers, drapers, grocers, merchants, exporters and importers, horse traders, wheel saleswomen and silk producers, barbers, apothecaries, armourers, shipwrights, tailors, spur-makers and water-deliverers.

Women were early surgeons, masons, carpenters, hat makers, artists, manuscript writers and illustrators, binders, portraitists, bakehouse managers, planters, winnowers, threshers, in rarer cases ploughwomen, but often gardeners, pig keepers, dairy-women, weavers and more.

Suffixes added to the end of a job title indicated women did them too, including the 'ster', 'wife', 'maiden', 'ess' or 'trix', 'lass', as in dairywife, hand-maiden, milleress, editrix, pit-lass (mining worker). A 'necessary woman' emptied chamber pots and a 'tweenymaid' was the youngest of female servants.

A list of common women's work from the 1600s and 1700s included spinster, weaver, brewster (beer maker), pub manager (alewife), baker, midwife, indentured farmer, broiderer, washerwoman, hairdresser (busker), cleaner, dairy manager, silk manager.

Some occupations so presumed to be women's jobs they have to gain a prefix when they're not: male nurse, manny (male nanny), male model, male stripper and, goodness me, man whore. Some jobs are so presumed to be men's that they get a qualifier as well: woman pilot, lady doctor, female jockey, woman astronaut and stay-at-home dad.

Somehow, women are always told they're lesser. Master (male) means to be in charge, or very experienced and skilled. Mistress (female) has come to mean a woman having an affair with a married man, often paid. Sir is a term of respect. Madam, its original equivalent, also means brothel keeper.

Saying 'guys' isn't always a dreadful offence, but it isn't a genderless word, either. I'm trying to give it up. It *is* a bit odd calling a woman a 'chair' (if not an occasional table), but it's less odd than calling her a chairman. And how about the word 'mankind' leaving out half of humanity?

Hire him. He's got great legs.

Equal employment rights poster, printed by Sydney University Feminists in 1974, after an original 1972 National Organisation of Women ad in Ms. *magazine. (Museum of Applied Arts and Sciences)*

'Working women power this country, through both paid and unpaid labour . . . women are paid 14.6 per cent less than men.' – ACTU president Michele O'Neil, 2018, pointing out that women retire with an average of 43 per cent less superannuation than men

'Women & Work' colour poster by Alison Alder, 1988. (Redback Graphix, Museum of Applied Arts and Sciences)

"Married women shouldn't have jobs."

Since the 1930s depression, the employment of women was seen by many as taking jobs from men who had more right to them. In his 1969 'maiden speech', (can we *please* just call it the first speech?), new member Paul Keating, aged 25, told the parliament that the government should be ashamed it boosted jobs for married women.

In 1932 a new law called the *Married Women (Teachers and Lecturers) Act* required women to resign when they were married. Laws were introduced to the same effect across the

Public Service. Decades followed wasting women's talents and university degrees. 'It is the woman's lot to marry and share the home with the breadwinner', dribbled the Director-General of Education, a man, at the time. The rules were relaxed for women during World War II, and imposed again straight afterwards.

In 1966 the ban was rescinded, after lobbying from public service employers including the ABC, banks, an airline, the military, and science laboratories, which had all suffered a ridiculous 'brain drain' of experienced, talented and indispensable women staff.

"Mothers are bad employees."

Women face extra challenges to stay in or return to the workforce: a lack of affordable childcare, a lack of support and training and available career paths, the fact that they are clustered in lower-paid jobs meaning it can seem more 'logical' for them to be the ones to 'stay home' with small children. Women are more likely to be doing part-time or casual jobs and 'freelance' jobs with no benefits such as sick pay or superannuation. This adds yet more disadvantage because their superannuation ends up, on average, far below a man's, which has caused homelessness and deprivation for many women later in life.

Every so often women are confronted with the smug face of a treasurer or prime minister who supports inadequate childcare funding, declaring that middle-class women (but not poor ones) should have more children to help the economy. This might change if every cabinet minister had to do a week's work with a toddler in the room at all times.

Men go to work. Women sweep the floor. Situational English for Newcomers to Australia, prepared by the Department of Education and Science for the Department of Immigration, 1969–1972. (National Library of Australia)

'Change is a long and frustrating and agonising process, I am afraid.' – Clare Petre, then Energy Industry Ombudsman, legal specialist, quoted in a 1998 NSW Government resource kit for women in management

'We apologise for the inconveniences, but they are murdering us.' – banner at Mexican women's strike, 2020

"Women are too timid & inferior to be bosses."

Arguments against promoting women to management positions include that we're too timid and that men don't like to be told what to do by women. Some women, nevertheless, rose through the ranks due to their superior management and organisational skills, and then hit a 'glass ceiling' – an invisible boundary above which they were hardly every promoted to chief executive officer or high-up positions.

Businesses that fail to include women on their boards are being challenged. Activists point to the commercial advantages brought to a company by better representation of women. They support the training and mentoring of women to become board members, suggest or enforce targets for women's inclusion, and call out the astonishing number of companies with no women, or only one woman on its board. Women make up about a quarter of members on large company boards.

A typing pool at chemist firm Rumbles, Perth, 1953. (State Library of Western Australia)

"Women are too aggressive to be managers."

Words used to put women in their place at work have included bitchy, aggressive, ambitious; qualities that in men have been described as tough, decisive and showing leadership. Women have always been convenient, low-paid workers doing the necessary jobs that allow whole industries to run.

"Women don't belong in politics."

We were told that being in politics would damage our brain, derange our uterus and deepen our voice. Traditional paths to politics were the bloke-fest union movement and a slide greased with the fermented slime of entitlement for private school boys who never took empathy lessons. Indigenous peoples' leadership roles for women were smashed and forbidden by colonisers. Globally, some women could only inherit power from a dead husband or father.

We're still shown a different road to men's: ours is blocked with a system that doesn't even bother to calculate how much official budgets disadvantage women; with tenacious sexism; and a discriminatory lack of training and support, childcare, opportunities, pre-selection, and promotion. If we do manage to make it to a leadership position we must be weird, ambitious harpies, and we're threatened and abused by men on social media. If we're in politics we must be neglecting our children, but if we don't have any children we're not proper women (Senator Bill Heffernan described Leader of the Opposition Julia Gillard as 'deliberately barren' in 2007). Politics is still run as if men should be living and working in another state while their wives do everything at home.

Women are scandalously under-represented in almost

Managers and workers at the Melbourne Telegraph Branch Office, 1949. The safest bet for a party would have been Thelma, I reckon. (Bob Kent's scrapbook, State Library Victoria)

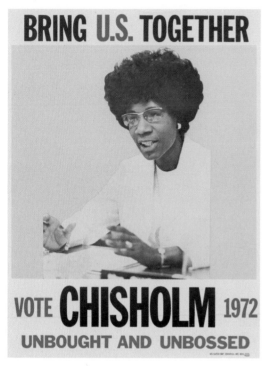

 inside the poster: **BRING U.S. TOGETHER** · VOTE **CHISHOLM** 1972 · **UNBOUGHT AND UNBOSSED**

Shirley Chisholm's US campaign poster when she ran for the Democratic presidential nomination. The motto was also the title of her autobiography.

'If they don't give you a seat at the table, bring a folding chair.' – Seven-term US Congress representative Shirley Chisholm, the first Black woman in Congress.

all political parties, governments and Oppositions, in democracies and military juntas – wherever there's no quota system requiring that at least half of the places go to women. (Yes, I might have just said it's a scandal there aren't more women in military juntas. Who wants a tea?)

Male party leaders and backroom spin-faffers who hate quotas tell us that candidates and cabinet ministers are chosen on merit. Presumably that's how we've end up with a representative rabble of mostly male dunderheads lit from within by the glow of misplaced self-worth beholden to tax-dodging squillionaires who run companies trying to hurtle faster towards climate destruction. Mate. Crème de la bloody crème.

"Women shouldn't have their own money."

You can outlaw education and better jobs for women, but how do you control them if they have their own money and possessions? Tell them it legally belongs to their father or husband.

In her book *A Woman's Work is Never Done: A History of Housework in the British Isles 1650–1950*, Caroline Davidson says the *English Married Women's Property Act* of 1883 – which also operated in some colonies – finally meant a woman could own her own property and money, without ceding control and ownership of it to a husband. Before that,

Don't Get Mad, Get Elected! Poster by Carol Porter, Red Planet Posters, 1997. (State Library Victoria)

only inheriting widows were likely to be able to legally run a business.

As Diane Bornstein tells it in *The Lady in the Tower: Medieval Courtesy Literature for Women*, laws had been passed in the 1800s specifically to stop women controlling or inheriting their own money and property, after so many of them, for hundreds of years, had been in charge of running and doing the accounts for small and family businesses.

My English-born great-great-great-great-grandmother Sarah Wills benefitted from a loophole in the law in the early 1800s in Australia: she could legally control money and run a business because her husband couldn't – in 1797 he was convicted of armed robbery and transported to Australia.

Sarah must have been pretty undauntable; after her husband's death sentence was commuted, she paid to come out to Australia a free woman, with a toddler, on the same ship that transported him in chains. She survived the nine-month journey aboard an infamous 'death ship', violent and riotous and typhoid-ridden, in which almost half the convicts died, arriving in 1799. Once in Sydney, her husband was assigned to her as convict labour. They set up a trading business, bought their own ships, ran a restaurant and warehouses.

Sarah was a canny businesswoman with a lot on. In 1808 she wrote to her mother to say she was 'making money very fast'. Her feet ached, she wrote, from standing and rocking a new baby, and she was running out of candle.

Soon after, she was a widow at 32 with 7 surviving children and one on the way, wealthy in her own right, inheriting an astonishing £15,000 of assets including three farms, a small ship, as well as 'two mares and two fillies; three cows and two calves'.

Mary Reibey on the Australian twenty-dollar note.

There's no surviving picture of Sarah, but her business partner Mary Reibey made it on to the twenty-dollar note. In what was almost certainly the first 'pre-nup' in Australian history, when set to be remarried to a rogue called George Howe in 1812, Sarah paid for a legal document to be drawn up to protect her money and property. She was unable to have the land-grant title in her own name to her house at 96 George St, The Rocks, near the edge of the harbour. Her new husband secretly changed his agreed will, and died leaving the house to his children and step-children, and nothing to his wife, causing Sarah to spend years contesting the will.

Up until the 1980s, most women found it impossible to borrow from banks – they only lent money to men. Even though laws and regulations have changed, many women are still denied the right to control their own finances: it's a key feature in many cases of partner abuse and control. Women are coerced and controlled, often having no access to or any say over money that they earn or inherit.

"Women aren't smart enough for interesting jobs."

Loïe Fuller invented revolving coloured spotlights for the theatre in the late 1800s – used until the digital era. Sister Rosetta Tharpe invented the style of electric guitar that began rock-and-roll. She was finally acknowledged in the Rock & Roll Hall of Fame in 2018, almost 50 years after she died.

Prevented from a science education or social status, the most significant early British palaeontologist Mary Anning found and studied dinosaur and other fossils in dangerous cliff conditions but was shut out of the Royal Geological Society, and any ability to publish, and she was forced to sell her discoveries to male scientists. Her intelligence was attributed to being struck by lightning as a child. Later, filmmakers spiced up her life with a lesbian subplot.

When women dared and achieved, it often caused redoubled efforts to keep others out. Hertha Ayrton became an electrical engineer in England in 1899. The next woman to be certified got through 17 years later. By 1922, only 22 of 18,000 members were women.

If you put 'Walyer the warrior' into a search engine, it asks 'Do you mean Walter the warrior?' No, I mean Tarenorerer, aka Waloa, who led guerrilla fighters in a resistance war against colonial invaders and the seal industry in Tasmania in the first half of the 19th century. When still a child, like so many Tasmanian Aboriginal women, she was kidnapped and enslaved for sex and ship work by sealers while the colonial government ignored it. She escaped and put together an army of men and women with some stolen weapons. Yellilong (Mary Ann Bugg) was one of several Aboriginal women who were bushrangers.

Gráinne Ní Mháille, aka Grace O'Malley, was an Irish pirate navy commander and politician of the 1500s. Her biographer Anne Chambers recounts how Grace, as a girl, was told she couldn't sail because her hair would get caught in the rigging, so she cut it all off. She negotiated in person with Queen Elizabeth, and once came up from below decks while in childbirth and shot at some attackers with two blunderbusses. Writing of her hundreds of years later, a male writer felt it seemly to observe she was not 'handsome'. I hope he promptly got cholera.

We know Marie Curie won a Nobel Prize – few know that she won two, in chemistry *and* physics, and her daughter Irène also won a Nobel Prize for chemistry. Both of them died after exposure to radiation.

Plucky reporter, sticky situation: Brenda Starr comics combined 'bad women', adventurous women and career women, 1950s.
(State Library Victoria)

Then there's Viking explorers Freydís Eiríksdóttir and the splendidly named Unn the Deep-Minded, one of the many known women to dress as a man so she could get on with things. And Spanish sailor and coloniser Catalina de Erauso, who invaded the country of the Araucanian Indians, whose womenfolk – names unrecorded – no doubt fought back by whatever means they could.

For every 'lady explorer' who had the means to a more interesting life, having her trunks lashed to camels, or posing with a rifle, in racy jodhpurs, next to a dead elephant or tiger, there were African, Indian and South American women who were forced into servitude to the one

Dashing pilots, 1930s–1950s, clockwise from top left: solo biplane flight pioneers Freda Thompson and Evelyn Koren; jet and bomber test pilot Cecil 'Teddy' Kenyon in her Lockheed Lightning; Grace Cavanagh and Marie Richardson. (National Library of Australia)

with the gun. For every singular botanist, entomologist and anthropologist, millions more women had no time, no money, no break from childbirth, no choices, no education to get there.

The golden age of women 'aviatrixes' and pilots who helped in war efforts wasn't driven by men offering women the opportunity. It happened because rich young women who had the means to buy or hire their own plane and pay for their own lessons proved themselves. War correspondent and White House reporter Fay Gillis Wells flew her own plane and reported the coronation of Emperor Pu Yi of Manchuria in 1934. (After taking time off to have a baby, in 1961 she invented a folding table for boats.)

When a newspaper reported in 1912 that the first flight of a woman pilot across the English Channel had been made by Miss Harriet Quimby, a male pilot's views were sought. Women were probably not suitable as pilots, he explained, because they have 'delicate throats' and may 'distract or be distracted'. He literally said a woman couldn't do something when asked to comment on the fact that she had just done it. He would have loved Twitter.

Zora Neale Hurston wrote beautifully, and helped to make Harlem a hub of African-American excellence in the arts and studied the cultural landscapes of the people with African heritage in the Caribbean. Geologist Kathy Sullivan was the first woman to 'walk' in space. Endurance skier Valentina Kuznetsova headed a women's scientific expedition to cross Antarctica on skis in the 1980s, when women were forbidden to enter Russian polar stations. Commodore Robyn Walker, a specialist in submarines and health, became the deputy fleet medical officer of the Royal Australian Navy in 2000.

Look at these gorgeous, comradely workers at an Australian munitions factory, undisclosed location, 1940s. (State Library Victoria)

Two unnamed workers at the same Geelong factory in the 1950s: one sealing oil barrels, and one in the office. (Helmut Newton, State Library Victoria)

'When she won they'd say, "The horse is very fast", and if she lost they'd say, '"Well, you shouldn't put women on horses in the first place".' – Aisling Bea on QI, 2020, talking about her mum, jockey Helen Maloney

Trifecta: Riders of the placegetters in the fifth at Warrnambool Races, 24 May 1996. From left, sisters Therese (1st) and Maree Payne (2nd), and teenager Clare Lindop (3rd). (Robin Sharrock)

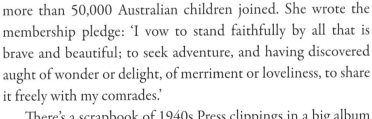

Writer and traveller Nina Murdoch invented the Argonauts Club on ABC Radio in 1933 for children, which ran for decades: more than 50,000 Australian children joined. She wrote the membership pledge: 'I vow to stand faithfully by all that is brave and beautiful; to seek adventure, and having discovered aught of wonder or delight, of merriment or loveliness, to share it freely with my comrades.'

There's a scrapbook of 1940s Press clippings in a big album at the National Library. Without it, we wouldn't know what a clever wartime newspaperwoman we had in Marjorie Goodison

Hedy Lamarr, actress and inventor, in the movie Ziegfeld Girl, *1941. Her invention 'frequency hopping' helped torpedo use in World War II. The technology eventually formed the basis for wireless Bluetooth. (It wasn't a helmet made of stars.) (Michael Ochs Archives/Getty Images)*

(aka McDonald). She conjured stories when there were none, and covered news in Australia and as a correspondent in London, Berlin and Malaya. She wrote about women maintaining engines and loading bombs in the Australian airforce, the damaging Sydney spread of VD by servicemen to young women, the patriotic women who still wore ankle-wrinkling pre-war rayon stockings, and the stagecraft of women escapologists. Marjorie kept and pasted the stories she wrote, almost all of them published without her name.

As so many Australian newspapers don't even have an obituary desk anymore, many fascinating women's stories will never be told to challenge the idea that every elderly woman we see is 'just' an 'old lady' or a 'nanna'.

"Women never invented anything."

Kettle's probably still warm. Take a break and Google 'women inventors'.

"Men's careers are ruined by accusations of harassment."

The fate of an 'unprotected' woman (without a father or husband and out of the house) has been assumed for centuries: at best she will be insulted and the target of sexual suggestions and threats, seen as fair game. At worst she'll be raped, and a pregnancy caused. As women joined the workplace, they were immediately targeted.

For a very long time workplace sexual harassment was

considered so normal that women left jobs and professions as the only way to get away from it. It's still hard to prove without witnesses. 'He said, she said' is just another way of saying whatever he said wins.

Feminist gains in the 1970s and '80s meant that regulators, laws and anti-discrimination laws improved things a little. But, without clear, protected lines of reporting and consequences for creeps, women are still being told in various ways that standing up for themselves will mean discrimination and recriminations, being labelled difficult, or denied promotion.

The same insulting scenarios have come up again and again for decades: a groper here, a leerer there. The advice is always to be quiet and to get out of the way – move cinema seats, rooms, jobs. It's hard enough for a woman to say loudly on a train, 'Stop touching me and move away!' – what if there's nobody else in the carriage? What if he turns violent? Did I mention he's my boss?

When she was in her 80s, I asked my mum about what it was like for her. She told me things about her life I never knew, from her first city job at a major bank headquarters around 1950. 'You just used to have to make yourself invisible when men were being revolting. I was 17. I didn't know what to do, I felt trapped. At work, next to your desk, on the stairs. I could never look men in the

'Garment industry workers, mostly young women, in their workplaces at lunchtime are "invaded by gangs of lecherous young hooligans – they pull about and maul the hoydens in the shop (factory floor)".'
– Brisbane's Truth newspaper, 1903

Actor Lily Brayton makes her feelings clear, c1890s. (Theatrical postcard, National Library of Australia)

eye on the tram because you couldn't trust them. They would occasionally try to put their knee between your knees when it was crowded; you had to keep moving. Their hands everywhere when it was crowded, being bothered by them rubbing against you – it was just the intimidation. Now I'm old I can talk to anyone.'

I asked Mum what she thought would change things. 'You can make lots of laws and they can't enforce them. But you have to start there, and then education – some devious people just look for the opportunities.'

Millions of women have been sexually harassed, many of them hounded out of professions, losing jobs and opportunities. The number of men whose careers have been derailed is so small that it doesn't even seem to have constituted a deterrent effect.

"Sexual harassment is over."

As I write, there are known, reported harassment cases in industries and institutions including universities, schools, financial management, journalism, the High Court, the military, medicine, cleaning crews, steel factory shift workers, aviation, office administration, stand-up comedy, restaurants, bakeries, sports reporting, wine-tasting, fine art, the music industry, the movie industry, front-line retail and backroom politics. Some industries and workplaces are getting better at lines of reporting and consequences. The law has yet to catch up.

It seems sexual harassment will continue anywhere and everywhere there is no active policy against it that involves investigation and proper consequences. Heroic young women are rejecting the idea that it's normal, and are speaking out.

Leave Us Alone poster by Marie McMahon for the NSW Women's Advisory Council Anti-Discrimination Board, 1984. (Museum of Applied Arts and Sciences)

'Was it even remotely plausible that (the applicant), as a consummate professional, would have taken such a risk for such a fleeting moment of supposed sexual gratification?' – Part of the legal finding in a 2019 libel case by Australian Federal Court judge Michael Whitney

'Dyson Heydon, a former Justice of the High Court of Australia, was a serial sexual harasser of his young female associates, an independent inquiry by the court has found.' – Sydney Morning Herald, 2020

(2) Round back, and bring knees together.   Relax.

EXERCISE 5.—On hands and knees.

a. (1) Head down, raise back, tightening abdomen.

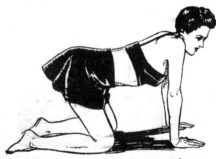

(2) Head up, lower waist, alternately.

Unless you'd rather spin on that piano stool.
(Pregnancy exercises, Pre-Natal Booklet, Department of Health, Victoria,
1946. Possibly by Betty Paterson, National Library of Australia)

6

BE A PERFECT MOTHER, WHICH IS IMPOSSIBLE

ONE OF THE NEW TRENDS IN MOTHERHOOD BOOKS is for 'hip mamas', a cultivated image of eerily calm women with beachy-waved hair, handknit jumpers and long skirts, still looking like sexy models even if a baby just threw up in their ear, who bake their own bread and do everything 'naturally', except for the bit where they put a curated view of their life on social media.

It's not so different from the equally unrealistic view of motherhood that was 'aspirational' in the 1950s, which required another sort of image: glamorous and bouffant-hairsprayed housewife wearing a hostess apron and disinfecting all available horizontal surfaces. Or further back, the angelic-looking mother of the 1890s with her long hair piled on her head, in a high lace collar and post-partum corset, bringing up baby to be a good Christian with the help of a maid-of-all-work.

The hairstyle has changed, as has the emphasis on staying 'sexy'. But the pressure of whatever the latest definition of 'perfect' is stays the same. Any nannies or helpers are out of frame. The sidelined male partner is still a feature: invisible in 1890; sitting in the corner smoking a pipe in the 1950s; now a blurred image of a dude surfing while the kids are on the beach with mum.

One of the more glamorous stay-sexy mother books I saw recently claimed to feature aspirational examples of ordinary mothers: they included heads of global PR for Adidas and Armani, a Nike work-out instructor with a 'bangin' body, super-toned but not ripped in a weird kind of way', a model and a 'muse for French DJs', none of whom were supposed to make me laugh out loud.

The problem with the great support and democracy of mothers and advice on social media is that a lot of it doesn't get filtered through a safety net of known medical and safety knowledge. Take the nonsense nutrition advice about post-baby diets and other fads, and new-mum exercise suggestions that will worsen a case of separated abdominal muscles, and the idea of squirting perfume up your vagina during the first six weeks after birth, which can cause an infection.

One of the 'natural remedies' for post-natal blues I've read was, 'Smiling can trick your brain into thinking you're happy. Give it a shot and see what happens.' Or, how about whoever wrote that can get entirely rooted? And please don't send me the website story suggesting mums with a tiny newborn should get their whole body waxed, buy a nice bottle of wine and 'try to feel sexy'. I mean, why not try pulling your perineum over your head and wearing it as a jaunty bonnet?

Due to the endless, nerve-wracking overhauls and new reprints for my own pregnancy book *Up The Duff* and its sequel *Babies & Toddlers* ('What have I missed, what have I missed? Arghhh!'), I lose sleep over changing medical and emotional advice to mums, terrified they'll read an old edition with outdated, possibly dangerous advice on sleeping positions, of the now defunct one called *Kidwrangling*. I can only soothe myself with the knowledge that I am at least not repeating motherhood advice from the further past, which said to give your baby poison for a cough and opium if they cry.

A stack of parenting books through the years have all conspired to tell mothers that they are the reason a child gets sick or dies. Women were urged to wrap babies in tight flannel binders *or* put babies outside naked; told to induce vomiting *or* induce diarrhoea; administer any amount of hot poultices *or* cold baths; give them vigorous rubbings *or* leave the baby to cry . . . the list of opposites was almost endless.

The self-dubbed Mere Man, author of *The Domestic Blunders of Women* in 1900, told mothers they were 'killing' their children through incompetence. 'Why do more children die every year than calves or lambs, or kittens or puppies, or anything else? . . . because they are managed by women . . . most children die of sweets.' Also, no pants. 'The absurd custom of stripping children half-naked and being surprised and crying floods of tears when they die . . .' It's difficult to have no pants, but it's sadder to have no empathy.

Such mother-botherers used the scarifying infant mortality statistics of, say, a London year in the late 1890s – 3191 deaths in every 10,000 births, and of the 6809 survivors, 1235 dead in their first year. Fifty per cent dead in their first 3 years. Many babies wore no knickers: therefore, cause proved. In fact the main causes were infections, diseases and malnutrition, and abysmal information from doctors.

Women have always been instructed to become mothers and then told they're bad at it. The first written guides were called things like *General Management of Infants* and their tone was as cold and grim as the title suggests. In the early days of verbal advice to mums, much of it was on how to keep babies and children alive: a task that was only achieved by luck: no amount of 'good management' could guarantee a baby's, or a child's, survival.

For a very long time, more babies died than survived. By the 19th century, despite being warned by midwives and common sense, doctors still conducted births in unsanitary ways that caused fatal infections for mothers after childbirth. Mothers were defenceless against vomiting illnesses that killed babies and bacterial infections and viral diseases before immunisation and antibiotics, and yet they were still blamed, whether accused of 'neglect' or 'over-fussiness'.

"All women should be mothers."

Poppycock. Next.

"Pregnancy is a married woman's glory."

Have all the children, wear all the aprons and do everything while a man sits in the corner. Even the baby is shocked. Liberal Party policy booklet, 1949. (National Library of Australia)

Before scientific explanations, pregnancy and the appearance of babies was linked to phases of the moon, animism, prayers, blessings and magic. In the 17th century the medical men of the day made firm and loud statements that they insisted people write down with a giant feather concepts such as each sperm has a miniscule tiny human in it and a woman is just the cupboard in which it grows.

The ideas about pregnancy and birth being a woman's purpose can be expressed in a circle. Imagine it on a clockface, we'll start at noon with 'women must create children to help support the family', travelling clockwise down past 'women must provide new Christians for the church', through 'women must provide new soldiers for war', hitting bottom with 'women must give birth to boys who are the important ones', coming up past 'women must provide more white children to entrench coloniser control and white supremacy', through 'women who don't have children are wrong or selfish', 'we need more children for the economy', and at five minutes to 12 please remember, 'if you do have children you are ruining the planet but it's your biological destiny.'

Would you be more careful if it was you that got pregnant?

'Pregnant man' used to advertise a contraceptive advice service, Family Planning Association of Victoria, 1970s. (State Library Victoria)

"An unmarried woman's pregnancy is her ruin."

If a man is described as 'fallen', he died in a war. If a woman is fallen, she's understood to be pregnant and unmarried, or a sex worker. The phrase 'fell pregnant' is a carryover from those years and I urge you to keep an umbrella about your person and use it to poke anyone who says it.

"Women have pregnancy instincts."

A man in a restaurant once said scornfully to me, 'Why would you bother writing a book about pregnancy? Women have known what to do for centuries, haven't they?' You should have seen the look on his wife's face. I kicked off with, 'A lot of women and a lot of babies have died so we can have the knowledge we have now.' He looked at his wife. She took a breath in. I imagine he's still sleeping in the garage.

"Pregnant women do all the wrong things."

Since the days of travelling tinkers and the contrivance of homeopathic 'remedies', advertisers have used the subtle or obvious blame on women for any perceived wants or faults in their children.

A lot information hard-won through difficulty and heart-ache is now used to help women protect their fetuses during pregnancy: we're told to take a folate supplement 3 months before, and during a pregnancy to avoid neural tube conditions such as spina bifida. Marketing of products to pregnant women and new mums still uses words about pure, safe and healthy.

All cultures had assumptions and warnings about food taboos during pregnancy. English women were told not to eat strawberries lest it cause a birthmark, some Aboriginal cultural rules prevent a pregnant woman eating hopping animals lest it cause lameness in a child, some Asian cultures forbade prawns and shrimp because the curve of their back was associated with disabilities, or because an animal was known to 'hide' from predators and eating it could cause a baby to not come out at the right time.

Some food recommendations were useful, but many worked against women getting the extra protein and other nutrients they need. Food and drink restrictions now are based on scientific studies, which have proved causational damage: from the lower risk of listeria in some foods, to the high risk of fetal brain damage caused by some alcohol use.

'Pregnant lady' c1870s. Either that or she's got a netball team under there. (I. J. Chidley, Melbourne Portrait Rooms studio, State Library Victoria)

"Maternity clothes must hide a pregnancy."

Visible pregnancy is of course evidence that you've probably HAD SEX, you slutburger. In the repressive English culture we inherited, women were expected not to appear in public in the last months of pregnancy – impossibly, of course, unless you were rich and had servants. Giant, hidey underskirts were employed, suspended from bodices with buttons, crinolines worked pretty well, and mid-to-late-20th-century maternity clothes resembled queen-size doona covers with a Peter Pan collar. The advent of stretchy jersey fabrics and new 'athleisure' clothes (yoga pants even if you're so not doing any yoga) and the acceptability of thongs or ugh-boots as day wear has been quite the boon for pregnant folk.

"In the past, women didn't mind miscarriages."

It seems to me a great libel on our ancestors to say that they didn't love their children as much then, because so many babies died and it was more common, so they didn't mind as much about miscarriage, stillbirth and the death of children. It was so common in centuries gone past that there is no special word for a parent whose child dies, as there are words for widow and orphan.

But an examination by women historians of the first-person diaries and letters going back hundreds of years disproves the idea that women didn't feel the same way about their children, even if they knew they were likely to lose them.

The intense grief of women who lose their babies and small children was everywhere anybody bothered to record it: from medieval Europe to the Central Desert of Australia. Varied beliefs and rituals were used to try to ward off miscarriage or death of babies, and to try to avoid what was believed to harm a fetus.

"Dancing causes miscarriages."

We now know that miscarriages – the termination of a pregnancy by a woman's body – are not rare, nor caused by the woman herself. It's only over the last hundred years that some of the real reasons for miscarriage have been identified, including syphilis, medical problems with the uterus or placenta; and chromosome or other genetic conditions.

'I know not what ocationed. But am jealous [worried] least it be a punishment of some particular sin.' – Elizabeth Turner looks for a reason for her miscarriage, 1662

'A day never to be forgotten; wherein I felt the bitter fruits of the sin of my grandmother Eve . . . Heaven is something fuller for my babe.' – Anne Hulton, 1695, whose baby died during childbirth, both quotes from Blood, Bodies and Families in Early Modern England by Patricia Crawford, 2004

When my great-great-grandmother Sarah Wills had a miscarriage in 1873, her mother-in-law, Elizabeth, sent a letter saying, 'You see, you are to blame,' because she rode a horse while pregnant. Sarah's wish to pursue her own freedom was the cause, Elizabeth chided. The baby, she said briskly, was 'in its heavenly home . . . I trust this lesson will be well remembered.'

Women have been given different reasons for miscarriage. The following list was compiled using an analysis of reasons mentioned in 19th-century Australian medical journals 1856–1921 by Eugenia Pacitti; Shannon Withycombe's book *Lost: Miscarriage in Nineteenth-Century America;* reasons given from the 1400s to the 20th century in textbooks for doctors and midwives and home medical books, as well as studies on assumed causes, from Qatar, Kenya, England, America and Australia. We now know a miscarriage is never a woman's 'fault' or the result of anything she thought or saw, and very, very rarely from anything she did 'wrong'.

Many miscarriages, stillbirths, cases of blindness and other medical conditions in babies and women were caused by the unchecked ravages of syphilis and gonorrhea. Some women were not told they had a venereal disease because it would be 'shameful' or implicate a husband. Until better screening and antibiotic treatments became available after World War II, pregnancies were routinely plagued by Sexually Transmitted Infections (STIs).

Wrong reasons given for miscarriage 1300s–2000s

Not eating enough

overnourishment of fetus

a mis-step on the stairs

operations

tired uterus

thin uterus

womb acquires a habit

excessive sex

anxiety

too many eggs

melancholy

excessive joy

a morbid state

high spirits

a pretend pregnancy

hysteria

inflammation

exhaustion

toothache

blows (being hit)

plegmatick humours of the
womb

lifting heavy weights

not enough exercise

constipation

being advanced in life

excessive youth

dancing

horseriding

tight clothes

intestinal irritants

haemorrhoids

having sex

tooth extraction

smallpox

grief

rage

sorrows of captivity

apprehension of death

scrofula

lead poisoning

anaemia

not weeing enough

a long walk

being sexually aroused

irritation of the nipples

supernatural forces

God's will

the evil eye

possession by a jinni

too much housework

using a fertility clinic

overhearing gossip

previous use of contraception

a dose of purgative

the jolting of a carriage

sea-bathing

seeing another woman in
labour

fright

shock or overwhelming grief

appalling sights

eating mould

hot climate in women
unaccustomed

cold climate in women
unaccustomed

over-indulgence in food

drink and exercise

weakness

reaching for something

a journey

being thin

being large

an episode of sex during a
period in your past

hunger

too much food

getting pregnant before a
bride-price was paid

taking a dangerous medication

not being vaccinated

rape

sorrow

running

lust

watchfulness

fullness

emptiness

infidelity

eating meat from a pregnant
cow

essential oil vapours

wearing high heels

something unknown that the
mother must have done

and . . . drastic cathartics.

"Doctors know about pregnancy; women don't."

The patronising tone of some obstetricians was commemorated by a rogue indexer of the fifteenth edition of the standard textbook, *Williams Obstetrics*, in 1976. Nestled among the entries for words starting with C the indexer inserted: 'Chauvinism, male, variable amounts, (pages)1–923.' By the sixteenth edition (1980) the index had been overhauled, amending the entry to 'Chauvinism, male, voluminous amounts (pages)1–1102.'

I am sorry to say subsequent editions are missing the entry. Still, tremendous while it lasted. (As Dr Diane Madlon-Kay pointed out in an article in the *New York Times* in 1991, the excision of the index line didn't mean the sexism itself was all removed.)

For decades, the Williams textbook said women's pregnancy nausea was due to their psychological condition: a woman who vomited had 'emotional instability'. Later, women were prescribed sedative drugs for the condition, including thalidomide, untested on pregnant women, which caused the death of fetuses, brain damage and many babies to be born with medical conditions and without limbs. The effects differed depending on which day of pregnancy the drug was taken.

Sister Pat Sparrow at the Crown St Women's Hospital in Sydney first raised the alarm with Dr William McBride, who was prescribing it. He ignored her, then later claimed credit for noticing the connection in a letter to a medical journal. He was later struck off as a registered doctor for medical research fraud.

The rogue indexer strikes again.

Chamberlen forceps, *887*
Chancroid, 631
Chauvinism, male, variable amounts, 1–923
Chemotherapy. *See also* Antibiotics.
  choriocarcinoma and, 465
  hydatidiform mole and, 461, 462
Chiari-Frommel syndrome, 782
  treatment, 782

"Childbirth hurts to punish women."

It's said that Queen Victoria's doctors initially refused to administer chloroform to her in childbirth, because it was believed the Bible instructed women to suffer for the sins of Eve (apple, snake, and so forth). The queen demanded it anyway for her eighth childbirth in 1853, later giving it a rave review: 'blessed chloroform, soothing, quieting and delightful beyond measure'.

Alice B. Stockham is best known for her contraceptive advice about abstinence called Karezza, in her 1883 book *Tokology*. She had a weird insistence that childbirth only hurt if pregnant women didn't get enough fresh air and eat fruit. This, she said, accounted for the (mythical) painless, short labour of women of 'savage nations', a commonly repeated racist assumption of ignorant advisors. The obstetric care, options and outcomes for women of colour, including Aboriginal women in Australia, and African-American women in the US and other countries remains consistently, statistically worse than those for white women.

The idea of an easy childbirth being guaranteed if a pregnant woman does yoga, eats organic food and has no medical intervention is still perpetuated now. Women are still being blamed, or blame themselves, for not having a lucky, 'perfect' birth.

"Women are designed to give birth."

Childbirth has always been dangerous for women, but it's far less dangerous now in places where full midwife services and obstetric emergency care facilities are available. The biggest killers of the past are 'solved': puerperal fever (infection caused by doctors and midwives not washing their hands), conditions such as placental abruption and placenta praevia (much more likely to be detected early by ultrasound, or managed better by hospitals), pre-eclampsia is (usually detected and managed

'If only we could have children without the help of women!' – Line in the play *Hippolytus* by Euripides, 428 BC

'I will greatly multiply your pain in childbearing; in pain you shall bring forth children; yet your desire shall be for your husband; and he shall rule over you.' – Genesis 3:16, Christian Bible

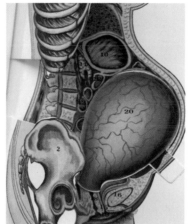 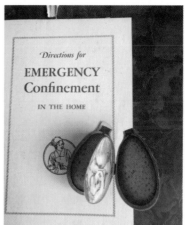

before it proceeds to eclampsia and uterine haemorrhaging can usually successfully treated quickly after a hospital birth).

If things go wrong in childbirth, it isn't the fault of the labouring woman. The biggest factor in having an easy birth isn't diet or exercise or whether there's a pool in the room: it's luck. High-quality pregnancy care and screening, and emergency medical help at hand are the next biggest factors.

"Recovering from childbirth is easy."

Most cultures have various recommendations for special food and care for new mothers, so they can concentrate on their babies. Broths, puddings, a festival of available protein, and various kinds of glop was the English way.

'The Maternal and Child Welfare Council was founded in 1928, the year 691 women died in childbirth in Australia. Half of them were under 20.' – Information given by councillor Mrs E. A. Waterworth, *Burnie Advocate* 1939

In her essay 'Two cultures and a baby', Alice Pung talked about the conflicting pregnancy and childbirth preparation advice from Australian medical experts and traditional Asian advice. The Chinese and South-Asian practice of *zuo yue zi* allows a new mum to stay in a heated room for a month and be fed 'special soups and tonics' by relatives. As she observes, it's a tradition that centres and supports the mum as much as the baby. 'When Kate Middleton brought baby (Prince) George out to the front steps of the hospital to show the world, the tone of Chinese and Taiwanese media's coverage of the event was not of excitement, but grave alarm,' Alice wrote.

Apart from not washing your hair for a month, this isn't unlike what richer women could afford in the English tradition of 'lying in' hospitals, or by employing a 'monthly' – a special maid with a specialty in baby care who came to live with you for a month. South American women have a similar tradition of '*cuarantena*' for a month to six weeks. It allows for family bonding, the bringing of meals by relatives and friends, and in some cases, requires a gate-keeping sister or partner to mitigate an avalanche of advice or expel gaggles of exhausting visitors.

"A post-baby body shouldn't look like one."

Looking like a mother when you're a mother has been forbidden since approximately 1991. You must fit any momentary definition of 'sexy' regardless of whether something the size of a shoebox has just come out of your vagina or been cut out of you using actual knives, or if you haven't had time for a shower since last Thursday nor slept more than a couple of hours at a time for a year. I hereby amend this advice to: if anyone uses the acronym MILF near you, you are allowed to hit them with some of the furniture.

If you don't worry, you're neglectful, and if you do worry you're neurotic. Advice for new mothers supplement. (Australian Women's Weekly *magazine, 1967*)

"Mothers worry too much."

On the birth of their baby in hospital, some mothers are given a showbag of wet wipes and baby massage lotion to promote brand loyalty. They're also handed a meta-phorical sample bag of guilt that they'll never be perfect enough, given a list of things to watch for which might be dangerous, and then told they're being too anxious if they worry about anything. I once asked an unkind eye specialist to be more gentle with my toddler, who he was examining. He said, 'Don't fuss, mother.' I said, 'I am not fussing and I am not your mother.' He nearly fell off his chair.

"Breastfeeding is easy."

Some mums have always had trouble breastfeeding; medieval writings include accounts of trying to spoon gruel into babies who couldn't suck, or when mums had trouble producing milk. Doctors and midwives knew babies were much more likely to survive if breastfed – there was no researched, regulated powdered formula milk then, only 'sugar water', dreadful glop with mashed grain, or fish oil in milk if you had a cow, or just water. Often, laudanum or brandy might be added to stop a baby crying (or living, by accident).

The original caption for this was: 'Baby-feeding machine at St Margaret's Hospital, 1967'. Well, it can't have been, can it? A baffling contraption at a hospital, which stole babies from unmarried mothers for 80 years. (Ern McQuillan, National Library of Australia)

By the late 1600s and 1700s, wet-nurses – paid, surrogate breast-feeders – were common, and records show that many nurses loved the babies they fed. In families, no doubt, sisters and others helped out if they could. It wasn't a bad job, and you got good meals with it – quite a lot of beer and stout with every meal as 'malt liquor' was considered the cure for exhaustion.

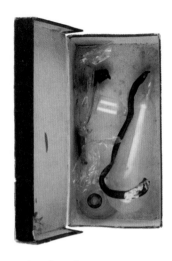

The Acme Improved Breast
Exhausters pumping set,
with various bits: a glass
bottle, teat, er . . . suction
thingy, rubber tubing
and a cellophane funnel,
1910. (Museum of Applied
Arts and Sciences)

There were all sorts of mad rules for choosing a wet-nurse based on assumptions that religion could be passed on in breast-milk, and that rosy cheeks meant good milk.

More recently, breastfeeding somehow became everyone's business, with some people demanding to know why you weren't doing it, or insisting you do it in private (such insistence is illegal) (and annoying).

As far back as the *Directory for Midwives* in 1651 by Nicolas Culpepper, breastfeeding advice was fraught: 'Oh! What a Racket do Authors make about this! What wharting and contradicting, not of others, but themselves?' Culpepper advised that some of his own children had died, and he recommended a wet-nurse who wasn't 'crump-shouldered, nor yellow-haired' and didn't have any black teeth. Guess what, this author of the *Directory for Midwives* NEVER ATTENDED A BIRTH.

The doctor-imposed breastfeeding schedules of European and colonial women were reflected in *Mrs Beeton's Book of*

'The tediousness
of nursing we owe
to sin.' – Mrs Ann
Hulton of Chester,
England, late 1600s

Mothers' advisor Truby King seems fun. (National Library of Australia)

Household Management's very strictypants rules, decreeing it to happen at 'six, ten, two, six and ten o'clock'.

Dr Warren in *The Wife's Guide & Friend* (1927) lied to mothers, saying, 'More infants die from too much food than from too little ... Feed every two hours for first 4 weeks, then every 2 and a half until 6 months then every 3 hours until 18 months. No night feeds between 11 pm and 5 or 6 am after first few weeks.'

Women were wrongly warned that their feelings were converted by breastmilk into the behaviour of a baby. Useless advice on breastfeeding and nipples through the years has included perfuming them (1905), cleaning them every day with a toothbrush (1965) and putting twirl tassels on them (1998 – oh, that was me.)

"Ignore your baby."

There is a long, disreputable tradition of mostly men telling mothers they're showing too much love to their babies and would 'spoil' them. Right from Nicolas Culpepper in the 1600s blathering that 'the fondness of Mothers to Children doth them more mischief than the Devil himself can do them' through to Scottish-New Zealander Truby King telling mothers to leave babies outdoors in a pram alone for hours.

A pie chart of '12 essentials' in Modern Mothercraft, *an official Plunket Society booklet given to most New Zealand mothers, 1945 to 1950s.*

"Weird schedules are good for babies."

By the early 1900s, especially by the 1920s, private nurses and charitable infant welfare services were trying to tackle high rates of baby death due to malnutrition and hygiene-related illnesses.

Dr Truby King's efforts to create the best baby formula of the day, while promoting breastfeeding when possible, and setting strict hygiene rules were believed to have lowered infant mortality rates in New Zealand, so his other advice was also adopted by early Plunket and Karitane homes and parenting advice services: his books were bestsellers.

King forbade mothers from cuddling their babies, apart from briefly at precisely spaced 4-hourly feedings. The psychological damage from all this is immeasurable. A Channel 4 UK parenting TV show in 2007 called *Bringing Up Baby* went for maximum controversy by contrasting the advice of an 'attachment parenting' advocate who said don't put the baby down until it's about 6 months old, with a woman who faithfully recycled King's advice from 1907.

The recycler's advice was wicked: mothers were not to make eye contact while feeding their baby, only cuddle for ten minutes a day, adopt the 4-hourly rigid feeding rule and leaving babies outside. Medical and psychology experts and

'Crying . . . is a means of exercise and expansion of the baby's lungs; therefore too much attention need not be paid to crying . . .'
– Dr Warren in Wife's Guide and Friend, 1927

Details of a baby show satire by Punch *cartoonist John Leech, with an award for having a charming child; the 'Natural Diet' is a jab at sober vegetarians. (National Library of Australia)*

parents alike were deeply upset. It revealed that the woman held not a single nursing or infant care qualification. The ABC in Australia broadcast this crap program in 2009, with a lame disclaimer.

By the late 1960s the NZ government threatened to pull funding and take over maternal and child services if the Plunket Society didn't update its advice and provide proper services to the less well-off, and to Maori and Islander mothers.

"Every woman has a mother's instinct."

Women have always been eager for information on motherhood, whether from home encyclopaedias, infant welfare clinics, or online. In the 1920s and '30s, hundreds of country women flocked to mobile lectures on the Better Farming Train. The train was a joint venture of the Victorian government railways and agriculture departments, and had carriages for

Pipe down, it's Sister Muriel Peck, the first infant welfare nurse in Victoria, lecturing in the mothercraft carriage of the Better Farming Train, 1927. (State Library Victoria)

the propagation and care of cattle, sheep, honey, poultry, potatoes, and babies.

Women's carriages were on each of the 38 tours of the trains between 1924 and 1935, with instructresses in needlework and cooking, recruited from the technical schools of Melbourne. Led by Sister Muriel Peck, the lessons in mothercraft included instruction on household hygiene designed to prevent illnesses, and tips on how to avoid the common rural problem of childhood malnutrition.

"Mothers should be alone with kids."

Part of the mad cruelty of the 'happy housewife' myth was the idea that women should be alone with small children. It broke thousands of years of tradition of women's camaraderie and closeness in Indigenous and village situations. It imposed a terrible loneliness and inbuilt insecurity, removing the natural human urge to share experiences, swap and assess advice. 'Housewives' weren't in village sewing circles, or going together to collect the water from the creek or pump, or handing off their babies to a neighbour when they were exhausted, or singing songs together to judge the right length a fabric had to be in the boiling dye pot.

Easier said than done: an official NSW pamphlet advised pregnant women eat lots of fresh foods and protein, during rationing in 1941. (Public Records Office Victoria)

"Mothers create their children's personality."

Miss Leslie's Behavior Book by Eliza Leslie came out in 1839 strongly in favour of the popular instruction of the day to start punishing babies at three months old.

Leslie said babies cried because their mothers dressed them in uncomfortable clothes or scratchy necklaces instead

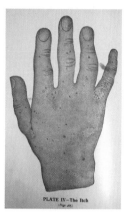

PLATE IV—The Itch
(Page 476)

A mother's guide to identifying an unspecific 'itch', Ladies' Home Handbook by Eulalia Richards, 1912.

of smooth coral beads (the idea of necklaces for babies is, needless to say, a Bad One). Babies with long hair look unruly and this should be stopped. Tight waists caused tuberculosis, as well as bad manners, in a baby. Be careful of Irish nannies who will secretly have a child baptised Catholic and European nannies who have been known to take babies into dirty alleys to meet other filthy immigrants. There is any amount of this rubbish to be had from Miss Leslie so I think we shall take our leave in high dudgeon, snapping our elasticised waists.

"If you're in paid work, you neglect your kids."

You can still get this sort of bilge in tabloid websites and social media comments, neither of them useful or supported by evidence. Society and the mindset of male politicians work against the needs of mothers, including school hours, working hours, public transport schedules, shop hours, product marketing, and childcare availability and subsidies. All of this works against modern mums.

"Single mothers are appalling."

Though statistics repeatedly show single mums stay on government entitlements for relatively short periods, provide endless and important work that is not recognised or paid, and contribute to current and future societies, they remain a common target for critics.

It's partly a moral hangover from the days when 'unmarried mother' was an insult and church and state alike provided no protection or respect to a mother without a partner to help her. A widow or abandoned woman was considered less immediately dreadful, but morally suspicious anyway.

In a 1940s book, *Sex Instruction for The Adolescent Girl and The Young Woman: The Facts Without the Humbug*, the targeted teen readers were warned: 'An unmarried mother...may die of starvation, or disease. Young girls finding themselves in this tragic position have sometimes gone insane with worry and killed themselves...any child of an unmarried mother is called illegitimate. The child having no rightful name, is almost a nobody. These unfortunate children, and their mothers, too, are often treated by unkind people as if they were mongrel dogs. How would you like to be the mother of one of these poor children?'

How would you like to go fu– oh, look, it's the end of the chapter.

A poor mother shuts her eyes against the photographer's flash in a kitchen without running water or a pantry; her three children may have measles, 1935. (Possibly Oswald Barnett, State Library Victoria)

*The scarifying winner of the Miss Tiny Tot beauty pageant,
3-year-old Debra Vincent, 1962.*
(Fred Boyle, State Library Victoria)

7

LOOK PRETTIER

AS A TEENAGER POISED ON THE BRINK OF WOMANHOOD, the poet Edith Sitwell was given a book by her father, about how to make the most of not being beautiful. *How to Be Pretty Though Plain* had been compiled from columns in *Truth* magazine by Mrs Humpry in 1899. Mr Sitwell was a barking rich aristocrat who invented a teensy gun for shooting wasps, and ordered his cows stencilled in a Willow pattern. Sadly, his eccentricities don't seem to have made him a kinder father.

Perhaps as a consequence of receiving the book, Edith later referred to herself as plain. In fact, she was the opposite – a fascinating-looking woman, with a nose like a spinnaker and a collection of wackadoodle outfits. She was most often photographed touching her face, to show her extraordinary rings.

Anyway, back to *How to Be Pretty Though Plain*. Mrs Humphry was yet another clergyman's daughter having a crack at earning her own money as a journalist-advisor. Under the pen-name 'Madge', she wrote about manners, household management, fashion, but most of all how to be 'pretty' without any 'elaboration of cosmetics and hair dyes – artifices to which no girls who are true would have recourse'.

How then was a woman to make herself beautiful? Industriousness, 'a pleasant expression, a bright countenance, a graceful figure, a charming manner and attention to details of toilet and dress'. Mrs Humphry was shortly thereafter swept away downstream by a billion-dollar beauty industry and that was the end of her.

"Make-up is the devil."

Saint Augustine denounced unmarried women who tried to make themselves 'prettier'. 'To dye oneself with paints in order to have a rosier or a paler complexion is a lying counterfeit.' They were terrible sinners if they wanted to attract men, but less sinny if they were just 'vain'. He also believed every act of sex was evil, so best we back away from him slowly with our hands in the air.

Edith Sitwell, at 75, possibly wearing a laundry basket on her head, with a ring the size of an emu egg, 1956. (Hulton Archive/Getty Images)

'I am an unpopular electric eel set in a pond of goldfish.'
– Edith Sitwell, 1963

Make-up was actually anti-God, said Cyprian, an early Christian bishop in the 200s, for whom a lick of mascara was 'an assault on the Divine handiwork, a distortion of the truth'.

Thomas Tuke let fly in 1616 with *A Discourse Against Painting and Tincturing of Women Wherein the abominable Sinnes of Murther and Poysoning, Pride and Ambition, Adultery and Witchcraft are Set Foorth & dicovered.* Painted faces were 'on earth the greatest counterfeit', he says before getting agitated on the subjects of visible 'papes' (bosoms). Women should put up with how they look naturally: 'The nature colour of face and haire is true and right . . . but false and wrong, that's dyed by art work of a lying, wanton hart.' Unless he meant tart. Either, or.

An even more unhinged dude called Ambrose Parey in 1665 went right off: 'This following discourse is not intended for those women which addicted to filthy lust, seek to beautifie their faces, as baits and allurements to filthy pleasures; but is intended for those onley, which the better to restraine the wandring lusts of their husbands, may endeavor by art to take away those spots and deformities which have happened to fall on their faces either by accident or age.'

An English law passed in 1770 said marriages would be annulled if the wife was convicted of 'witchcraft and like misdemeanours', which included the pretenses of 'scent, paints, cosmetics, washes, artificial teeth...iron stays, hoops, high-heeled shoes or bolstered hips.'

Knowing her murder was afoot, Jezebel in the Bible 'painted her face and tied her head', which is variously interpreted as make-up and a wig but might just have been a high pony. It took a few hundred years for the word jezebel to be more associated with sexual immorality and vanity, and cosmetics.

In the US, the term was often used to slander African-American women. Bette Davis wore a scandalous red dress in the 1939 movie *Jezebel*. Margaret Atwood uses jezebel as the word for sex worker in The Handmaid's Tale novels. When Kamala Harris, a woman of colour, became the Vice President of the United States, male evangelical church officials immediately called her a 'godless Jezebel'.

Music Hall and vaudeville performers used blush and eyeliner on stage, for the same reason costumes often used gaudy colours, large spots and stripes: good visibility from the back row. Later, make-up became associated with sex workers.

An elderly man at a tram stop once piped up out of the blue and told my 18-year-old daughter her red lipstick would cause some people to see her as a 'loose woman'.

Capitalism put an end to the Jezebel business fairly quickly; you don't build the Revlon empire by telling women that lipstick makes them look like the devil's whore.

'An orange-tinged lipstick, so popular these days, is wrong with lamé. The tone should incline rather to the crimson.' – The Daily News, Perth, 1934

Unusual early visible lipstick on 'Australia's Sweetheart', stage actress Nellie Stewart, 1906. (N. J. Caire, State Library Victoria)

The Mary Lou cosmetics line of 'Outdoor Girl' make-up for younger customers, with a golfer in a short skirt logo, 1920s, USA. (Museum of Applied Arts and Sciences)

"You need to spend money to express yourself."

Savvier modern cosmetic companies are being much nicer to us these days instead of telling us to camouflage facial differences or hide 'flaws'. They've recognised that many of us, including LGBTQI+ people, wear make-up to express ourselves, and relate to the 'self-care' part of skin products. Modern girls are far more likely to please themselves with make-up than to use it as the 1950s advice to help 'find a boyfriend'.

In the 1970s, L'Oreal capitalised on the ability of women to spend money on themselves. As capitalism met the Women's Liberation movement the idea of 'be more beautiful for men' took a backseat, and the slogan became 'Because I'm Worth It', then 'Because You're Worth It', and finally the more inclusive, 'Because We're Worth It'.

"Make-up is compulsory."

The idea that a man's plain face is fine, and a woman's is not, is something few men think about. Every day and every night, men just get up and go out the door wearing their very own face. But women are somehow supposed to visibly 'make an effort', which then looks 'effortless'.

The online world is full of blog posts from women who wear make-up to work because otherwise they're told they look too young, too tired or have 'let themselves go'. The grooming tax refers to the hundreds of dollars a year we can spend on make-up, manicures, eyebrow wrangling, body-hair removal methods, haircuts and styling products.

Some workplaces stipulate the use of make-up, others have an unspoken requirement 'policed' by people shrieking, 'You look tired, are you *all right*?!' if you don't have any on. We're so used to the default normality of make-up that the sight of a woman with wildly running mascara and skewiff lipstick is shorthand for drunk, or not in her right mind.

Glamorous face powder packaging for 'Evening in Paris' features tiny images of dining, dancing, a carriage ride and … posing nude for a painter. (Museum of Applied Arts and Sciences)

"Put make-up on in secret."

Putting on make-up in public was considered vulgar, mainly because it was vaguely shameful. It had to be done in secret even if everyone knew you were doing it. 'I just need to powder my nose' and 'powder room' became euphemisms for going to the loo.

"Your eyelashes aren't hairy enough."

Originally, black chemicals were mixed with water and painted on as eyeliner and eyelash colouring. In the early 1900s, some

False eyelashes and an eyelash curler, 1965. (Museum of Applied Arts and Sciences)

women had fringes of false eyelashes sewn to the base of their own. More recently, we've had dyed eyelashes, eyelash perming and glued-in false eyelashes designed to last a few weeks.

At some point in the early '90s I noticed during irregular appearances to promote books that TV lady-hosts now, almost to a woman, have started to wear false eyelashes, like chorus lines of high-kicking spiders.

"Blush."

As the array of make-up we 'need' becomes ever-larger (you'll be needing a base under that primer before your foundation, love), rouge has been joined by bronzers and highlighters. Originally, girls would walk briskly or pinch their cheeks. Depending on who you asked, red cheeks meant youthful vigour or virginal blushing (rouge is also called blush) or orgasmic. (Two top-selling rouge names are 'Virgin Blush' and 'Orgasm'.)

Rouge was applied as a paint powder, or a liquid rubbed in. Other rouges were carmine preparations made from crushed up cochineal beetles. Chalk was soon recommended as a base, rather than dangerous lead.

"It's your duty to buy face creams."

In her 1913 book *How to Be Beautiful*, Marie Montaigne was relieved to know what was expected of her: 'There is a certain satisfaction about the thought that in conserving and enhancing one's personal attractions one is performing a sacred duty, and this belief lends zest to the practice of facial massage and the application of beautifying emollients.'

After years of being told that any make-up or primping made you a frightful Jezebel, making an effort was greenlit, and

A tin of 'undetectable
colliandum'; a fancy-name
for rouge, 20th century,
Dearborn company.
(Museum of Applied
Arts and Sciences)

in swept the beauty advisors in newspaper columns and books, and a capitalist empire of cosmetics.

In 1908 ads for Helena Rubinstein's 'Valaze' beauty cream (said to be Hungarian for 'from heaven'), the first smash-hit brand moisturiser, decreed, 'Woman's duty is to be beautiful. That is her place in Nature . . . Vivacity and personal charm are not enough.'

The motto of beauty duty was summed up even earlier by Lola Montez in 1858: 'Every woman owes it not only to herself, but to society, to be as beautiful and charming as she possibly can.' That's from her book *The Arts of Beauty or Secrets of a Lady's Toilet*, which included a satirical section called 'Hints to Gentlemen on the Art of Fascinating', covering the perennial problems of mansplaining, manspreading and leering, not to mention being 'triflers and danglers'.

Lola had quite the life: born Irish, married at 16, the lover of Ludwig I, King of Bavaria, who made her a countess and a baroness. She fled upheaval and a riot against her, and started over. Within a decade, she'd written her beauty book, danced the saucy tarantella (pretending to search her skirts for a spider; it was possibly danced without pants, or at least some tickets

Lola Montez's portrait
was used as an emblem
of sluttiness on the cover
of a 1979 book about
colonial recreation,
called . . . good Lord.

were sold with this hope in mind) and attacked a *Ballarat* newspaper editor in the street with a whip during a tour of Australian goldfield town stages.

A haughty *Argus* reviewer frothed of her Melbourne performance in 1855: 'utterly subversive of all ideas of public morality.' The *Argus* advised Lola she was an unwelcome scarlet woman, and she was having none of it. She had a letter delivered in time for the next day's more supportive *Herald*: 'Theirs is the indelicacy.' Why, her act was as tasteful as nude statues, she said. And furthermore she would do it all again that night.

Her *Arts of Beauty* is mostly the usual exhortations for plain

Don't let the breeze up: an interpretation of Lola's spider dance 100 years after she wrote the beauty hints book. (National Library of Australia)

A GAY ···· VIRILE · Lola An AUSTRALIAN ELIZABETHAN
AUSTRALIAN MUSICAL Montez THEATRE TRUST PRODUCTION

food, light exercise and tepid baths. It's inconceivable that Lola used no make-up on stage – she'd have wanted her eyebrows and lips accentuated in case nobody was looking up her gown. She said lipstick is disgusting, but was a fan of rouge: 'This allowable artifice must be used with the most delicate taste and discretion . . . always be fainter than what nature's palette would have painted . . . A violently rouged woman is a disgusting sight.'

"Cosmetics work miracles."

I'll say it again, because it's still true. They don't sell us anti-ageing creams because they work, they sell them because we buy them. And they're called that because women don't want to see or hear the word wrinkles. The same cream can be separately marketed as eye cream, neck cream, décolletage cream, day cream or night cream. My favourite is the stuff marketed as a 'vanishing cream', which must be dangerous to put on your feet.

The names of products echo what we want as we get older: revitalising, anti-ageing, repair, rejuvenation. Helena Rubinstein asked what women said they didn't want in the early 1900s: red noses, wrinkles, spots, blackheads, freckles, dry skin. Then she sold products that claimed to fix them.

"Firming creams make your skin firmer."

Nope. That there is no such thing as a lifting and firming cream doesn't stop people from claiming it in ads and on packaging. Look closely and you'll see the ads dodge legal problems by saying it 'creates the appearance of' or some such other meaningless phrase. Last time I was in a Sephora it was selling 'Black Tea Firming Corset Cream for Face and Neck', and just as absurdly, my local pharmacy sells a 'bust firming cream'.

'Wrap your hands in chicken skin at night, to keep them soft.' – The Ladies Dressing-Room Unlock'd, 1690

'When the skin is inclined to be oily, bathe the face daily in orange juice.' – 'Novel Beauty Hints' by Mildred St. Aubyn, supplement to The Lady's Realm, 1912

'No cosmetician has ever been known to compliment a client on the state of her complexion. To do so would contradict the mysterious faith-healing aura which is the essence of their craft.' – Mary Tuck, The Intelligent Woman's Guide to Good Taste, 1958

"Wrinkle creams work."

Wrinkles are caused by age, gravity, the changing effect of hormones on the skin, sun-exposure damage, and having facial expressions. Wrinkles are caused by staying alive.

Various celebrities or those who claimed to know them gave out recipes. Sarah Bernhardt's Wrinkle Eradicator recipe used alum, almond milk and rosewater. (Her Beauty Bath was basically porridge: oats, rice, bran and pulverised lupin seed.)

Although the only proven wrinkle-reducer is digitally altering a photograph, the claims in advertisements have done nothing but multiply, without the addition of any new 'proofs'. Advertisers claim their own research and surveys prove things like a '37 per cent reduced appearance' of wrinkles.

"Sciencey cosmetics are the best."

Cosmetic names have always been made up to evoke a feeling: delicate daintypants names from the 1700s, such as rosaline, blanc de perle, rose-leaf powder, magnolia and velvetine, which gave way to early-20th-century sciencey-discovery type ones like jettoline, palerium, onalite, tennaline and collandium. The science-name caper is still on today, with serums, peptides and brands such as PhytoSpecific and Cellular Swiss sold as 'cosmeceuticals'.

Sciencey-sounding products often have extra gimmicks – they must be dispensed in droplets with a squeeze-dropper, or teensy rollers, and they have labels that scream 'laboratory'.

A Malaysian cosmetics brand, among others, has taken to claiming it contains synthetic snake venom and snail slime, 'enzymes . . . proteins, glycoloc acides and elastin'. The 'viper' cream is said to relax the muscles that cause wrinkles, but to use another popular slogan, yeah, nah.

'The right of every woman – loveliness.'
– Helena Rubinstein slogan, 1906

Helena Rubinstein being sciencey.

252

"Beauty is medical."

Many newspaper magazines and websites have acquiesced in calling beauty salons 'offices', 'clinics' and 'medical spas', despite them having no qualified medical staff. (Some do have a doctor on the premises and nurses qualified to inject fillers and Botox.) If you don't like the science slant, you can attend a 'wellness and aesthetics centre'. Customers became clients and sometimes even 'patients', while services are called 'treatments'. When it became legal for doctors to advertise, in the late 20th century, the number of cosmetic 'clinics' increased exponentially.

Bronze Roman tools: an arrowhead for shooting things, and wee spoons for getting cosmetics out of bottles. Not sure which was messier. Before 410 BC. (Museum of Applied Arts and Sciences)

"If it's expensive, it works."

William Alexander set the bar pretty high already in the 1700s, claiming that Roman Empress Poppaea Sabina 'had every day the milk of five hundred asses made into a bath, which she supposed gave her skin a softness and polish beyond that of any other woman'.

You can make something seem exclusive by upping the price and using a tiny bottle made of a heavy substance and adding a few words like 'luxe', 'platinum-infused' and including ingredients like caviar and gold, even though they don't 'do' anything.

Our old mate, Polish-Australian forged beauty entrepreneur Helena Rubenstein launched many enduring genius marketing moves in her early salon days in the first decade of the 1900s. She invented the idea of a skin type and selling products for dry, oily and normal skin; and she lied about their origins and ingredients. But her big move was selling a cheap cream with a fancy label, and when it didn't sell well at first, she did nothing except *double the price*. Suddenly, it was a premium product that rich people could afford. It had cachet, it had aspirational appeal. It had sheep fat.

'Now why do you wrinkle your face by thinking. Nothing ages a face more, not even an out-of-date hat.' – Ad for a Brisbane millinery shop, *The Telegraph*, 1914

"If the label is in French, it's better."

La Prairie, De la Mer, Crème hydratante. There's no reason except marketing to have labels translated into French as well as English. Most cosmetics are made in China, with a registered office in France or Switzerland (ah, Switzerland: it's France, only sciencier).

"Beauty ads are so true."

One can only imagine the unhinged glee of the person who put some kind of perfumed gravel and oil into a packet and sold it as a butt exfoliating mask. Cosmetics are often relatively cheap ingredients sold at high prices using a variety of buzzwords and concepts: novelty, science, naturalness, pretty packaging, fun joke names, and expensive fanciness.

I said something like this in my book *Real Gorgeous* way back in 1994, but here's a little recap: skin has evolved to keep stuff out of its lower levels, and that's why you don't dissolve in the bath. A cream can contain nice smelling oils, or 'botanicals' and vitamins, antioxidants and amino acids or animal collagen, or elastin, but it doesn't change your actual skin. Your body has to make the elastic and collagen that does that.

The molecules of cosmetic ingredients are just too big to get down into your body from the top layer of your skin. It's like trying to fit a chair down a funnel into a jar. Won't go. And even if it did go, it wouldn't change what your skin is made of when it got there. Which it doesn't.

The useful stuff almost all cosmetics do is wash your face (a cleanser, or soap) and then put a barrier cream on it so it sinks into the very top layer a little, and prevents too much evaporation from the skin (a moisturiser).

The same company will sell you something sciencey under one brand name, and a 'natural organic botanical not tested on animals' from a nearby shelf.

Some sellers of supplements claim that they're selling you powders or capsules with elastin and collagen and vitamins in them that make skin supple. And, yes, there might be those things in their product. But it doesn't follow that the product is changing your skin any more than normal eating is.

"You can feel it working."

A perennial trick of the cosmetic industry is the 'I can feel it working' principle – manufacturers use basic ingredients that may cause tingling, or a tightening feeling, which don't do anything else. House-paint will cause a tightened feeling when it dries, peppermint as an ingredient will make the skin tingle and is associated with a fresh smell because companies have already trained us into this association with toothpaste. Alcohol-based products will also cause tingling on a slightly exfoliated skin, while doing nothing useful to your skin.

"Damage yourself."

A handful of salt or sand rubbed vigorously into skin will cause your face to glow, caused by a chemical reaction that causes a warm feeling, or because the top layer of skin is abraded and the lower level is inflamed. The plumping – swelling of the skin – is caused by low-level bruising and inflammation as it begins to heal itself.

Acid-based products using citrus extracts or other chemicals can also create a skin peel, taking off the very top level of skin, which makes facial lines less obvious as the skin slightly swells

'The species of beauty showing the thinking system.' (What she's thinking is: 'Why has this old perv got me holding one bosom?') from Beauty *by Alexander Walker, drawing by Henry Howard, 1836. (National Library of Australia)*

and grows its new cover. Some examples of this deliberate short-term slight damage is caused by mild chemical acids, blade needles, vigorous massage or exfoliants. Many lip plumpers trigger swelling by using known irritants such as cinnamon and the aforementioned mint family.

In the 1700s, the poet Lady Mary Wortley Montagu encouraged new skin growth to resurface her skin by taking off the top layer with a sulphuric acid solution. 'Lady Mary records that she had to shut herself up most of a week, and her face meantime was blistered shockingly.' The poor woman eloped to avoid an arranged marriage with a man called Clotworthy Skeffington, wrote a satire on the sexual double standards imposed on men who could cheat on their wives, and popularised the smallpox vaccine, so yay her.

On the whole, concluded another beauty advisor to women, Shirley Dare Power, 'Typhoid fever is preferable as an agent for clearing the complexion, being perhaps less dangerous and more effective.'

"Beauty experts are trained."

A beauty expert is traditionally anyone who's considered pretty and who's asked, and a journalist who's interested. The *Australian Women's Weekly Good Grooming Guide* published in 1963 quoted a few with their hints, including Eunice Bevege, a 'Sydney fashion compere', who scrubs her face with soap and water 'until it tingles'.

By the 2000s, the favourite beauty journalism method was the 'road test': the beauty columnist and perhaps some other women in the office would try a free sample. Astonishingly, some even tried procedures such as the 'vampire facial' and other roller-based facials that punctured the skin with 'microneedling', without warning of the possible side effects, including scarring or a blood-borne disease infection. (At least two customers at a US 'vampire facial' salon contracted HIV.)

If you can find me a beauty writer who admits that all the procedures and products she 'tests' are a baroque waste of time and money, I shall buy you a banana daiquiri.

"Men get to define beauty."

Insufferable author Alexander Walker was fuuurious in 1836 that women had just been judged only on their attractiveness, rather than also using 'anatomical and physiological knowledge' to assess their 'locomotive system'.

So he wrote a book, *Beauty: Illustrated Chiefly by an Analysis and Classification of Beauty in Woman*, in which he quoted a whole bunch of other blokes about how important women's beauty is, because it matters to men. He said that a beautiful woman is necessarily a good one. He perpetuated common myths such as hip-size being important to fertility: 'Consequent breadth of the haunches are necessary to all those functions which are most essentially feminine: impregnantion, gestation and parturition and a live birth with a surviving mother.' What an old romantic.

Because men do the 'selecting' of women to breed with, there would be more beautiful women as the generations passed, he assured his readers, forgetting, for one thing, the effect of the participation of men who looked a bit like toads. Or Alexander Walker.

Another illustrative woman from the same book (this one is thinking, 'No, but I mean seriously, when do I get to stop holding one bosom?').

A man who draws beautiful naked women, or who looks at their nude pictures will become more moral, he said, though it was a morality not extended to women, who weren't allowed to draw a naked male figure at European art schools until only about 120 years ago.

Walker's book has a list of the defects of women, which include (you may need to sit down) too tall, too wide, not wide enough, too plump, not plump enough, having a brain larger than a man's (I am not making this up) and a mouth wider than the nose.

"Be born white."

It can be quite a shock to see pimple cream and orthopaedic stockings, described as 'skin-coloured' – usually a ghastly pink. In the 1980s, 'beauty' books and magazine columns clacked on with quite the bizarre level of racism. Asian girls and women were told to give themselves an 'oriental look', while those with dark skin were advised to 'tame' their 'wayward' hair, and spray 'fun colours' on their hair for a 'jungle effect'.

More recently, photographs of fashion models (not to mention actors, comedians and writers) who have African or Asian heritage are routinely published with the wrong names.

Daintee brand 'Witchhazel Snow', the first and not the last of cosmetics claimed to make skin whiter, c1930. (National Museum of Australia)

"Make your skin whiter."

The pervasive idea about whiter or lighter skin being closer to the pinnacle of beauty is just historical racism, with some poisonous dollops of class in the mix. One theory is that having a tan, or freckles, or a healthy strong body and muscles meant you marked yourself as a worker in the fields, rather than a woman of idle, housebound leisure and high status.

Lead-based paints and chalky minerals were originally used: arsenic and the effects of tuberculosis were both praised as the way to get the desired, whiter effect, at least until you died.

Poorer women were told to use lemon juice and scrubs of bicarb soda to lighten their skins. Some over-the-counter corrosive creams have caused burns and other side effects.

Expensive skin-lightening and whitening creams – often now called brightening, clarifying or radiant to try to seem less racist – are still a billion-dollar industry across India, Africa and Asia.

"Make your skin darker."

There's a pretty weird space where the racism Venn diagram overlaps the wellness Venn diagram, and it's coloured in a biscuity fake tan. In a colour-coded version of the 'you can't win' game for women, some of us are told to use creams to make us lighter, others are told to buy stuff to make us look darker, and everyone is supposed to use sunscreen.

"Do face exercises."

The splendidly named Dorothy Drain took issue with beauty advice in the *Australian Women's Weekly* on 7 March 1956, pointing out some flaws in the scheme to cure eyebags which involved either standing on your head or lying down with your head upside down over the side of the bed. She quite sensibly suggested bulldog clips attached above the front of the ears to hold your face up. Funny Dorothy was also a war correspondent, and I rather adore her.

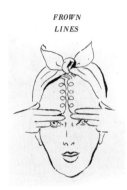

FROWN LINES

FOREHEAD LINES

Swirly face exercises from Be Beautiful: A Complete Guide to Beauty for Women of all Ages *by Jean Cleland, 1970. (This is now called face yoga.) (National Library of Australia)*

"Botox is no big deal."

As with the 'undetectable rouge' of the past, the prevailing idea of having Botox now is to get away with it. In 20 years, Botox and other paralyser products have become normalised, and these days, it doesn't even rate a mention that Botox, a trademark of the Allergan company, is a poison. It's administered and costed in units – one unit of Botox is exactly enough to kill one mouse.

So within 20 years the argument has moved from 'Why would you get toxins injected into your *face*?' to 'Make sure you go to someone qualified.' It's now considered normal for women to pay tens of thousands of dollars in their lifetime so they don't have to be so confronted with their own actual face.

We all make decisions about wearing lipstick, and having our eyebrows professionally shaped and dyed, and whether we get a hair-do instead of a hair-cut; decisions based on self-image, available cash and employment prospects. So I don't begrudge women their Botox, but let's not pretend. The women who say they're doing it to look 'relaxed' or 'refreshed' are injecting relatively safe poison into their face to look younger.

"Use poisonous cosmetics."

Eyedrops made from the poisonous plant belladonna (deadly nightshade) once used to make the pupil bigger, but also caused blurred vision, possible hallucinations, heart arrhythmia, seizures and blindness.

Lead and arsenic have already been mentioned; other heavy metals in dangerous concentrations have been used in cosmetics, including antimony eyeliner in ye olde times.

Western regulations prevent dangerous ingredients being used in mainstream cosmetics, although many companies still face accusations of using poison and toxins in mainstream cosmetics. Some ingredients are totally banned, or their dose levels regulated in some countries but not others, including phthalates, parabens, formaldehyde and coal tar. Many people are allergic or have reactions to common ingredients, including cinnamon, fragrances and essential oils, among others.

A correspondent called Barbara to the showbiz world's *Everyone's Magazine* in 1921 was advised to rub the popular product called mercolised wax daily into her face and neck, as were other women for decades. The most important ingredient was mercury. She was also advised to take her 'weight loss' laxative pill and put it on her hair roots. Poor Barbara.

They were dreadfully obstructive at the storage facility of the National Museum of Australia stores when I visited: they wouldn't let me try out some sealed, decades-old hair remover called Pheminol (barium sulphide, which can cause alkaline burns) on my underarms. Not as dangerous, apparently, as the deadly poison thallium used as a depilatory in the late 1800s.

Deadly radium was a popular ingredient in some cosmetics, and Lucy Jane Santos has written a whole book about that and others with radium-related bizzo called *Half Lives*. Several companies applied to be allowed to patent and import cosmetics containing radium in Australia, but after testing 'Radema' in 1939, the Physicist-in-Charge of the Commonwealth X-Ray and Radium Laboratory said there wasn't a trace of radium in it anyway.

Other documents in the National Archives of Australia also show that, after testing, would-be importers of Kemolite, Genuine Nature's Own Radio-Active Beauty Plasma from the Volcanic Wells of the Carpathians, and the more prosaic 'Radioactive mask

Pheminol: very pheminine, aside from the burns. (National Museum of Australia)

for greasy, sallow and wrinkled skins' weren't allowed to advertise their products as containing real radium either.

"Beauty contests are perfectly sane."

The idea of beauty pageants comes directly from livestock parades at agricultural shows, during which the fattest or woolliest animals were paraded, and then judged. Winners were first given a medal on a neck ribbon, then later a sash with room for the name of the prize. In 1968, feminists protested at the Miss America Pageant, holding signs saying women were being judged like farm animals. In an excellent move, they crowned a sheep.

The beauty pageant, prevented by propriety from making women parade while naked, added high heels, tiaras, and the most revealing swimsuits allowed by the convention of the era.

The pictures of South Korean pageant contestants that were altered without their permission.

Miss World claims to have raised hundreds of millions for charity since 1951 but it is not a public company with transparent records. The Miss America Pageant's claims to have delivered $45 million in scholarships has been debunked.

Women have been forced to withdraw from pageants because they are mothers, married or had posed for 'revealing' model photos in the past, but the organisations themselves are . . . questionable. In 2017 emails between the CEO of the US Miss World organisation and other officials called contestants the 'c-word' and also 'snakes', which is weirder but no more respectful, frankly.

Miss Universe USA is now run by a talent agency but for two decades was owned by a sleazy New York real estate developer . . . called Donald Trump. The Miss Universe Australia competition is run by a West Australian boxing match promoter and is part-sponsored by a mine equipment spare parts company.

Miss Australia doesn't exist anymore and Miss World Australia has an anti-trans entry criteria, and other weird entry requirements, such as 'never given birth to a child'. Or a rabbit?

It's widely believed that Miss Universe Venezuela candidates have all had facial and breast cosmetic surgery. The organisation there was run for 40 years by a man who had on-staff dental and cosmetic surgeons to alter women, and required contestants to undergo restriction diets. He explained that darker-skinned girls had to have 'a white girl's features' to advance. In 1994, 17 of the 26 candidates had gum surgery to show bigger teeth. The official orthodontist described his aim as 'Farrah Fawcett teeth that are toilet-bowl white.'

Pop-star Ross D. Wylie's knee is a perfectly normal place for teenage girls to be asked to sit, thought a photographer in 1968.
(State Library Victoria)

When a compilation emerged of official photos taken of the 2013 contestants in the Miss Daegu feeder contest to the Miss Korea pageant, people were shocked at how similar they all looked, and accusations of plastic surgery bounced around social media. The women were trolled but it turned out that their photographs had been digitally altered by someone else, after they'd supplied their own real portraits.

And here, a respectful pause, please, while I repeat my own old joke from the 1980s (and who amongst you will try to stop me?).

Miss Universe is always better than Miss World because people from other planets can enter.

A Berlei corsetry model, admiring her fine self in a hand-mirror, about 1930.
(Museum of Applied Arts and Sciences)

8

YOUR BODY SHAPE IS WRONG

WHAT WE NOW CALL A BODY USED TO BE CALLED A FIGURE, OR FORM. As fashions for the 'perfect figure' changed, we were supposed to change our bodies. When flesh and bones could not conform, clothes, devices and surgical implants would be used to try to squeeze women into templates of the times.

I remember a fashion headline in the 1980s, 'Breasts are back.' Great, I said, I think I left mine in the cutlery drawer, I shall dig them out.

For decades now, as women in the 'developed' world are getting larger in average size, the models for expensive brands have remained dangerously thin, often with visible individual ribs showing front and back. I have watched beautiful young female graphic designers erase the jutting bones on models' clavicles and backs, so that it didn't look so scary. And then heard them talk about how confused it made them feel about their own bodies.

If you're convinced it only matters what your body looks like, you forget to ask what your body needs; to marvel at your own strength and the mystery of how your body works. We're distracted from what our bodies can *do* – kick goals, create life or dance.

"Your body is your enemy."

'When you're seventeen, and a girl, you have the whole world telling you what to do with your body.' – Writer-director Tayarisha Poe, 2020

In the fifth book of her 1983 'Fit Self-Improvement Series', *Waist and Stomach*, Dorothy Herman wrote to encourage some extra self-loathing: 'Being critical also helps us fuel the fire within us to do something about what we see, to push ourselves through that exercise class or to push ourselves away from the restaurant table . . . It is a constant battle to keep the waist wispy and the stomach taut.'

Poor Dorothy wrote that she kept the 1982 *Time* magazine cover called 'Body of the 80s' on her fridge for inspiration. The cover, emblematic of the aerobics era, featured an unknown model in a red leotard with matching leg-warmers, because if there's one thing you want to wear during vigorous exercise it's knitwear.

Dorothy disparaged women who'd had children and then didn't wear restricting rubber under-suits and attend steam rooms in an effort to make them dehydrate and look smaller. Quoted advisors included a Jane Fonda workout instructor (this was years before Jane Fonda explained she was bulimic, miserable and over-exercised in those years) and an Olympic figure skater.

"Disguise your body shape."

Every woman is given insulting labels for their body. Every school bully tries to make a girl flinch with 'fatty' or 'stick'. We've been told to categorise ourselves as ectomorphs or endomorphs, or hourglasses, or curvy, or a number on a bathroom scale, or a medium, or a '16'.

'To minimise or camouflage the fullness of the (bottom) cheeks . . . wear shoes with heels.' – Hot Stuff: The Ultimate Guide to Style for Women of a Certain Age by Penelope Jane Whitely, 2008

In the early 2000s, 'dress for your shape' advice was all the rage. Transformation-harpies Trinny & Susannah from the English TV show *What Not to Wear* sadly pre-dated the inclusive kindness of the post-2018 *Queer Eye* makeover shows. They subjected women to inspections under stadium-strength lighting and harsh assessments. Their book, *The Body Shape Bible*, told women how to conjure visual effects using the cut of clothes.

The optical illusions worked using their clever, illustrative photos of themselves in 'wrong' and 'right' styles (and suitably glum or thrilled expressions) to disguise 'figure flaws'. Trinny & Susannah spoke to the women they were to make-over in a brutal way they would call honest: on television, some of the women cried. The books employed indelibly hurtful phrases such as 'no tits', 'flabby tummy', 'uncontrollable girth', 'criminal calves' and 'saddlebags'.

And the *pièce de résistance*: 'If you are single, take heart from the fact that men are more likely to talk to a pair of tits than to a flat stomach.' Those guys are keepers. *What Not to Wear* was a hit because they were right about the many optical illusions that could be created. But one wonders how much self-confidence was shredded rather than boosted along the way, and why an optical illusion was necessary anyway.

Women used fashion engineering to alter the shape of their bodies: iron cages in the shape of hips and bottoms strapped to their waist, swagged-draping for a bustle, a false bottom. We've also strapped on farthingales – hoop skirts and layered petti-coats, cage-shaped crinolines the size of yurts. Body-shaping

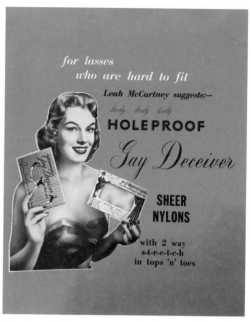

Stockings ad for women who were 'hard to fit'. They weren't, of course. Always blame yourself, not the garment, ladies. (National Library of Australia)

Madame Weigel brand dressmaking patterns showed quintessential body shapes, 1870–1960s. Plus, bonus convertible bag/ hat. (National Library of Australia)

devices and garments helped take the weight of madly heavy skirts or massively beaded gowns. Corsets were used to cinch in the waist and hoist up bosoms. We've had rubber girdles, padded bras, cosmetic surgery, and then 'shapewear' and digital 'filters' and the alteration of photographs. (There's more crinoline bizzo in the 'Dress Up, Dress Down' chapter.)

The ideal shape of the 1890s was exemplified in the exaggerated proportions of the Principal Boy, a male role in a pantomime always played by a woman plump of thigh and hip, corseted of waist, bunched of bloomer and voluminous of sleeve and hat. Marie Luella, who starred as Prince Lionel in *Beauty and the Beast* in 1895, was universally said to have a 'splendid physique'; one male reporter said she had the 'unstudied ease and grace of a perfectly developed woman', in other words: phwoarrr.

Two 'ideal' shapes: Marie Luella as Prince Lionel in the 1890s and the 1960s 'fashionable' shape personified by Lesley Hornby ('Twiggy'). (State Library Victoria and Bettmann Collection/Getty Images)

Typical late-1800s corset shapes, from Corsets and Crinolines *by Norah Waugh, 1954.*

'To make what is called a 'handsome couple' the female should be about three inches less than the male . . .' · The Book of Nature: A Complete Marriage Guide for Men and Women by Dr Thomas Faulkner, printed by The Sex Knowledge Publishing Company, 1930s. (Three inches where?)

Where women now digitally alter their social media pictures to manufacture a 'thigh gap', Music Hall actresses used to stuff padding down their tights to erase one, and padded their hips and bottoms. The ideal shape of the 1960s was said to be boyish (not even mannish), and women 'bound' their breasts to flatten them.

"Make your waist look small."

We're now being sold a modern version of corsets called a waist-trainer: a restrictive, super-elastic bandage belt. Most waist-trainers are just bands made of wetsuit that make you sweaty and uncomfortable. You take it off, your waist goes back to what is it. It doesn't train your waist to be smaller unless it damages your ribs or internal organs. Nevertheless, people who profit from them suggest long hours of wear: if you took advice from a Kardashian who makes money from it, you'd wear it all day and then to bed. Because of the displacement effect, while they're on, they can make a perfectly normally shaped woman look like a bison wearing a tin-can around her middle.

One article copied and repasted on several women's websites in the late 2010s said, 'You've probably seen all sorts of celebrities . . . sporting the (waist) trainers, plus a plethora of girls young and old all hoping to widdle their waistlines.' (This is what happens when you spend too much time using a big fancy word like 'plethora' instead of 'lots': you don't notice you've replaced whittling with widdling, which means weeing.)

"Shapewear is modern."

The ubiquity of 'shapewear' means a sort of Russian doll situation is going on. For argument's sake we will use American sizes and pretend we're at the Oscars – a size-10 woman wears uncomfortable pants so she looks a size 8, and a size-6 woman wears uncomfortable pants so she looks a size 4 and so on, until we are at the equally absurd situation of a 'size 0' woman wearing uncomfy pants to make her look like she doesn't exist.

In a similar vein, if the women who are 162 cm tall wear high heels so they look 168 cm tall and the women who are 168 cm tall wear high heels to look 2 metres tall and the women who are 2 metres tall bring a library step ladder then . . . I've lost my train of thought.

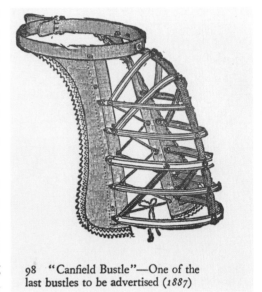

98 "Canfield Bustle"—One of the last bustles to be advertised (1887)

Generally, shapewear is just corsets and tight underpants made with fancier new fabrics, sometimes with a celebrity label on it. It's doing exactly the same thing, for exactly the same reason: to modify a natural shape.

Modern corseted bodies get clicks on social media precisely because nobody looks like that naturally. But some corsets didn't nip in the waist at all because it wasn't a fashionable look at the time. The high-waisted Regency Era (roughly just after 1800), the drop-waisted flapper frocks of the 1920s, and the mini-shift frocks of the '60s are the few brief fashion eras in modern history that shrouded, rather than emphasised, the waist. In the 2000s, fashion has shattered into a mosaic of personal choice, mass production and the rise of mass leisure wear, which means fashion eras, like waists, will perhaps never be so tightly defined again.

A bustle: it would have been indelicate to call it a strap-on arse. Nora Waugh's Crinolines and Corsets *book, 1954. (National Library of Australia)*
It was usually easier to adjust clothes than change your shape: Mary Brooks Picken's illustration of different silhouettes in The Fashion Dictionary, *1973. (National Library of Australia)*

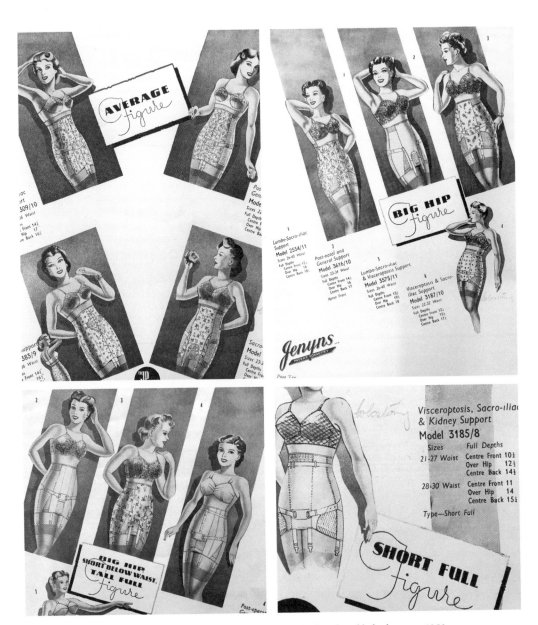

BIG HIP *Figure*

1
Lumbo-Sacro-iliac
Support
Model 2554/11
Sizes 26-40 Waist
Full Depths
Centre Front 15½
Over Hip 18
Centre Back 18½

2
Post-natal and
General Support
Model 3616/10
Sizes 23-34 Waist
Full Depths
Centre Front 14½
Over Hip 16
Centre Back 17
Apron Front

3
Lumbo-Sacro-iliac Support
Model 3575/11
Sizes 26-40 Waist
Full Depths
Centre Front 15½
Over Hip 19
Centre Back 18

4
Visceroptosis & Sacro-
iliac Support
Model 3187/10
Sizes 22-32 Waist
Full Depths
Centre Front 12½
Over Hip 15½
Centre Back 17½

iliac
rt
309/10
6 Waist
Front 14½
Hip 17
e Back 16½

Pos-
Gen-
Model
Sizes 24
Full Depth
Centre F
Over Hip
Centre Back

Sacro-
Model
Sizes 23-
Full Depths
Centre Fron
Over

upport
385/9
6 Waist
Full Depths
Front 14½
16½

Jenyns
PATENT CORSETRY

Page Ten

2   3   4
BIG HIP
SHORT BELOW WAIST.
TALL FULL
Figure
1
Post-opera-
Ge-

Visceroptosis, Sacro-iliac
& Kidney Support
Model 3185/8

Sizes   Full Depths
21-27 Waist   Centre Front 10½
               Over Hip   12½
               Centre Back 14½

28-30 Waist   Centre Front 11
               Over Hip   14
               Centre Back 15½

Type—Short Full

SHORT FULL
Figure

Catalogue for Jenyn's corsets with two purposes: medical needs and lady-changing, 1950.
(National Library of Australia)

"Corsets are necessary."

While some corsets can be used for medical reasons, the vast majority weren't. Girls and women were assumed to be frail and defective, in need of support. Plus, corsets restrained bosoms from looking loose and real. Breasts were not to move independently. At some points in fashion history, breasts were only allowed to appear as one shelf-like 'bust'. Diet advisors in 1970s girls' magazines told girls to see if they jiggled when they moved parts of their body, and if so, that was a problem. (If no part of you ever jiggles, you might be dead.)

In 2019, the Mothercare website in the UK advertised a post-baby corset, pictured on a woman wearing high heels.

Remember the 19th-century physiologist Alexander Walker? I should hope not, the dismissible buffoon. In his book on beauty, he advises women plainly to employ the arts of deception. 'Those who have the bosom too small, enlarge it by the oblique folds of the dress. Those who have the lower part of the body too prominent anteriorly, elevate it by the top of the skirt being gathered behind.' Anteriorly my arse.

"All corsets are dangerous."

As many fashion historians will tell you – quite shoutily if they've had a champagne – historical corsets weren't all tight-laced affairs that caused fainty

Eeeek. The E.E.E corset advertising poster, from the Troedel Company, 1890s.
(State Library Victoria)

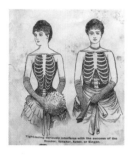

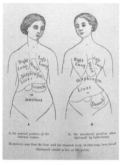

Imagined damage from tight-lacing: Mr E. W. Cole, owner of Cole's Book Arcade, published many warning booklets, 1890s. (National Library of Australia)

fall-abouts. Some were useful supports, some were just another form of underpantery.

Just like 120 years ago, if people overdo the restriction, it can cause breathlessness, pain, extra sweating, rashes, digestive disruption and, over time, displaced internal organs, wasted muscles and forever being uncomfortable. Hardly anyone does, though. One online commenter pointed out crossly that being very pregnant also causes the same things, so it didn't matter if shapewear was doing it.

Mainly, women suited themselves, as they do now: they found their own trade-off point between comfort and how they wanted to look. Many trans women and others use a version of a corset to change their silhouette, some people do it for fun, or for cosplay. Few take it to the sad lengths of squillionaire shapewear-seller Kim Kardashian, who had to stand up without a seatbelt in a special car and hold onto a pole to be delivered in her weird corset dress to the Met Gala in 2019, dehydrated so she wouldn't need to wee because she couldn't sit down.

When Ms Kardashian was first famous, she was a welcome role model to many girls with a different shape to the usual white mainstream models. Sadly, her families' surgically changed, digitally altered look and promotional profiteering from products such as useless laxative teas and bruise-inducing lip-suctioners has resulted in an auto-removal from the usefulness arena.

In a 1914 short film written and directed by Mabel Normand, starring herself and Charlie Chaplin, called *Caught in a Cabaret*, there's a woman in the background of a café who comes to the centre of the screen and does something shocking. She is obviously encased in a stiff bosom-to-thigh corset underneath her dress. But she's freeform dancing, as sprightly and expansive as any girl at a night club last Friday night, waving her arms around, wiggling her bum, quickstepping and twirling.

Ads for Berlei corset products in the second half of the 20th century featured women dancing, as well as playing golf, to show the freedom the girdles allowed (indistinguishable from 1980s and '90s tampon ads, trying to evoke the same idea).

"You can always tell who's wearing a corset."

The author of the sumptuous *Dress in the Age of Jane Austen* book, Hilary Davidson, revealed a little secret about those supposedly floaty, muslin Empire-waist Regency gowns. Underneath, a corset probably provided scaffolding to pin something diaphanous to. It's what she calls the 'illusion of naturalness' – a low, bare neckline and two clearly defined breasts, but no floppeting allowed. The idea was to look like a classical statue wafting about in a diaphanous frock while being invisibly hoisted underneath.

Not much engineering is obvious in this 1920s 'corset', from Norah Waugh's definitive book Corsets and Crinolines, *1954.*

They were marvels of design disguise. Different shapes required changes in buttressing. Berlei's long-time chief designer Desolie Richardson said in 1955, 'It's like building a bridge ... there are strains ... and stresses. And you've got to know just where they come, otherwise your bridge – or your foundation garment – soon collapses.' In a 1961 interview, she added, 'The job's rather like accountancy and engineering, with a dash of fashion thrown in.'

"You are your dress size."

You don't even *have* a dress size. You just fit into stuff that manufacturers put a label on: originally this was to be a convenient way of deciding what to try on, and then became increasingly

85 Corselet in pink or white (1927)

unpredictable as a dress that was once a size 14 became a 10 because clothing companies assumed that everyone wants to be 'smaller'.

Women's clothes were not sold by number until the 1950s. Before that, rich women had clothes made to order and many middle-class and poor women made their own or altered their own second-hand clothes. Clothes-sizes standards for women were originally backed by a government-approved system of measurements. They were supposed to have a handful of general sizes plus variations for hip, waist and bust: the same garment might have a size-14 bum, a size-10 chest and a size-12 waist, plus different lengths of shoulder-to-bust, arm- and leg-length.

A standardised hodge-podge ensued that described very few women. A size-10 model, for example, might be 30 cm taller than another size-10 woman. In the US sizes were calculated by guessing and using past research. In Australia they were set after combining US research and 1920s measurements by Berlei company representatives working with University of Sydney science researchers who spent a summer measuring 6000 girls and women at factories and beaches.

*Another elegant model
displays the middle-
engineering of Berlei
undergarmentry, c1930.
(Museum of Applied
Arts and Sciences)*

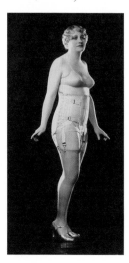

Using the measurements, Berlei began manufacturing figure-type calculators – flat cardboard devices, half a metre tall. Wielded by a corsetiere, who twirled cardboard circles into a position using your measurements, it would align on a colour, and the colour told which one of five shapes you were: Sway Back; Average; Big Hips; Big Abdomen; and Short Below Waist. From 1930 to the 1960s, tens of thousands of women were assessed and fitted using these devices.

Fashion industry measurements were set for a standard size 8, 10, 12 and so on, but because no woman was exactly 'average'

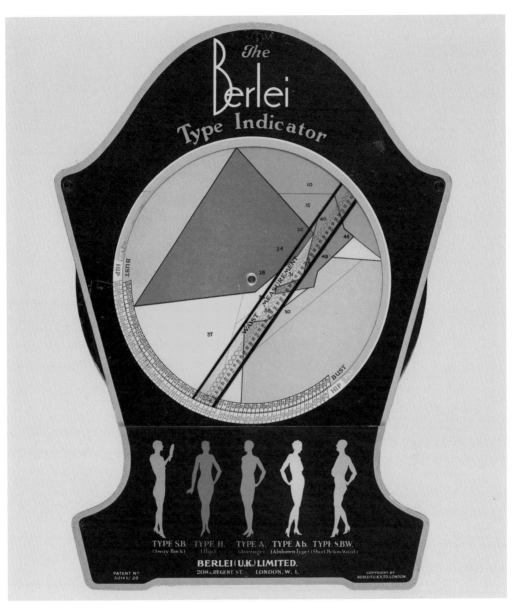

Only five possible types of women are shown on the Berlei figure calculator: Large Hip, Sway Back, Large Abdomen, Average and Short Below Waist, 1930s. (Museum of Applied Arts and Sciences)

and no account was taken for height, or say, thigh size, and then manufacturers started dicking about, by the end of the 20th century it was a shambles. The thoughtless term 'plus size' and 'one size fits all' (ha!) didn't help.

Countless women have clothes in their wardrobes that are the same size, but are labelled with numbers. The marketing use of size labels that vary from the standard was immediately blamed on women. Rather than being called inaccurate predatory marketing sizing, it was called 'vanity' sizing.

"Aim to be thin."

In her 2019 book *Fearing the Black Body: The Racial Origins of Fat Phobia*, assistant sociology professor Sabrina Strings wrote that slimness became and remained fashionable from about 1800, long before mainstream medical advice connected it with health. In many cultures, plump was often seen as healthier, stronger and safer. Strings points out that larger bodies, often along with darker skin, were commonly seen by racist colonists as connected to sensuality and 'sexual appetite'.

In the Australian colony, Aboriginal and Torres Strait Islander women, though usually lean, were wrongly seen as having race-based strength (in order to do menial, heavy tasks) with bodies that more easily produced children (medical help and early maternal and child services they had a right to were withheld from them). There was no logic or truth to the assessments of Indigenous women's bodies, because the underlying assumptions were not about health but about exploitation and cruelty.

Rosie Waterland says in the 2016 anthology *Better Than Sex* that if she showed the amount of skin other women do on their Instagram feed, she'd be called brave – 'because I'm fat'. She identifies some of the deeply knitted-in prejudice of society: women who aren't thin are often considered brave for wearing nice clothes, having a job, having a sex life. For daring to exist.

"Thinner is always better."

Nothing is nuttier than the history of advice to girls and women about eating, not even nuts. The fraught business of disordered eating behaviours and the damage they do to bodies and minds is now so normalised it's impossible for girls not to absorb it, no matter how hard we try to mitigate it.

Some research and analysis shows that some badly designed anti-eating-disorder programs can even give girls ideas and methods that they may not have had before. Teachers and parents can send confused messages, including 'healthy eating is so you don't get fat', if they don't fully recognise that eating disorders are complex mental health issues and they're untrained about cultural issues relating to size and weight.

What definitely helps is learning to see one's body as a friend and an ally, to appreciate it for what it can do, not just what it looks like; to learn about nutrition and food without an emphasis on weight, and especially to question social media, family attitudes and statements, and advertising images and messages.

Sometime in 2019, girls searching for hashtags on Instagram that encouraged eating disorders were greeted with a pop-up intervention window, which asked, 'Can we help?' Instagram was responding to fierce criticism that self-harm and othorexia and fasting messages on its platform were damaging young girls, leading them into eating disorders and encouraging them not to get treatment. That's the beauty and the horror of social media – you can find any advice you want, and filter out the rest.

'Be wise and join the National Slimming Campaign . . . the famous Bread & Butter Diet. Write for full particulars . . .' – Ad in UK magazine My Home, *1938*

'Three-Day Milk and Banana Diet. Setting aside three days in which (to) eat just 6 ripe bananas and drink 2½ cups of milk a day.' – Marjorie Bligh

'Norwegian Ice Cream Two-Day Diet. Stay on it for two days only. For each of the two days you are allowed 5 cups of vanilla ice-cream . . . You are also allowed 6 cups of tea, coffee or fruit juice daily.' – At Home With Marjorie Bligh, third edition, 1982

'Breakfast: 2 hardboiled eggs; Lunch: 6 dried prunes; Dinner: steak – all you can eat but must be grilled.' – Marjorie Bligh

After the Instagram pop-up asking if you'd rather see posts that might help with an eating disorder, and be redirected, searchers of a pro-anorexia hashtag were asked, 'See posts anyway?'

"Thin isn't womanly enough."

'Men like women to be curvier.' 'Men like something to hold onto.' (Why not get some handles implanted?) This is the only time I'm ever going to say 'not all men'. This is the kind of statement used to reassure 'curvy' women that men will want them. It's not true and it's rude to thin women, who are just as much 'all woman' and as cuddly, if they feel like cuddling, as anybody else.

"Go on mad diets."

Every short-term diet for hundreds of years has claimed it would 'work' and that this one is different because (blood groups, magic eggs, doing stuff after 11 am, juice, as seen on TV, is a bestselling doctor-author, these graphs here). I shall say it again: it's proven that short-term restrictive diets don't work long-term; they can stuff up your metabolism and make you cranky, farty and miserable.

"There's a perfect weight to be, which varies."

There has been *a lot* of popular formulas of how to judge 'ideal weight' – none of which have been useful. Most have been based on young men, who have different muscle to fat ratios.

The Ladies' Book of Home Treatment, first published in 1905, told women if they were 5'6" (170.7 cm) tall they should be 143 pounds (65 kilos), and if they were 5'2" (158.5 cm) they should weigh just under 50 kilos.

Guthrie's Formula, dispensed to US army members during World War II and later recommended to women, was to subtract 60 inches from your total height, multiply the difference by 5.5 then add 110, and that number, in pounds, is your ideal weight. (Miraculously, doing the hokey-pokey was not also a requirement for the calculation.)

The Body Mass Index calculation was popular for a while in the 1980s, but it made no consideration for the difference between fat and muscle as weight, or the age of the person calculating it. Its categorisations included hurtful words such as obese, and its inaccuracies caused much misunderstanding and alarm.

Medical height-and-weight charts now carry the more sensible nuance of a healthy possible range rather than a target number of kilos.

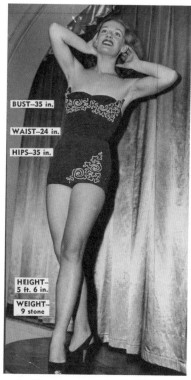

"There's a perfect figure & you don't have it."

A twit called Félibien, the official court historian to Louis XIV of France in the 1600s, published a long list of requirements for a woman: a specific head and forehead size, shaped eyebrows, narrow cheeks, ears 'with an agreeable tinge of red', a small mouth that is like a rosebud ready to bloom, 'middle-sized' teeth, a hand that 'unites insensibly with the Arm' (as opposed to . . . a hinge?), a 'white bosom' with 'breasts . . . rising gently and very distinctly separated', the knees should be 'even', and hips wider than the shoulders.

Nineteenth-century physiologist Alexander Walker – him again, the utter nincompoop – had the usual impertinent

Who was she? Who loved her? What was she good at? Oh, who cares – we have her 'vital statistics'. Model Leah McCartney, c1952. (State Library Victoria)

opinions: 'A well-formed woman should have her head, shoulders and chest small and compact, arms and limbs relatively short; her haunches apart; and her hips elevated; her abdomen large and her thighs voluminous . . . Plumpness is essential to beauty . . . an excess of plumpness, however, is to be guarded against. Young women who are very fat are cold and prone to barrenness.' Absurdly, Wikipedia calls him an 'aesthetician' – a fancy word for misogynist arse.

"Annette Kellermann had the perfect figure."

One of the most photographed women of her day, Annette Kellermann successfully promoted herself as having 'the perfect figure' and lived to regret it.

Annette's career as a Music Hall performer had taught her valuable marketing tricks. She did wire-walking and light comedy singing, graduated to swimming and tank-diving exhibitions and then had a 'mermaid' career in silent films.

She was a strapping young teenager when first photographed around 1900 in one-piece swimsuits and black tights, and much leaner in 1905, after training to swim lengths of the Yarra and the Thames rivers; she attempted the English Channel three times. She had the endurance, she said, but not 'the brute strength', losing 3 kilos a go. By 1907, she was world famous, staging a clever stunt near Boston where she was arrested for indecency

Postcard comparing Annette Kellermann's wrist measurements to the Venus de Milo statue, which had no arms, c1914. (National Library of Australia)

282

Annette Kellermann poised 'twixt sky and sea, aged about 18, England, 1905.
(Cricketer Frank Laver's album, Melbourne Cricket Club Museum)

Annette Kellermann's hibiscus print cozzie, custom-made for her 'perfect figure', date unknown. (Museum of Applied Arts and Sciences)

See? Totally armless.

because of her form-fitting swimsuit, with handy newspaper reporters on scene. Annette immediately started her own line of swimwear, a side-hustle that endured beyond her film and book career.

She was assessed by the gymnasium operator at Harvard University, 'Under-Professor' and one-man travelling creepoid Dudley Sargent, who visited girls' schools for 3000 comparison measurements (or maybe 10,000: the claims changed). He concluded that Annette's proportions were so similar to those of the Venus de Milo statue, she had the perfect figure. Annette took on the story, and the title.

A promotional postcard to advertise the 1914 film *Neptune's Daughter* shows Annette in diving mode alongside an exhaustive list of Measurements That Almost Surpass Belief.

As well as some water ballet footage of Annette Kellermann in a bubble costume, the National Film and Sound Archive holds a silent 1912 newsreel footage of her with a Gibson-girl roll hair-do diving in cap-sleeve swimsuit and black tights with a slide informing viewers of the Venus de Milo comparison. A snippet of sound from an interview in 1974 reveals that as a male reporter talks over her, she says, 'It's the most ghastly thing in the world to be called the perfect woman.'

In her 2007 essay, *The Transit of Venus*, in *Southerly Magazine*, Anita Callaway discusses different Venus statues that personified the 'perfect figure' or standards of beauty. Callaway points out that the Venus de Milo is more than 6 feet tall, so the measurements would seem a bit skewiff, wrists aside.

Like many women and doctors of her day, Annette was unaware of the role of hormones in muscle mass and fat distribution. Her book *Physical Beauty, How to Keep It*, in 1918 was a strange mix of white supremacy, nascent feminism, and advice to 'keep your figure' using diet and exercise.

'You want slender ankles, tapering wrists and a supple waist, and you cannot grow excess of muscles there. And you want a full chest, well-rounded arms and plump calves – or ought to – and muscular development will give these to you in just the right degree . . . If women would as fully recognise their right and duty to be permanently attractive to mankind as they do the immediate necessity of personal cleanliness, there would be little occasion to write this book,' she sniped.

"No, Pansy & Muriel had the perfect figure."

A while ago State Library Victoria librarian Katie Flack alerted me to her work on Pansy Montague, aka The Modern Milo. In the first decade of the 1900s, Pansy posed on Music Hall stages as the human statue, employing white body-paint, blackout lighting and long black gloves (for the no-arms effect). Anita Callaway found Pansy's alleged proportions in a theatre program: height, 5'8"; bust, 37 inches; waist, 26 inches; hips, 42 inches.

Other eminences were trotted out to variously define the perfect body, including London surgeon Dr Forbes-Ross, who said the perfect woman was 'medium sized', 5 feet 5 to 7 inches tall, knock-kneed, with hips broader than her shoulders and a 'symmetrical' nose.

Up popped creepy Harvard tape-measure boy Dudley Sargent again in 1912: he said a woman should walk 6 or 7 miles a day (10–11 kilometres) and only eat twice a day to 'maintain a figure'. In running Sargent's opinions, Adelaide's

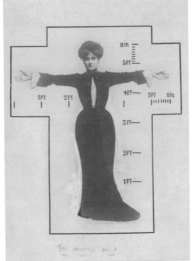

Pansy posing as a statue; a photo showing her 'proportions', which have been altered with white paint; and with lovely visible tum in a publicity postcard, c1905. (State Library Victoria)

Evening Journal lamented that girls don't scrub the floor enough, or have to go up and down the servant stairs in a large house.

Miss Muriel Cadogan of the Dupain's School of Physical Culture in Sydney entered the fray, theorising that Kellermann was shorter than the perceived perfect height of 5'4" and a quarter inches, had larger upper arms due to swimming, and that the larger hip measurement was due to fat being redistributed because of artificial waist constriction – fightin' words, considering Kellermann stated opposition to 'fiendish' corsets. Further she said Kellermann had 'faulty points' in comparison with the perfect Venus de Milo. You're terrible, Muriel.

"Scientific studies prove what's attractive."

A few university psychology departments around the world churn out what in my opinion (hello again, lawyers) are crappy studies in medical and behavioural journals, many of which are now pay-to-publish organs. Many such researchers then quote their own studies in subsequent studies, giving themselves more citations.

David Lewis of Murdoch University in WA has been a researcher and lead author on several studies with click-bait theories such as a 2016 one suggesting 'physically attractive' women have gay male friends to prevent the attention of predatory straight males or 'competition' from other women.

And another one about men 'judging' the 'attractiveness' of women by the angle of women's backs when wearing high heels. The world is now adorned by countless studies in which 'attractiveness' is taken as a central idea of the research.

For one study, the researchers made 68 women (uni students) into 'study stimuli'. 'These women were asked to come to the laboratory wearing form-fitting clothes...and no make-up.' They were photographed. Then their photographs were judged by male students 'on a 10-point scale (1 = very unattractive, 10 = very attractive)'.

Mr Lewis was lead author on the 2017 study 'Why Women Wear High Heels: Evolution, Lumbar Curvature, and Attractiveness', which said it was testing the 'hypothesis' that women are more 'attractive' in high heels due to the angle it causes in their spine, because of evolution. FFS. Again, they got men to rate the 'attractiveness' of women by looking at pictures. It used photos of celebrities, and also photos of recruited students who were photographed in 'form-fitting clothes'; then 126 men were told to 'rate' their 'attractiveness' from 1 to 10. The study says it found 'documented evidence of high heels on women's attractiveness.' I beg to differ unto infinity.

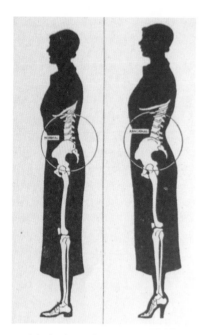

High heels rob you of grace and derange your pelvis, according to the Ladies' Handbook of Home Treatment *by Eulalia Richards, 1912 edition.*

This study quoted a 2014 one by Mr Lewis and others about 'evolved mate preference', suggesting that men's interest in women 'peaks' when the angle of their lumbar curvature is approximately 45.5 degrees – which would account for all the unevolved men dashing about with protractors. You know the type.

Mr Lewis concluded, 'This spinal structure would have enabled pregnant women to balance their weight over the hips . . . These women would have been more effective at foraging during pregnancy and less likely to suffer spinal injuries. In turn, men who preferred these women would have had mates who were better able to provide for fetus and offspring, and who would have been able to carry out multiple pregnancies without injury.' Oh my freaking god. Foraging bodies. Also, rubbish assumptions.

There's a lot of diagrams and science talk of 'vertebral wedging' and 'buttock protrusion', which led a *Washington Post* story in 2015 to report on the research called 'butt science'. Reader, it is not.

As one journalist commented on the research, 'But perhaps most problematic of all is that the average condition is often rated as most attractive, and it is unclear what this means.' It means pull yourselves together. When young male students are being told to choose what's attractive, and only given body shapes to choose from, and female students are asked to turn up wearing tight clothes to be photographed, you're just re-reinforcing a load of crap that's insulting to both men and women. And gay people, and possibly parrots.

Studies like these tend to have a few things in common: a small sample size, the aim to prove a theory, no double-blind element, run by a senior researcher, essentially pervy, and they give me the irrits.

A seminal (sorry) study, 'Adaptive Significance of Female Physical Attractiveness: Role of Waist-to-Hip Ratio' by Devendra Singh, published in the *Journal of Personality and Social Psychology* in 1993 purported to show that men judge women by a hip-to-waist ratio because it's an indicator of fertility (which it isn't).

This one asked young men at a university to judge pictures of 'Miss America winners', 'fashion magazine models' and '*Playboy* playmate . . . centrefolds [sic]'. It 'found' that women are only attractive if they seem 'fertile' and likely to breastfeed (what on earth), and this is how men choose their girlfriends (I do not think so). Pageant winners are listed by their chest, waist and hip measurements.

The study concludes, 'Cross-cultural studies would be needed to test the validity of these suggestions.' A har har har. Har.

But who amongst us is not persuaded by the science of the study called 'What Makes Buttocks Beautiful? A Review and Classification of the Determinants of Gluteal Beauty and the Surgical Techniques to Achieve Them' in the *Aesthetic Plastic Surgery* journal, 2002. The authors (cosmetic surgeons) looked at 1320 photographs of nude women and measured 132 female patients ages 16 to 62. The study 'found' that in the absence of globally recognised standards in judging buttock size, buttock implant surgeons such as themselves should judge what was needed in a false buttock.

The study concluded, 'Most importantly, the surgeon should

'The artificial India-rubber bosoms are not only ridiculous contrivances, but they are absolutely ruinous to the beauty of the part.' – Lola Montez in The Arts of Beauty, 1858

'[Critics] have always said we have big butts. We have big butts. The point is: WHO CARES.' – Choreographer and dance troupe director Mark Morris

Sabrina, aka Norma Sykes, poor darling, made a career out of her notorious bosoms: she was constantly surrounded by men ogling during her 1958–59 tour of Australia. (News Ltd/Newspix)

achieve buttocks with projection and volume.' By all means, let us all aspire to audible buttocks.

A study published in then-respected medical journal *Fertility and Sterility* in 2013 purported to measure the 'attractiveness of women with recto-vaginal endometriosis'. The study was not retracted until 2020, after years of fury from medical researchers and specialists and patients. The journal did not apologise and the authors of the study sullenly said, 'We conducted the study in good faith and according to correct methodology.' Bollocks to that. The women in the study were not told they'd be rated for 'attractiveness' and the concept contributes nothing to medical knowledge. Stop. Judging. Us.

"Even if you're gorgeous, hate bits of you."

Even the women held up as the most beautiful – models – are self-conscious about something they've been told is wrong. Women have been encouraged to feel bad about every part of their body, and invented problems from ugly elbow creases (caused by having a moveable arm), armpit wrinkles, back fat, cankles, wrinkly knees, cellulite (the normal dimpled appearance on thighs, named by advertisers in the 1920s), and toes that are considered the wrong length for sandal exposure.

Beauty requirements are like the demands of an abuser – a woman never knows whether she'll be considered acceptable or condemned for something she couldn't possibly get right, even if she tried. Many models have explained that at the height of their fashionable appearance, agents, clients and photographers made them feel miserably freakish and wrong for some body part or another.

290

"Your breasts are public property."

Sometime in the 1980s and '90s, profiteering cosmetic surgeons took advantage of relaxed regulation on advertising of medical services, glommed onto the term 'breast enhancement' and away they went. Many women since have been plagued with the side-effects and damage from cosmetic surgeries (and, of course, many women have been grateful for reconstructive surgeries after mastectomies).

Women with small breasts are confronted about it by perfect strangers: when footballer Wayne Carey randomly assaulted a woman in the street in 1995 he said to her, 'Why don't you get a bigger set of tits?' Women with large breasts, even from the time they were in their early teens, have been subject to insulting stares and groping.

The American La Resista Corset Company's inflatable bra was launched in the early 1950s with the slogan 'Blowup!! To be the size you want.' (State Library Victoria)

"You can't have a good face & arse."

Actress Courtney Cox from the sitcom *Friends* lamented, 'In Hollywood, to get your bottom half to be the right size, your face may have to be a little gaunt.' This was dubbed 'diet face'. The Mamamia website asked in 2010, 'Which do you choose, face or ass?'

The solution women were given was generally to starve themselves and use facial fillers. The people approached for comment and recommendation in stories are cosmetic physicians and dermatologists who make money out of cosmetic procedures. Nobody who makes a profit from this sort of stuff is ever quoted as saying what a lot of rubbish, have some cake and go for a walk with somebody who makes you laugh.

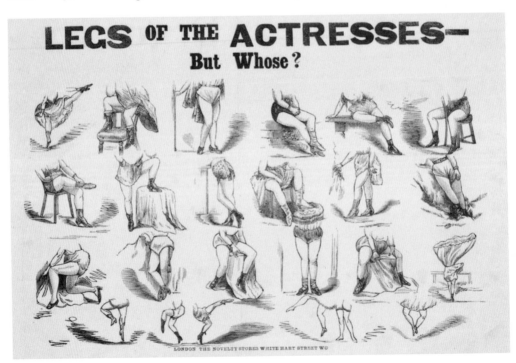

292

"Your lips are too thin. Or too plump."

Whatever size your lips are, I think you'll find you need special make-up fillers and surgery to make them look bigger or smaller. Or take Marie Montaigne's advice from the 1913 edition of *How to Be Beautiful* and, 'Say the words peas, papa, prunes, prisms' just as you enter a drawing room to make your lips into the right shape.

"There's something wrong with your nose."

It's in the middle of your face, for a start.

"Your neck is unacceptable."

A concept that appears again and again in beauty writing for a century or so was a dingy neck, which gave way to a wrinkled one. In 1934 when Europe was on the brink of war, women were told to worry about their dingy necks. A neck ought to be bleached – yes, with bleach – so it would be 'a real beauty asset and not merely a means of attaching your head to your body', the *Charleville Times* told Brisbane women. In other articles women were advised to exercise the neck: 'Swing the head in a circle as many times as this can be done without causing dizziness.'

"Ugh, your hair."

It will be too frizzy, too limp, too 'Black', not blonde enough, too grey, offensively straight, appallingly curly, and you will need some stuff to combat its general dreadfulness, plus rollers, straighteners, spray, mouse, mud, masks and a perm. Also, it is too short, or too long, or too stiff or not stiff enough, or there's too much of it or not enough.

'I feel bad about my neck.' – Nora Ephron, 2006

'Women with kinky or curly hair should not be treated like a problem . . . Women who want to straighten their natural coils should be able to. No one else's opinions should matter.' – Lauren McEwan, The Tempest website, 2015

'The perks of short hair are many. It's fun, low maintenance and comfortable. There is no reason that access to this should be limited by gender, sexual orientation or the failure of a person's face to perfectly align with a particular geometric shape.' – Sam Langford, Honi Soit, 2014

"Women shouldn't have body hair."

The real craze for body-hair removal didn't start until companies manufactured depilatory creams and shaving products. By the early 2000s, the Nair company began marketing directly to girls as young as 10.

The craze or expectation for removing pubic hair didn't start until pornography was more readily available online. Before that, sex-film actors were more likely to wear merkins – pubic wigs, as well as head-hair wigs – to appear as different characters.

Hair-removal product companies have relatively little success marketing to menopausal women, who are generally too overcome with rage to want to succumb to the pain of leg waxing anymore, but also because the lack of estrogen tends to make most of their leg hairs disappear and turn up on their chin, which they can plait at will.

First statues, then the pornography industry popularised the idea of women's bodies not having pubic hair. The first happened because it's really hard to sculpt pubic hair out of marble, and the second happened so that vaginas were easier to see in the hurly burly of the vulva area, to film a penis going into it.

Even though the opposite is true, it has come to be believed by many younger women that removing pubic hair is cleaner. Sadly, the process of removing hair

Even looking at this photo of a 1945 women's razor will cause audible ingrown hairs to form. (Museum of Applied Arts and Sciences)

accounts for many vulval infections, skin irritations, ingrown hairs, and allergic reactions. In some cases, laser hair-removal has led to burns, scarring and more serious infections.

"Your feet are gigantic."

Little feet have been huge for centuries, if you know what I mean. Even though feet on average used to be a couple of sizes smaller a generation or two ago, this was still not small enough. The original Cinderella story has the stepsisters hacking off pieces of their feet to try to fit into the shoes that are perfect for Cinderella.

The comparison has been made countless times between high heels and the old Chinese cultural practice of footbinding to force the feet to become deformed and folded over time into 'lotus feet' on which it is impossible to walk properly. Later, Chinese women were told by nationalists that they should participate in sports and physical activity to make them stronger mothers.

In a tale of the many Nellies, a newspaper notice of Nellie Stewart's 1903 performance of Nell Gwynne reviewed her feet: 'much too big', while another reporter's review of Nell Fleming as Bo Peep at the Opera House in Sydney in 1923 opened with,

These boots were made for mincing. 'March of the Amazons' from a Christmas pantomime, 1875 woodcut by Hugh George, The Australasian Sketcher. *(State Library Victoria)*

'No one . . . can forget Nell Fleming's dainty feet.' Her singing skills were dispatched in the second par.

In 1915 the female readers of country newspapers nation-wide, including the *Gippsland Independent* and the *Buln, Warragul, Berwick, Poowong and Jeetho Shire Advocate* were chided for not having 'French enough' feet, which should be disguised by optical-illusory shoes with 'rounded toe-caps . . . without straps'.

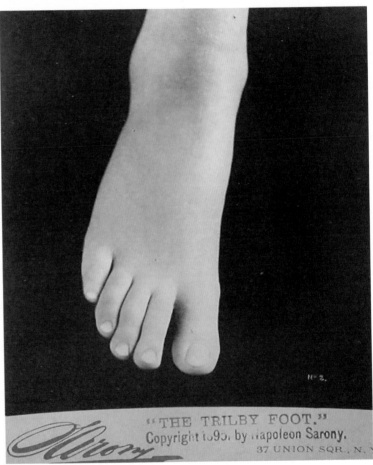

The 1890s novel and smash-hit play, Trilby, spawned a new name for hats, and controlling men (with the character Svengali), but originally created a craze for foot-shaped jewellery and slender shoes to fit the 'perfect foot', in response to the heroine's scandalously bare 'Trilby feet'. Theatrical photograph, 1895, found on a foot fetish website. (The things I do for research, honestly. You're welcome.)

"THE TRILBY FOOT."
Copyright 1895 by Napoleon Sarony.
37 UNION SQR., N. Y

Nº 2.

"Pose."

Traditionally, boys and men pose to make themselves look bigger in photos. But since photography started, women have used it to make themselves look smaller.

Side-on is always a favourite. Here's a photo of Miss Dorothy Woolley, a 'girl' the Sydney *Sun* says might have a better body than the 'girl' they featured the previous week, Carmel de Smythe, because Miss de Smythe's bust was half an inch smaller (yes, really).

Women are not supposed to take up space – elbows in at the table, said June Dally-Watkins, and never sit with your legs apart – not just because you might show your knickers (this was not of such concern when, for example, starlets of the 1990s began to be photographed exiting from cars practically perineum-first). It's also because women mustn't be WIDE, mustn't take up space.

That looks natural, Dorothy. 1922.
(Trove newspaper archives)

Soldiers-turned-exhibition-divers do goofy he-man poses with 'Hazel, a pretty aquaballerina'. Leon Marco's Water Spectacle at the Morecambe Baths, Lancashire, 1950.
(State Library Victoria)

Left, top: Australian dancers for the 'Folies Bergère' season at the Melbourne Tivoli, 1940: Joy Gibbs, Dawn Raines, Margaret Dianne, Beverley Strang, Helen Brown, Pat Doucey, Dawn Snedpon and Val Stedford. (State Library Victoria)

*Right, top: a professional in a 1956 Balmain outfit with a hobble-skirt, using the classic perfect front-foot pose. If she moves a muscle, she will fall right down those stairs. (*The Argus, State Library Victoria)

Right: sisters Glenda, Wanda and my mum, Linda, on her wedding day in 1961: guess which two had recently attended posing lessons at a deportment school by a well-known model? (They can't remember now if it was Bambi Shmith or Elly Lucas.)

Every day on public transport, millions of men sit lolling with their legs wide open taking up way more than half a seat while women, knees together, are squashed into a third or quarter of the available space. I'm sure you don't need me to authorsplain that this is called manspreading.

A standard pose for women to take up less space and seem slimmer was invented by fashion models, adopted by showgirls, and taught at deportment schools: one foot in front of the other to make the body have the smallest – and least stable – footing, as if taking a step forward.

Modern social media pose variations include 'The Invisible Tightrope' with both feet pointing forward, one in front of the other and the ankles crossed; the 'Beyoncé Triangle'; the 'Flexed Calf'; the 'Skinny Flee'; the 'Teeny Lady Head Toss'; and the 'Disappearing Pineapple' . . . all right, I'm just making stuff up now.

PEOPLE

A man is a person.
A child is a person.

Even if you don't exist, ladies, be sure to take up less room. Well done, fictitious drawing woman. Language lessons book produced by the Australian Government, c1970. (National Library of Australia)

The opposite of posing: Janina Green's photograph of women in the nuddy at the baths, 'Collingwood', 1989. (Courtesy of the artist and M.33, Melbourne)

Dr Belva Lockwood, a lawyer who judges refused to hear in court, and Dr Mary Walker,
Civil War surgeon, prisoner of the Confederate Army, and pants wearer, c1912.
(US Library of Congress)

9

DRESS UP, DRESS DOWN

WE'VE BEEN THUNDERED AT FOR A FEW CENTURIES, warned that a love of fashion and fripperies betrays a trivial character, one of forbidden pride and vanity. But being dowdy is also a sin. Fashion was supposed to render us decorative. Too plain of cloth and with less complicated skirts that allowed free movement, and we looked, after all, like servants. Your clothes immediately marked your class.

In the same way that we're now supposed to be good at sex but express no interest in it, we're required to take enough of an interest to look fashionable, but not *too* fashionable, and to do it rather magically with hardly any money, and to seem unconcerned about it.

Society is still struggling to make the transition from being told what to wear, and everyone wearing sort of the same thing, to a free-for-all. While some of us still want to follow rules and trends, we now please ourselves – wear clothes for our own spiritual or religious reasons, express our politics or mood, defiantly enjoy cosplay, work out our own style and ignore new seasonal trends based on what the fashion industry wants to sell.

"Only idiots are interested in clothes."

A book said to be written by a Stephen Gosson in 1595 furiously denounced women who cared about clothes, otherwise known as having a 'greedy lust (for) hellish toyes'. He wrote this in his mad book, *Pleasant Quippes for Upstart New-fangled Gentlewomen A Glasse (Mirror) To View the Pride of vainglorious WOMEN containing a Pleasant Invective Against the Fantastical Foreigne Toyes Daylie used in Womens Apparell.*

Society demanded crinolines; cartoonists ridiculed them. This send-up of an inflatable cage is a detail of John Leech's 'Follies of the Year', 1860s. (National Library of Australia)

Fashionable outfits, Gosson said, would trap young men who would then get 'poxe and pyles' from 'whores', and he was *very* cross that a big hoop skirt would hide a 'synne', in other words, a pregnancy. He doesn't sound very nice.

The UK Costume Society republished a satirical poem written in the 1680s by a writer called Mary Evelyn who died when she was 20 of smallpox, called *The Ladies Dressing-Room*. Her fond father published it, having once described her in a letter as 'my fardle of impertinences'.

Mary's comic list of accoutrements a man must provide a wife includes 4 petticoats, a black rich silk gown, three pairs of embroidered shoes, various undergarments, garters, diamond buckles, 12 day smocks, 12 Flanders lace night smocks, hankies a dozen laced, a dozen plain, embroidered velvet slippers, girdle with ruby buckle, diamond rings, three painted and perfumed fans, sables (fur cloaks), diamond and sapphire hair ornaments, diamond and pearl earrings, necklaces, bracelets, cuffs, manteaux about her neck, ruby locket, ribbons and 12 pairs of gloves.

Women have often been mocked for presuming to follow fashion, or for enjoying it. They have often been portrayed as 'fashion victims' rather than people trying to enjoy themselves.

The crinoline, undeniably absurd, ramped up the double standard for women: they were expected to be fashionable, but ridiculed for it. In her 2014 essay '(Ad)dressing Women: Fashion and Body Image in Punch, 1850s–1860s', Shu-Chuan Yan quotes Charles Dickens's satirical journal, *All the Year Round* in 1863, saying 'Ladies are found doing the best they can to make themselves look like beehives and trees.'

Weirdly, the crinoline was easier than the old style of several petticoats and skirts: lighter, often on a collapsible frame. Underneath their skirt, women might have worn long, loose undies – bloomer trousers, in effect.

This made movement for rich women much easier than it sometimes was before, though it was harder to go through

Crinoline as cage, by John Leech, 1857.

'A Woman is Not to be proud of her fine Gown.' – The Lady's New Year's Gift or Advice to a Daughter by George Lord Saville, Late Marquis and Earl of Saville, 1688

doors and into carriages and do much except stand too close to the fire and be burned to death – the fate of hundreds of women a year.

"Only frumps ignore fashion."

To this day it sets my teeth on edge to hear the word mumsy as an insult. An exhausted woman who wears comfortable and low-maintenance clothes and might have a Vegemite sandwich in her cross-body bag ought not to be mum-shamed. And you don't have to be a mum to get shamed for not being a style icon.

When researching, I hate looking at microfilm, with its windy-on spools, dragged through a projector screen light-thingy, old-fashioned technology; I can't feel it's quaint and charming, just annoying. But it was worth it at the National Library to have a squiz at the 1839 book *The Art of Dress; Or, Guide to the Toilette: with Directions for Adapting the Various Parts of the Female Costume to the Complexion and Figure, Hints on Cosmetics, & etc.*

'How often,' it asked, 'do we observe the finest faces spoiled by ignorance and want of taste in the selection of the colour and style of the headdress, and figures which . . . would be all but charming, distorted and destroyed by an ill-considered costume!' And then it went on to recommend the bustle.

DIY bloomers pattern in The Cutters Practical Guide to the Cutting of All Kinds of Ladies' Garments Including Bodices, Habits, Jackets, Coats, Ulsters, Vests, Blouses, Skirts, Equestriennes, Cycling and Walking Skirts, Trousers, Breeches, Knickers, Leggings, Gaiters Underclothing, Etc. *by William Vincent, c1900. (State Library Victoria)*

"Your trousers are outrageous."

It's hard for us to imagine now that women wearing trousers was once illegal and then extraordinarily rare. Before pants were trousers, they were called bifurcated garments or freedom dress.

The organised movement for more sensible clothes for women came around the 1850s, after the mad panniers and false bottoms, as well as the giant collapsible crinolines, were fashionable. It was as much a backlash against all the wide, multi-petticoatery folderol as it was against the tight-lacing of corsets.

It was also a big feature of the new health campaigners like vegetarians, hydrotherapy hotel patrons, physical education enthusiasts, gymnasium fanciers, calisthenics cosplayers, bicycle enthusiasts and anti-corset doctors. Being healthy was another way to require people to be religious and do their duty.

In America, women organised as the National Dress Reform Association. Gayle Fischer's 2001 book *Pantaloons and Power* suggests that pants aka 'Turkish trousers' were adopted by European and American women first as novelty costumes, worn underneath skirts: turbans also featured.

The poster woman for bloomers, in countless Press engravings, was the eponymous Amelia Jenks Bloomer. She shortened her skirt to a mid-calf length and wore trousers with a ruffle cuff to the ankle underneath. Women who literally followed suit were Bloomerites, practising Bloomerism. In England, the idea of bloomers was immediately ridiculed as much as crinoline cages had been for the opposite reason – they were too practical.

Mrs Bloomer was a political activist ally of Elizabeth Cady Stanton, and they related freedom of dress to some of the women's issues of the day – freedom of women to vote, their right to have an equal say in their family – and the banning of alcohol and the emancipation of enslaved people.

A betrousered Amelia Bloomer, drawn for the sheet music of 'The Bloomer Polka', c1860. (National Library of Australia)

'I don't wear men's clothes, I wear my own clothes.'
– Dr Mary Walker

Geraldine Hargrave, 17, a teenager dressed as a 'masherette', a female rake, at a Children's Fancy Dress Ball in Adelaide, 1887. (State Library of South Australia)

Bloomers were treated by the wider world as another fashion fad. A lot of women went back to skirts, because trousers were considered foreign or associated with manual and male work, some to avoid the abuse they copped in public, or because they didn't want to be seen to make a political statement. Many rural women wore trousers in private to work on farms. But bloomers proved bifurcation was possible, and set a precedent that made trousers less shocking in later decades. The notion of 'Who wears the pants in that family?' is still a recognisable reminder of what trousers can signal: power.

"Skirts are compulsory."

When I was a teenager working as a reporter at the Melbourne stock exchange in the 1980s, women were not permitted to wear trousers in the room. Most schools still also required girls to wear a uniform skirt, never trousers. Public schools have finally got with the new century and most now allow trousers for girls.

Though written policies forcing women to wear skirts (and high heels) at work are becoming anachronistic, many women report that unwritten rules still require it, especially in legal and some political settings.

Lola Montez (in wrong-era fishnets) played by Mary Preston, Elizabethan Theatre Trust play, 1958. (National Library of Australia)

"You look like an aristocrat. Or a stripper."

After a big night out at a 19th-century ball, the requisite accoutrements worn by an English duchess were gently returned to their perfumed drawers by her 'lady's maid', or sent back to the family bank vault: a tiara, stonking great blingy earrings and necklaces, an extra-long ostrich feather fan with a tassel on its handle that could be opened for full phooofy effect, perhaps a feather boa and long white gloves with many buttons. And yet the same accessories, by the 1950s, were all firmly associated with striptease acts.

Strippers took off the ultimate respectable rig to make their salacious showgirl display even naughtier. Fishnet stockings weren't widely adopted, probably because they weren't easy to make, until the 1920s. They were a handy cross between the flesh-peeking, the removable, and the respectable cachet of proper stockings. From a distance they might look black or grey, but under a theatre light, the theory goes, hundreds of glimpses of skin showed through. The mathematically minded have pointed out that the geometric change in mesh size accentuates curves where the leg changes shape.

Lady Tweedsmuir is simply livid that her accessories have become a staple of the burlesque circuit. Her over-wrought husband concurs, 1930s. (City of Vancouver Archives)

The Rocky Horror Show added some extra kink to the fishnets, punk rock ripped them, and roller derby added danger and speed.

Prototype scarlet woman Lola Montez and her scandalous dancing and propensity to whip editors (now there's an idea) predated the general use of fishnets by decades, but she was portrayed wearing them in various theatrical productions of the 20th century. In its own way, this was advice to respectable women not to wear them.

When English light opera singer Suzanne Steele arrived at Essendon airport in the mid-1960s to play Lola Montez in a musical she was snapped by a Press photographer. The pictures

were captioned, 'Suzanne Steele . . . 5 ft. 1 in. and red-haired, arrived at Essendon in a mini frock – without stockings'.

"A skirt worn without stockings is a scandal."

In 1965, Jean Shrimpton, a famous 22-year old London model, went to the Derby Day races in Melbourne wearing a white, sleeveless mini-dress, about 12 cm above the knee, provided by the fabric company that sponsored her trip, Orlon.

Her lack of gloves and stockings and hat became a front-page newspaper scandal, described as a disgrace. She was shaken by catcalls from men and abuse from women at Flemington Racecourse. Her companion, actor Terence Stamp, drew no ire with his needle-cord suit.

Jean Shrimpton later said she hadn't been told that gloves, stockings and hats were required. A spokeswoman for the Melbourne Bureau of Meteorology recently confirmed that the unseasonable top temperature on that October day at Flemington was probably between 32 and 35 degrees, and added that she hated stockings.

Had Melbournians absorbed what every etiquette book said we ought to have, the social set should have reefed up their hems and whipped off their stockings to make Miss Shrimpton feel welcome. Instead, the posh ladies' brigade was merciless in their humid gussets. The Lord Mayor's wife, Lady Nathan, hissed to a newspaper: 'This Shrimpton is a child and she showed very bad manners . . . it's not done here. I feel we do know so much better than Miss Shrimpton . . . we all dress correctly here.'

Jean Shrimpton and Terence Stamp on arrival to her scandalous, stockingless visit to Australia, 1965.(Photo by News Ltd/Newspix)

Like most etiquette books of the 20th century, Amy Vanderbilt's 1950s editions of *Everyday Etiquette* says an employed 'girl' must wear stockings even in the hottest weather but provides no reason. That's pretty much the size of it. Nobody even knew why.

Ladies with hats, gloves, and handbags that may have bricks in them, Country Women's Association fashion show, Wangaratta, 1970. (Bob Beel, State Library Victoria)

"You dress like a tart."

Clothes that reveal the shape of a woman's body have been both required and denounced, from the over-corset bodices with hardly room for another stitch to tight stretch-jersey dresses that hug a pregnant belly. Tight clothes were first blamed for breathing restriction, then for being lewd. Women in Egypt have more recently been arrested, despite being fully clothed in Instagram posts.

Pregnant women, primary school girls and older women in bikinis have all been told off, publicly or privately, for wearing 'revealing clothes'. Many US schools have rules that forbid girls, but not boys, from showing any shoulders or 'too much' leg in shorts. Sometimes the reason given is that it's not modest, and sometimes that it 'distracts boys'.

Neck-to-knee bathing suits were denounced as 'indecent'. English men of the 1800s who came to Australia were scandalised at the bright colours of women's dresses. A contemporary tabloid newspaper website is constantly saying that celebrities are 'flaunting' their legs, arms or 'figure'.

My nanna told me I looked like a 'streetwalker' when I wore a black lace dress to the Year 12 dance. Nearly three decades later, I drove with my 10-year-old daughter past a couple of women dressed in short skirts and high-heeled boots on a well-known sex-worker beat corner. My daughter looked out the window and asked me, 'Mum what's a street walker?' I launched into 20 minutes of socio-economic history of sex work and how we must respect women who did this work, and how some of them had difficult childhoods and drug problems, and some didn't, and maybe no ability to earn higher pay (wage gap) and that what they wear didn't change how we should see them as people. My kid looked out the window again. 'Really? Then why are they on stilts?' She had been talking about circus parades.

"Wear lingerie, not undies."

A lace bra trimmed with real mink fur and a fur bustier nestle in their bespoke archive boxes at the State Library of New South Wales. They were designed by Miss Desolie Minnie Richardson (later Lady Hurley), the company's chief designer from 1954 to 1970. In 1962 it was used as a promotional item for the Berlei company.

When researching her book *Out of Shape, Debunking Myths About Fashion and Fit*, Mel Campbell found that Berlei's Head of Training, Clare Stevenson, held equivalent rank to a British general as Group Officer of the Women's Auxiliary Australian Airforce from 1940. *The Sydney Morning Herald* headlined an article about her: 'Director of WAAFs approves lipstick. Smokes, too.'

Bet this was ticklish: Desolie Richardson's mink-trimmed bra – a flung view. (B. VanOver, State Library of NSW)

But back to the fur-trimmed bra: the library catalogue says it has never been worn – but I bet it *was* worn at least once, even just for fun to dance around in in the design studio. In 1952 it was dangled in front of a *Daily Telegraph* columnist, who obligingly ran a story, saying, 'It is WORN ON TOP' (that is, outside a blouse) and made much of a fictitious 50-guinea price tag – in today's money a bit over $1500.

The sturdy methods used, of machine-stitch edge overlocking and the metal 'hook and eyelet' bra fastener, still endure – no amount of hope or Velcro has bettered them. What makes the bra glamorous? The use of mink, but not ferret. Beige, not red lace. And yet, all these years later, it doesn't read the same to modern eyes. It's now a diverting item of second-hand lingerie, rather than glamorous.

"Don't go out in your work clothes."

Nanna, my mum's mum, worked very long, hard hours on a farm usually in a sturdy bib-and-brace denim overalls big enough to go over warm clothes for a 4 am winter milking. When her

Nanna, Lil Jones, on the farm with a bullocky whip, 1940s.

husband was off shearing she'd wear them for weeks to work, but never wore them away from the farm or to receive visitors.

Her daughters remember Nanna's off-work clothes in the 1950s being emblematic of frugal, unshowy, neat, respectable items: a twinset and a tailored skirt or trousers in pale autumnal colours that wouldn't show the dirt. She had one black day-frock with a matching hat for 'good'. She had lost all her jewellery in bushfires.

In her 70s, Nanna was baffled by anyone who would wear denim in public because she saw it as workwear. Durable fabrics were considered lower class, or only for coats, and had names like fustian and dreadnought. Well-off women and their seamstresses found ways to engineer and employ light, ephemeral-looking fabrics, soufflé-like gauzy voile and muslins and their sister fabrics called tissue and zephyr, after the word for breeze.

"Wear stuff that might kill you."

So many women died when their wide skirts brushed near a fire as their tight clothes, impossible to strip off quickly, went up in flames. Queen Victoria instructed chemists to conduct experiments in fire-retardant fabric: the idea of not wearing the cumbersome skirts was not considered. (In the first decade of the 20th century, girls aged 15–20 died of burns at eight times the rate of boys.)

A rare surviving colonial denim work outfit: a machine-stitched shirt with shell buttons and a gored skirt with a pocket and matching belt, 1890s. (Museum of Applied Arts and Sciences)

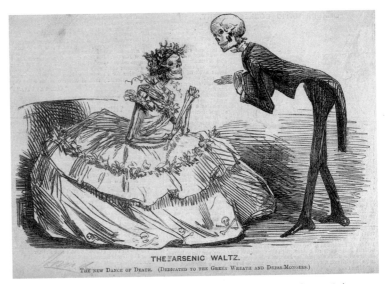

THE ARSENIC WALTZ.
THE NEW DANCE OF DEATH. (DEDICATED TO THE GREEN WREATH AND DRESS-MONGERS.)

In the 19th century, women and children (mostly) were poisoned with the green dyes made of arsenic used in dresses and jackets, fake-flower hair-wreaths and even wallpapers. Delta Airlines staff sued a clothing company in 2018 because their uniforms had been chemically treated to resist stains, be waterproof and resist wrinkles. They caused skin rashes, headaches, fatigue and other health problems.

"Dress in frothy frills."

The stage actresses in souvenir postcards of the Victorian and Edwardian eras show a 'pile it on' approach to hats, jewellery, braid, trim, sequins, shawls, tassels, lace and whatever else they could find. Display and abundance were all the go.

"Look in the mirror & take one thing off."

Fond of a fashion aphorism, this quote is alleged to be from designer Coco Chanel. It exemplified the requirements for

20th-century elegance: clean lines and minimum frippery. Mind you, she hung about with Nazis, so that's enough out of her.

"Clothes must be flattering."

Many years ago, when I was a satirical etiquette columnist writing 'Keep Yourself Nice' in *The Age*, a perennial, cross complaint would appear every few weeks from a different man who'd found some paper and a pen, and bought a stamp and driven the Holden to the post office to send me a letter, furious about women who wore jeans, which he felt were unfeminine and made a woman's bottom looked bigger. It did not occur to Ken of Glen Iris and his ilk that women wearing jeans did not care a jot whether their bottom looked large enough to suffocate Ken of Glen Iris (and all of his ilk) in a hatchback.

Actress Edna May wore everything but the kitchen sink, in the Victorian style of well-upholstered and enthusiastically decorated actresses. Souvenir postcard, early 1900s. (State Library Victoria)

'Flattering' has been generally understood to mean making you look taller and slimmer, or in some way less like yourself.

"Create an optical illusion."

In WWI the British navy created 'dazzleships' by painting their ships with sprauncy, bold stripes and patterns to confuse the enemy, who found it hard to estimate size and shape from a distance. Women have similarly been advised to avoid or adopt certain patterns, and use clever engineering and visual artistry to 'reshape' themselves.

A dazzleship.

The same base principle of clothes that disguise-and-distract had been used for more than a century: big hats, shoulders, sleeves, hips, and bums make waists look smaller. A photograph of a woman called Lillian May Bruce in 1904 shows her multi-pronged efforts: angled lines of the lapel and peplum created

arrows pointing at her corsetted waist; her 'leg-o-mutton' phouffed sleeves made her shoulders wider to further minimise her waist; and she stood with her upper body angled away from the camera to look narrower.

Lillian May Bruce (left) simply insists you notice her waist, 1904. Lillian again (top right) in quite the spinnaker sleeves, and some other unnamed American ladies who might be smuggling pumpkins. (Lillian pics: Mark Daniels, State Library Victoria)

Cabaret artist Jane Morgan, in a hat called 'Ruined'; Schiaparelli beach hat, 1950s. (The Argus, State Library Victoria)

"Hats are compulsory & also stupid."

A woman without a hat used to be considered disrespectable. But a woman could expect no approval for wearing a hat: it was bound to be either too fancy, too frivolous, too small, or too big, or too revealing of character, or age.

We can still indicate something of who we are by our hats and headwear, but it isn't always easy to decode. There's little difference between Queen Elizabeth II's chin-tied headscarf and a hijab, at least in terms of appearance, but the Queen was never abused in the street for wearing one.

Valiant Iris Edwards (centre) keeps a straight face despite her hat, with the Lanyon girls, 1904. (Mark Daniels, State Library Victoria)

In 1910 *Punch* columnist 'Sibyl' recorded the passing of hats which told the age of their wearers: a 'princesse bonnet' said 'I'm 17', a cap was the uniform for 'matronhood or old maidism'.

By the turn of the 1900s, the respectable little conical-shaped hats of the 1880s gave way to the fancy fripperiness of large 'picture' hats, which blocked out the view of anyone sitting behind them at the Music Hall.

Last-ditch attempts were made in the 1950s to entice women back to hats with novelty headwear, but by the end of the 1960s, millinery was firmly out of fashion for most people except for functions at Government Houses, attending a European royal wedding, and getting shickered at the races.

Mrs Helen Rutherford with unfortunate moustache-suggesting lace-trimmed veil, dressmaker Madame Elise, and Naomi McQuoin, a single mum with five kids. Stallholder security photos, Centennial Exhibition, Melbourne, 1888. (State Library Victoria)

Grand ladies throwing literal shade on a posh ladies' committee, Government House, 1906. (State Library Victoria)

"Hatpins make you stabby."

In the early 1900s newspapers called women hatpin fiends, and ran stories of the hatpin menace and the solution: hatpin suppression. Ten-pound fines were issued to women caught in public who had their hats anchored to their hair with a long, skinny, sharp pin stabbed through their hat and into their bun (the bun was often filled with a pad made from their own discarded hair called a 'rat').

Women were instructed to shorten pins and use a metal protector on the end of them. Instead, women advised each other to stab the hand or thigh of a frotter or assaulter on a cable tram.

New laws required blunted hat pins: not as good for stabbing, early 1900s. (Beyer collection, State Library Victoria)

"You're sending secret messages with your fan."

The House of Duvellroy, a fan-maker selling to the Paris and London markets in the 19th century, printed a clever piece of marketing – a list of secret gestures to use with a fan: drawing the fan through the hand meant 'I hate you', placed behind the head meant 'don't forget me' (or, surely, 'I am behaving like an unhinged person with a fan'). Any poor woman sitting there fiddling her fan might be accidentally shouting, 'I love you I hate you yes No You are cruel Kiss Me I am Married I Wish to Get Rid Of You Follow Me.'

Alexandra Starp declared secret fan talk to be a myth, in an article called 'The Secret Language of Fans' for auctioneers Sotheby's in London in 2018. One has to agree with her that even if a woman did have a complicated series of more than two dozen fan moves, what sort of straight man would be likely to notice, or be able to interpret them? No, fans, like most other accessories and clothes, let women say things to each other that were not much more complicated than, 'I'm making an effort', 'I have a lot of money' and 'Christ, I'm having another hot flush.'

"High heels always look better."

High heels might be the most tenacious, everyday emblem of the idea that women must 'suffer for beauty'. Hospital emergency rooms get a big uptick in ankle and foot injuries caused by high heels on weekend nights. Partly because of twists and falls from dancing and walking, partly because women take their shoes off because they're hurting towards the end of the night, and step on broken glass.

Some feminists love high heels, for the fashionable look, or because they 'make me feel powerful'. Others use them as a sort of work uniform – kicking them off under desks, changing into sport shoes to walk home.

Although Cannes Film Festival organisers denied an official policy, many women continue to be turned away from film premieres because they were not wearing high heels. In many Japanese workplaces, heels are still mandatory, with a stipulation of height (between 5 and 7 centimetres). The Japanese Minister for Labour responded to a 2019 petition he received asking for the regulations to be made illegal, saying that high heels were 'necessary' for women. I hope they stand on him.

"Women don't wear tool belts."

Before cross-body bags and bumbags and celebrity handbag collections allegedly worth hundreds of thousands of dollars, women used kangaroo-style pinny pockets, 'equipages', which were the equivalent of a lanyard, and chatelaines, a belt hung about with accoutrements to-hand, especially favoured by

Bemused footy players in heels; 1994 poster by Carol Porter, Red Planet Posters. (State Library Victoria)

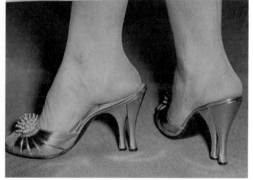

(Clockwise from top left)

Women wearing high heels and stockings in the bush, 1920s. (State Library Victoria)

Poor feet: 'Sketches on the Block' illustrated the unofficial fashion parades of ladies on Melbourne's Collins St, 1881. (May and Ebsworth, The Australasian, *State Library Victoria)*

*The double-heeled shoe never caught on. Fashions in Footwear Exhibition, London, 1955. (*The Argus, *State Library Victoria)*

Young women at the Road Traffic Authority in NSW took off their platform shoes to walk down several flights of stairs during a fire drill, 1975.

housekeepers, nurses and the rich, who had fancy silver ones. It was named after the French word for the 'lady of the house'.

A head servant's chatelaine was festooned with sensible things, such as keys, a whistle to summon under-servants, perhaps a needle, thimble and thread case, a pencil and little notepad, and weeny scissors. A fashionable lady's might have a watch, a perfume bottle, a powder puff, a fan, even a small painting pallet and brushes – hence satirical cartoons of ladies with giant clinky-clanky chatelaines. Early colonial artist Georgina MacCrae had a nutmeg container with a grater-lid, engraved with her initials, on hers. I sniffed it at State Library Victoria, but the scent had departed.

Georgiana McCrae's 19th-century nutmeg holder for her chatelaine (now non-whiffy). (State Library Victoria)

One lovely chatelaine nestles in its custom-shaped dent in archival foam inside a gunmetal-grey cardboard box at the Library. It belonged to the Beyer family of St Kilda, who owned tearooms at the end of Acland Street with tables on a platform in a tree. The chatelaine, probably owned by Janet Beyer, has a little photo of her children, the later champion rollerskaters Hilda and Ruby, as well as a tiny perfume bottle, a tea spoon, a pencil case, a tiny fleece powder puff with a mirror on the lid, a metal mesh purse, a watch, a needle case, and a key.

"Women don't need pockets."

There are fewer quicker ways to induce incandescent fury in a woman than the moment she tries on a garment only to find that it has a 'false' pocket – a useless, decorative flap or slit. Pictures of a dress supplied with capacious pockets, on the other hand, or women's jeans with a front pocket deep enough for a phone, will be shared triumphantly (#pockets), (#womenneedpockets).

The Beyer chatelaine with a forerunner of the 'Glomesh' handbag, in its preservation box. (State Library Victoria)

Punch *magazine cartoonist
John Leech ridiculed
chatelaines, showing a
woman hung about with
a teapot, kettle, corkscrew
and carpet brooms, 1849.*

Laura. " Oh ! Look, Ma' dear; see what a *love* of a Chatelaine Edward
has given me."

Women and other social commentators have been cross
about the sexist history of pockets for a long time and taken
matters into their own hands: when they could, women have
always made sure they had a lot of pockets.

*Blurry Sarah Sophia Banks
with clouds of grey curls and
lace, and no visable pockets.*

Lots of patents for extra pocket arrangements are filed
at the National Archives in Canberra. Only the envelope
remains which once held Esther Noble's 1900 design for
'Improvements in Garment Pockets'. Victorian dressmaker
Ellen Carroll's 1909 application to patent an overskirt with
12 pockets is missing its illustration. If that's not a conspiracy
I don't know what is.

The Pocket: A Hidden History of Women's Lives by Barbara Burman and Ariane Fennetaux has many beautiful colour photos of 'tie-on pockets' back to the 1700s, some gorgeously embroidered to carry treasures, some plain and white to hide under filmy muslin. They were like little flat bags that women tied onto their waist, underneath or between layers of skirts and petticoats, which had slits in them to get at the pouches underneath. People left their detachable pockets and contents in their wills.

Later, women who could afford tailors ordered riding habits – sensible tight jackets with pockets and big full skirts easy for striding in. One riding habit fan was Sarah Sophia Banks, a collector of coins, visiting cards, and hot-air ballooning ephemera, sister of the depraved, racist Pacific looter and profiteering botanist Joseph Banks.

Miss Banks was one of those women who were privileged enough to break many prevailing societal rules, protected by a father's or dead husband's money (or in Miss Banks's case, her brother's). Such rich women could chose to be carriage drivers, motorists or pilots. Miss Banks drove her own carriage with four horses.

Sparse paperwork remains for ambitious pocket patents, c1900. (National Archives of Australia)

A gallery curator's memoir from Miss Banks's day remembers that she used her skirt to carry things, as well as having several close-fitting riding-habit-style overall-coverings, which she had made three at a time. She called them Hightem (for best) Tightem (for day) and Scrub (the equivalent of trackie dacks at home).

She also had quilted petticoats made with especially large pockets, sturdy and large enough to carry several books. To supplement the pockets, she was often followed by a footman

'If women would change the position and plan of their pockets they would not so frequently suffer from the depredations of light-fingered thieves.'
– London magistrate to woman who'd been robbed, reported in The Fitzroy Mercury, 1877

to carry extra parcels. (Annette Kellermann had observed that her grandmother's generation had petticoats that could 'stand up by themselves'.)

Some of the books Miss Banks might have carried in her pockets were the advice manuals of the day, several of which she had in her collection, now held at the British Museum and the British Library, which has been studied by Dr Arlene Leis. These were literally called 'pocket books' and contained calendars with marked holidays, fashions for the year, how to update hats and frocks with new trims, lists of average prices and frugal tips and parlour games.

'If we give women pockets they can use they abuse them . . . stuff them full of all sorts of things, making ugly bulges.' – London manager of a dressmaking shop quoted in the *Daily Mail*, Brisbane, 1923

In a poignant appendix to her marvellous book *The Five*, which re-examines the lives of the women murdered by 'Jack the Ripper', Hallie Rubenhold lists the contents of the pockets of each of them, recorded by the police. For homeless or largely destitute women, their pockets and a little bundle might have been all they owned, hidden under several layers of clothes.

Their pocketed possessions included hankies (also used as scarves), 'piece of a looking glass', pieces of comb, and a knife.

In her satirical book *Are Women People?* published in 1915, New Yorker Alice Duer Miller wrote a much-plagiarised poem comparing the arguments against women having the vote to being allowed to have pockets. It said women didn't really need pockets, because their husbands had some, and if women had their own they wouldn't use them wisely. At about the same time, Sydney's *Globe and Sunday Times War Pictorial* campaigned, 'As women are doing the work of men they must have one of man's privileges – namely, pockets.'

The *Wagga Advertiser* claimed in 1906 that women's dresses used to have pockets – 'sometimes even as many as three'. Women were advised to tell their dressmakers to add pockets to dresses, 'good and deep'. Around 1920 women wore elasticised stocking garters with a small pocket attached at the back of the knee. In 1923 the *Adelaide Chronicle* reported that women's clothes had pockets for the first time in 20 years. Modern mothers regularly report on social media that their boy children's school uniforms come with pockets, and their girls' don't.

Lack of pockets has become the emblematic annoyance for women. For centuries we've been told we don't want them, and if we do want them, we can't have them. It's the quintessential bad and bonkers advice.

A 1950 Pierre Balmain knickerbocker suit in violet jersey had a pocket for a packet of fags. (The Argus, State Library Victoria)

That's enough now . . .

WE KNOW THAT EVERY HEADING IN THIS BOOK IS A LIE. We know that so much of what we've been told is just bonkers or bad advice. We know so much time has been wasted, while we've been shamed and belittled and plagued by these wrong assumptions and rules to keep us 'in our place'.

We've been harangued by fathers, boyfriends and husbands, and then pamphlets, and all manner of cops, and governments, and doctors, and various 'wellness' grifters and other advertisers. For centuries we heard these messages, absorbed them, and told them to ourselves, and our friends and our daughters and nieces.

We've disproven the inferiority of women in every realm, and still we get centuries-old versions of wrong advice repackaged and delivered through new technology. It's still the same message: sit down and shoosh, stop being hysterical about your health, you need a man, do all the housework, think less of disadvantaged women, pretend white women are better than other women, get paid less for harder work, be a good mother, the standards of which are impossible, buy clothes but you'll never look good in them, feel bad about your body shape, feel worse about your face. And furthermore, pretend none of this is happening.

So, from now on we can murmur it like a 19th-century girl: 'We shall no longer countenance this preposterous state of affairs', or we can, indelicately, stand up and shout: 'Bullshit!'

Up to you.

ACKNOWLEDGEMENTS

Aboriginal and Torres Strait Islander notes

Thank you to everyone who helped me try to find those who could speak for the Aboriginal people in photos from Cullinlaringo Station and Koonibba Mission, including Lenore Blair at Woorabinda Shire Council in Queensland, the Koonibba Community Aboriginal Corporation in South Australia and Marcus Hughes, Director of Indigenous Engagement at the National Library of Australia.

Thank you to the Aboriginal people who spoke to me about the content of the 'domestic service' section. As they know, I won't name them here, to avoid any inference that they endorse anything in the book.

As a gesture to reflect some of the contents of this book, and to honour the memory of Aboriginal people in some of the photographs, a donation has been made by the author to the Aboriginal and Torres Strait Islander Healing Foundation website, at healingfoundation.org.au.

NEXT TIME YOU READ that an author has 'discovered' or 'unearthed' something in a 'dusty archive', cock an ear for the distant screaming of thousands of donors, bequeathers, archivists, cataloguers, librarians, preservationists, digitisers, photographers, menders, curators, climate-controlled storage experts and retrieval staff.

Thank you to all of them, for making it easy for me – and you – to waltz into a public institution and see a splendidly tatty book with powdering edges that's hundreds of years old, or an aviatrix's goggles, or a pristine, shouty 1980s anti-sexual harassment poster.

The National Library of Australia An intensive 12-weeks fellowship here in 2019 formed a core of research. The fellowship was funded by the Ryan Stokes family. Thank you to Director-General Marie-Louise Ayres, librarians and specialist staff; Catriona Anderson, Catherine Aldersley, Andrew Sergeant, Damian Cole, Fiona Milway, Shirleene Robinson, Marty Spencer, Michael Herlihy, Nat Williams, Narelle Marlow, Kevin Bradley, and Elizabeth Robinson. Thank you to Rebecca Bateman, the Indigenous Curator, and Eileen Schmitt, Special Materials Cataloguing Team Leader, for talking to me about the history of Aboriginal girls who were stolen and kept at missions or state 'homes' and 'put out to service'.

Thanks to Di Pin Ouyang, Bing Zheng, Rika Wright and Mayumi Shinozaki, of the much-missed Asian Reading Room. Jessica Coates, the Copyright Law and Policy Adviser of the Australian Libraries Copyright Committee, helped with matters of reproduction rights, and public domain; Susan Newberry, the Integrated Library Management System administrator, magicked a spreadsheet of nearly 200 books I consulted; librarian volunteers Suzanne Morris and Regina Scanlon pre-jooshed relevant newspaper-cuttings files.

I'm indebted to the fellows with whom I shared an office, especially Ellen Smith, Andrea Gaynor and Ashley Barnwell, for their camaraderie.

Museum of Applied Arts & Sciences The Powerhouse in Sydney has generously allowed me to showcase objects from its collection. When my visit to the museum to take pictures was banjaxed due to pandemic lockdown, staff arranged for a professional to take new ones – a mammoth and delicate task at a difficult time – and helped find copyright owners. I still feel a bit emotional about it. Take a twirl, Rights and Permissions Officer Harry Rees.

Senior Curator Roger Leong wrangled a huge number of items from storage (and forensically inspected Annette Kellermann's hibiscus two-piece). Thanks to photographer Marinco Kojdanovski, the digitising team, and Kathy Hackett.

Artists & other copyright holders Thanks to everyone who gave permission for their work to appear. The linocut *Wawulak Wulay Ga Wititji* is used by permission of the office of Dr Banduk Marika AO, Senior of the Year Northern Territory 2020, artist and an Indigenous land management and cultural advisor, and the Art Gallery of NSW; Alison Alder for *Women Workers*; Marie McMahon for *Sexual Harassment Is Not a Compliment!*; Toni Robertson, formerly of Sydney University Feminists 1974 for *Hire Him He's Got Great Legs,* SHINE SA (formerly Family Planning SA) and Victoria Paterson for *Do You Know About the Emergency Contraception Pill;* Louise Mayhew (for the hand-pass) and the Estate of Frances Phoenix and her sister Sally Cantrill for *Dig For Victory*; and the Wollongong Women's Information Service and Anne Jarvis for *End the Silence About Domestic Violence.* Thanks to Ann Stephen and the late Di Holdway for donating posters. Thank you Berlei Australia and Andrea Mitchell for permission to use the Berlei figure calculator and 1930s photos. Photographs by Janina Green and Peter Milne appear courtesy of the artists and the M.33 photographic agency.

State Library Victoria An unrelated 2013 fellowship produced some useful ideas, images, and clever friends who've continued to help me. Thank you Senior Curator Carolyn Fraser, and Pictures Collection specialist librarian Gerard Hayes, who I bombard with many difficult queries often only answerable with knowledge inside his head. I imagine, given the vast culling of images and captions for this book, I'll have made some mistakes. Gerard will pretend not to notice them, or be terribly diplomatic about it, and on we shall go.

Thanks to all the retrieval, curatorial, and rights staff at the **Australian Institute of Aboriginal & Torres Strait Islander Studies** (especially Lisa Marcussen and Kylie Moloney); **National Museum of Australia** (Sarah Streatfeild and Sharon Goddard), **National Archives of Australia; Public Record Office Victoria** and **University of Melbourne Archives** (Georgina Ward). Vanessa Fleming-Baillie, the Executive Coordinator of the **Monash Indigenous Studies Centre** helped locate resources by Gurindji women.

Family My uncle Terry Wills Cooke, author of *The Currency Lad,* collected and catalogued papers and objects relating to Wills family history over decades; now at the National Library. His 'translations' of handwritten diaries and documents over generations are invaluable. He very kindly answered my questions about them, while knowing that my conclusions, emphases and opinions may differ markedly from his. Thanks to my mum, Linda, and her sisters Glenda and Wanda for family stories and the photo of Nanna with her whip.

Science and medical consultants included the author and Professor of History and Philosophy of Science, Doctor of Psychology and neuroethics specialist Cordelia Fine; Professor Susan Davis; Dr Gemma Sharp,

Kate Young, and Monica Cronin at the **Geoffrey Kay Museum of Anaesthetic History**, who introduced me to 'bicycle face'. **Melbourne Bureau of Meteorology Climate Data Services** staffer Cathy Toby confirmed that it was a hot day on 30 October 1965 at Flemington race course and shared her opinion of wearing tights.

Good folk Kay Craddock Antiquarian Bookseller shop staff let me photograph a page of flower meanings in the 1857 first edition *Bridal Souvenir* book, because I couldn't afford to buy it. A telepathic crocus to them. Denise Scott and Sue Ingleton answered impertinent questions. Costume designer Kitty Stuckey and the Clarke family allowed the inclusion of the photo of Mr John Clarke. Wendy Harmer retrieved some nonsense from her files for me.

Hat tips Gideon Haigh volunteered the unpublished 1905 shot of Annette Kellermann, from cricketer's Frank Laver's private photo album, held at the Melbourne Cricket Club museum. He also put me in touch with a member of Lillian Pyke's family, John Pyke, who ponied up the only known photograph of her. Geoffrey Blainey confirmed a quote in his 1994 book *A Shorter History of Australia*, which is commonly misreported. The Pental company elucidated the commercial Martha Gardener wool wash story. I nicked the bicycle hoyden photograph from a Bob Nicholson tweet.

Spelling No correspondence will be entered into about the spelling of Annette Kellermann, as it is the subject of an unseemly squabble between national institutions and their catalogues. Take it up with them, do.

Publishing It's a privilege to have a good editor. Thank you, Brandon VanOver, for helping me make a bag of broken biscuits into a proper cake – and for agreeing to enter a large public building to photograph a furry bra. Thanks to Penguin Random House Publishing Director Justin Ractliffe; Production Manager Nikla Martin; marketing and publicity mavens Heidi Camilleri, Hannah Ludbrook and Bec Howard; data diva Charlotte Saunders; cover collaborators Sandy Cull and the ever-patient Adam Laszczuk. The typesetters at Post Pre-Press we drove mad are the fabulous Renée Bahr, Julian Mole and Ann Wilson.

Escorting Flotilla Ms Lucy, Mrs Maver, Mrs Davidson and Mrs Riley; Kevin Whyte, Georgina Ogilvie and Claire Harrison; Gabrielle Coyne; Cousin Suze, Brother John; Jane Nicholls, Lily Brett, Mercy-dashers Audette & Anna; Lorin Clarke; Philippa Hawker, Fiona Wood and The Other Women of Reading Group; Kay Hartley; Mark Parry; Penelope Durston; Lyndal Thorne; Sonia; Anyez and Clare Lindop; and the requisite and rescue-y computer-wrangler, Kai Howells.

Attribution and availability of photos

Many photos in this book are yet to be digitised or individually catalogued by the National Library of Australia or State Library Victoria, including those related to the Argus fashion files, the Wills family, theatrical postcards, Emily McPherson College of Domestic Economy and the Tivoli Theatre.

If there's an object, photograph, artwork, or image that you feel has not been correctly credited in this book, please contact the publisher, or Copyright Australia, so we may amend future editions.

MADAME DARTO.

Kaz Cooke is a woman.

VIKING

UK | USA | Canada | Ireland | Australia
India | New Zealand | South Africa | China

Viking is part of the Penguin Random House group of companies whose
addresses can be found at global.penguinrandomhouse.com

First published by Viking in 2021

Cover and internal design by Sandy Cull, Kaz Cooke and Adam Laszczuk
© Penguin Random House Australia Pty Ltd
Cover image adapted from 'Sir Thomas Mansel and his wife Jane', 1625, artist
unknown. Courtesy Heritage Image Partnership Ltd/Alamy Stock Photo

Typeset in 11/16 pt Garamond Premier Pro by Post Pre-press
Printed and bound in China by RR Donnelley

 A catalogue record for this
book is available from the
NATIONAL LIBRARY OF AUSTRALIA National Library of Australia

ISBN 978 1 76089 697 3

penguin.com.au